China's Intellectual Property Regime for Innovation

Dan Prud'homme · Taolue Zhang

China's Intellectual Property Regime for Innovation

Risks to Business and National Development

Springer

Dan Prud'homme
EMLV Business School
Léonard de Vinci Pôle Universitaire
Paris, France

Taolue Zhang
Law School of Tongji University
Shanghai, China

ISBN 978-3-030-10403-0 ISBN 978-3-030-10404-7 (eBook)
https://doi.org/10.1007/978-3-030-10404-7

Library of Congress Control Number: 2019934525

This Springer imprint is published by the registered company Springer Nature Switzerland AG.
The registered company address is: Gewerbestrasse 11, 6330 Cham, Switzerland

Preface

Countries in the middle-income stage of development require a smart approach to their intellectual property (IP) regime that effectively stimulates genuine technological innovation, not just imitation. This strategic shift can allow a latecomer nation to avoid being perpetually stuck in the middle-income stage of development unable to transition to higher income levels (a situation called the "middle-income trap") and to catch up with forerunners. China, which is currently an upper middle-income country, is grappling with how to best make this transition. Over the last decade, China has embarked on a state-led "indigenous innovation" and intertwined IP development strategy. However, despite this new strategic approach to catch up, China has not yet landed among the ranks of high-income economies and the country's IP regime has increasingly found itself under fire by foreign governments, firms, and other stakeholders.

Amidst this backdrop, this book provides a timely and up-to-date evaluation of the risks that China's IP regime poses to innovation. Our central finding is that China's IP regime for innovation has improved notably over time, and therefore is more conducive to innovation than many believe, but it still poses a range of risks. The presence of these risks may, to varying degrees, negatively influence the innovation activities of both foreign and domestic firms, as well as other actors participating in the innovation process. In turn, this poses a larger set of risks to China's national development. However, with sufficient buy-in from the state, we do not believe that these factors will prohibit a number of smart reforms from being made to improve the ability of China's IP regime to foster innovation and entrepreneurship.

This book is based upon a report commissioned to the authors by the World Bank in 2017. The authors are indebted to Hoon Sahib Soh of the World Bank for his support for the project, as well as his valuable comments on early draft versions of this manuscript. We also much appreciate the support that Justin Hill of the World Bank lent to the project. Parts of the work produced by Taolue Zhang for this book were additionally funded by China's National Planning Office of Philosophy and Social

Science (I5BFX170) and China's Ministry of Education (14YJC820077). The authors are also grateful to Fengmei Peng for collecting some data for the book's IP enforcement chapter and to Yaoyao Jiang for her help formatting the manuscript.

Paris, France Dan Prud'homme
Shanghai, China Taolue Zhang

Contents

List of Figures

List of Tables

Chapter 1
Introduction

This book evaluates the risks that China's intellectual property (IP)[1] regime poses to innovation. The regime has been heavily criticized in recent years as potentially stifling innovation (e.g., Linton and Hammer 2010; Prud'homme 2012; US Chamber 2017; USTR 2018). Further, disputes over China's allegedly inadequate IP regime and IP "theft" have contributed to one of the biggest trade wars in modern history (e.g., Wong and Coty 2019). However, at the same time, China's innovation capabilities have risen significantly and major reforms have recently been made to the country's IP regime (e.g., Prud'homme and von Zedtwitz 2018). How risky, really, is China's IP regime for innovation? This book evaluates this important and timely question based on a multidisciplinary analysis involving law, management, economics, and political science.

A few of the book's terms and parameters are worth defining up front. By "innovation" we broadly mean new solutions that have clear commercial or otherwise practical applications, and the process of developing these solutions (e.g., Schumpeter 1912; OECD 1992). By "risk" we broadly mean potential hazards and costs that China's IP regime presents to firms and other actors (stakeholders) in the country's national innovation system (NIS). A country's NIS is its network for diffusion of knowledge and other resources among firms, universities, public research institutions (PRIs), customers, associations, government bodies, and other actors needed to stimulate innovation (e.g., Freeman, 1987; Lundvall, 1992; Nelson, 1993). Further, we focus exclusively on important risks that may make China's NIS actors less likely to innovate to the extent they would if the regime were reformed. In doing so, we do not simply repeat all aspects of China's IP regime that we have heard foreign businesses complain about over the years. Instead, we focus on select aspects of the regime that we believe currently deserve reform to better foster innovation by all actors in China's NIS (i.e., both domestic and foreign businesses, and the other actors shaping China's national development). More about our analytical approach is discussed later in this chapter.

[1]Hereafter "IP" and "IPR" are used interchangeably.

D. Prud'homme and T. Zhang, *China's Intellectual Property Regime for Innovation*, https://doi.org/10.1007/978-3-030-10404-7_1

We evaluate the riskiness of China's IP regime for innovation across several dimensions. We critically appraise China's substantive IP laws, policies for boosting patent quantity and quality, policies and other measures for transmitting and exploiting technological knowledge, new experimental IP policies and measures, China's system for administering patents, and the country's system for patent enforcement. In doing so, our book covers the multiplicity of need-to-know institutional risks that China's IP regime poses to innovation. Although an important risk receiving increased attention recently, we consider cyber-intrusions/hacking a separate issue not primarily governed by China's IP regime. Given that innovation is a core driver of productivity-based economic growth in middle- and high-income economies (e.g., Fagerberg et al. 2010), this book indirectly evaluates the ability of China's IP regime to help support future economic growth.

Our central finding is that China's IP regime for innovation has improved notably over time, and therefore is more conducive to innovation than many believe, but it still poses a range of risks. The presence of these risks may, to varying degrees, negatively influence the innovation activities of both foreign and domestic firms, as well as other actors participating in the innovation process. In turn, this poses a larger set of risks to China's national development. However, with sufficient buy-in from the state, we do not believe that these factors will prohibit a number of smart reforms from being made to improve the ability of China's IP regime to foster innovation and entrepreneurship.

We focus largely on China's patent regime (including invention patents,[2] utility models,[3] and registered designs[4]) because it is traditionally considered the most important institutional pillar for innovation. However, we also discuss China's regime

[2]Invention patents in China can be granted to both products and processes, and must meet a standard for absolute novelty, inventiveness, and practical use as determined by a Substantive Examination. Their duration of protection is 20 years.

[3]Utility models in China can be granted on the shape and/or structure of a product, and do not undergo a Substantive Examination but are required to be novel, meet a lower level of inventiveness than invention patents, and must meet criteria for practical use. Their duration of protection is 10 years.

[4]Registered designs/design patents in China are granted on the aesthetic aspects of an item used in commerce. They do not undergo a Substantive Examination nor have to meet any inventive step/technical function thresholds; however, they must be distinct from prior designs, and should not conflict with prior rights like copyrights or trademarks. Their current duration of protection is 10 years (although it has recently been proposed, in a draft revisions to the patent law, to protect them for 15 years).

for trade secrets,[5] trademarks,[6] copyrights,[7] plant varieties,[8] geographical indications,[9] and integrated circuits[10]—all of which can be useful for innovation and/or entrepreneurship. Our work culminates in several practical tools, including risk assessment matrices for businesses and recommendations for institutional reform.

1.1 Strategic IP Policy for China's Current Stage of Development

The theoretical arguments for instituting at least some type of IP protection are relatively well understood, albeit not always agreed upon (e.g., Machlup 1958; Arrow 1962; Maskus 2000; World Bank; Fink and Maskus 2005; Odagiri et al. 2010a; Gans and Stern 2010). Proponents of IP protection regimes suggest that they (i) provide a mechanism to legally codify the natural rights of creators (inventors, artists, designers, and performers) to be identified/attributed as such; (ii) provide a legal monopoly via which economic agents can charge rents on their intangible property, thereby correcting the market failure of free-riding and potentially encouraging investment; (iii) address the "information paradox" (where sellers of information are dis-incentivized from entering into meaningful transactions with potential buyers in the absence of a system of legal appropriability); (iv) enhance diffusion of knowledge and ideas in an economy (e.g., by making inventions in patent applications public); (v) enhance efficiency in the economy by limiting redundant investments (e.g., by making patented inventions public so it is clear what has already been invented); (vi) safeguard the public interest by providing a mechanism that may limit product information asymmetries and help dis-incentivize low quality and unsafe imitations; and (viii) optimize competition and safeguard the public interest by providing a mechanism to dis-incentivize unfair competition. At the same time, many criticize

[5]Trade secrets in China protect valuable non-public information guarded with confidentiality measures. They remain protected indefinitely as long as they meet their corresponding legal requirements.

[6]Trademarks in China are granted on identifying and distinguishing signs or symbols in goods and services. Their duration of protection is 10 years, which is extendable indefinitely upon renewal every 10 years.

[7]Copyrights in China are granted on original authored or otherwise created creative work. The duration of protection of the copyright depends on the type of creative work at hand, for example an authored work is protected for the lifetime of the author plus 50 years after his/her death.

[8]Plant variety rights/protection (PVP) in China refers to improved plant varieties developed by breeders that possess novelty, distinctness, uniformity and stability, as well as an appropriate denomination. The duration of PVP in China is 15 years for most crops and 20 years for trees and vines.

[9]Geographical indications (GIs) in China are granted on signs on goods with a specific geographical origin and qualities or reputation mainly derived from natural or cultural factors from that origin. As with trademarks, GIs duration of protection is 10 years, which is extendable indefinitely upon renewal every 10 years.

[10]Integrated circuits in China are granted on the layout-design/typography of semi-conductors. Their duration of protection is 10 years.

the modern IP regime. For example, some suggest that the monopolies the system affords can actually stifle innovation, make economic catch-up difficult, increase inequality, make medicines unaffordable, amongst creating other negative impacts on society (e.g., see Oddi 1996; Lall 2003; Boldrin and Levine 2005; Baker et al. 2017).

Regardless of what position one takes in theoretical discussions on IP regimes, it is difficult to make a conclusive case for abolishing them (Penrose 1951) and it remains an inescapable fact that they will remain in our economies for the foreseeable future. Moreover, IP regimes are increasingly used today by incumbent firms to maintain their lead over latecomers (e.g., Xiao et al. 2013; Song 2013). Further, the composition of IP regimes in many countries is not infrequently determined by the interests of incumbent firms via pressure they exert on IP lawmaking/policymaking in the form of global, regional, and bilateral trade agreements, and national law (e.g., see Drahos 2001; Dinwoodie 2006; Reichman 2009). As such, in the interest of pragmatism, policymakers in latecomer nations such as China need to develop a smart approach to governing IP that considers the sometimes asymmetric interests of forerunners while also, in the long term, incentivizes the majority of actors in their NIS to innovate.

Many Chinese policymakers have demonstrated an intimate understanding of this dynamic. As a rule of thumb, latecomer nations have found it useful to maintain relatively lax IP regimes in the early stage of their catch-up process in order to facilitate technological learning (Ginarte and Park 1997; Park 2008). Without this learning process, a nation cannot efficiently build the fundamental knowledge capabilities needed to indigenously innovate—which is essential to sustain economic growth in the long-run (Kim 1997; Odagiri et al. 2010a ; Kim et al. 2012). This strategic approach to IP regimes is well documented in the context of East Asian countries (e.g., see Kumar 2003; Odagiri et al. 2010b) as well as currently innovative Western nations, for example Germany and the US (Raustiala and Sprigman 2013; Peng et al. 2017a, b). China has generally followed a similar approach to its IP regime to date (Yu 2007; Lee 2015; Peng et al. 2017a, b; Huang 2017).

However, once a nation moves into the middle-income stage of development, there is much more room for debate about what constitutes an optimal IP policy (Ginarte and Park 1997; Park 2008).[11] At this stage—as economies' face diminishing marginal returns from reliance on labor and capital, and approach the technological frontier—innovation is needed to drive productivity (Fagerberg et al. 2010). In turn, these productivity gains drive economic growth (Schumpeter 1942; Acemoglu et al. 2006). This strategic shift can allow a latecomer nation to avoid being perpetually stuck in the middle-income stage of development, unable to transition to higher income levels (a situation called the "middle-income trap"). Generally speaking, strategic government decisions are needed to help middle-income latecomers transition from traditional trade specialization and reliance on imitation of imported

[11] Also, in high-income countries there remains room for debate about how exactly to design an IP regime that optimally encourages technological development and economic growth (e.g., see Mazzoleni and Nelson 1998; Jaffe and Lerner 2004; Encaoua et al. 2006).

knowledge to domestic technological innovation in order to avoid the middle-income trap and successfully catch up with industrial leaders (Lee 2013a, b; Lee and Mathews 2010; Kharas and Kohli 2011).

Smart governance of an IP regime, in particular, can be one useful tool to help latecomers avoid this middle-income trap (e.g., World Bank 2001[12]; Odagiri et al. 2010a; Ahn et al. 2014; Song 2013; Prud'homme 2017). On one hand, there is some evidence that increasing the appropriability offered by IP regimes in the middle-income phase is not always conducive to increasing innovation (Maskus and Penubarti 1995; Allred and Park 2007). On the other hand, research suggests that if middle-income countries—especially as they move closer to high-income status—offer insufficient appropriability for IP rights, this can be counterproductive to facilitating innovation and economic growth (e.g., generally on this subject see World Bank 2001; Falvey and Foster 2006; Lopez 2009; Hall 2014; Kim et al. 2012). Countries in this latter group require a smart approach to their IP regimes that moves them away from path dependency on imitation and towards genuine technological innovation. China, which is currently an upper middle-income country,[13] is currently at this difficult junction in its development process.

In response to these dynamics, China has embarked on a state-led approach over the last decade to avoid the middle-income trap and catch up with forerunner nations via a complex "indigenous innovation" (自主创新/*zizhu chuangxin*) and intertwined IP development strategy (Suttmeier and Yao 2011; Shao and Feng 2014). As proposed in the 2006–2020 National Medium to Long-term Plan for the Development of Science & Technology (S&T MLP), state-led IP strategy is now a core facet of China's indigenous innovation strategy (State Council 2006).[14] The guidance in the S&T MLP led to the creation of the National IP Strategy (2008–2020) issued by China's State Council in 2008, the first multi-faceted IP strategy of its kind in China. This strategy—and the plethora of supporting central-level, as well as provincial-level and county-level policies, plans, and other measures that have followed—aim at improving the IP framework in China by fostering the creation, utilization, management, and protection of IP (Suttmeier and Yao 2011). Most recently, China's central level government has also issued the National IP Strategy (2014–2020), the main targets from which are depicted in Table 1.1.

Further, in November 2016, the Central Committee of the Communist Party of China (CPC) and State Council issued a set of opinions on improving property rights protection in China, which includes a section specific to IPR.[15] This is the highest-

[12]World Bank (2001, p. 141–142), provides a typology of different IP policies that are both consistent with the WTO's Trade-Related Aspects of Intellectual Property (TRIPs) Agreement and are recommended for countries in the low-income vs. middle-income vs. high-income stages of development.

[13]See http://data.worldbank.org/country.china.

[14]The S&T MLP set-forth the goals for China to become an "innovation-oriented" country by 2020 and a "leading science power" by 2050, as well as to reduce China's dependence on technology from other countries to 30 percent or less.

[15]Full text (in Chinese) of opinions available at http://www.gov.cn/xinwen/2016-11/27/content_5138533.htm.

Table 1.1 Targets in China's 2014–2020 IP strategy

Targets	2013	2015	2020
Invention patents per every 10,000 people (number)	4	6	14
Number of patent applications submitted via the PCT (in 10,000s)	2.2	3.0	7.5
Average maintenance period of domestic invention patents (in years)	5.8	6.4	9.0
Number of registered copyrights of works (in 10,000s)	84.5	90	100
Number of registered copyrights on computer software (in 10,000s)	16.4	17.2	20
Total transaction amount of the technology contracts registered on the national technology market (in trillions of yuan)	0.8	1.0	2.0
Annual amount of IP pledge financing (in 100 millions of yuan)	687.5	750	1800
Export income from royalties and franchise fees from proprietary rights (in 100 millions of USD)	13.6	20	80
Average annual growth rate of the operating income of the IP service industry (%)	18	20	20
Social satisfaction with IP protection levels (rating points)	65	70	80
Average substantive examination period for invention patent applications (in months)	22.3	21.7	20.2
Average examination period for trademark registration (in months)	10	9	9

Source China's National IP Strategy (2014–2020)

level policy on the subject issued at the time of writing this book (Xinhua 2016), which is important because policies issued at higher-levels of government may be more influential in the Chinese system of governance (Liu et al. 2011).

1.2 Survey Data About Foreign and Chinese Firms' Perceptions of China's Current IP Regime

Much of the quantitative data readily available about businesses' perceptions of China's current IP regime is from foreign firms, although some data is also available from Chinese firms. Although subject to potential methodological shortcomings,[16] chamber of commerce/business confidence surveys can provide some insights into firms' perceptions about risks in China's IP environment. We provide a brief overview of some current data in this section.

On one hand, according to some indicators, foreign firms view China's IP regime quite negatively. Recent business confidence surveys of European and US firms show that China's policies, regulations, and other legal measures (i.e., legal instruments

[16]For example, these shortcomings include high subjectivity in survey questions, potential sampling bias, selection bias in terms of the type of staff responding within the firms to the survey, etc. Also, given differences in sampling size and method from year-to-year there is some difficulty comparing these survey results over time.

outside statutory laws per se) are not always optimal for encouraging innovation investment and technology transfer (Cohen 2015, 2016a). Approximately 55% of US firms recently surveyed by AmCham believe that China's laws and regulations for trade secrets are not effective (AmCham 2016a). IP infringement in China has long been said to negatively affect the technology transfer and R&D investment decisions of many foreign firms (AmCham 2006, p. 29, 33; Chan and Daim 2011; Brander et al. 2017) and is currently considered the tenth most significant concern of US businesses operating in China (AmCham 2016a, p. 19). Similarly, a 2016 US-China Business Council (USCBC) survey finds that IPR enforcement is one of the top ten biggest challenges of doing business in China (USCBC 2016). And a 2016 survey by the European Union Chamber of Commerce in China (EU Chamber) finds that 59% of respondent firms believe IP enforcement in China is inadequate (EU Chamber 2016, p. 40).

On the other hand, according to other indicators, China's IP regime is currently viewed by foreign firms more positively. US firms surveyed by Amcham in 2016 appeared generally much more confident in China's IP protection environment (the IP regime in its entirety) than ever before (AmCham 2016b).[17] In terms of more specific components of the regime, over 50% of US firms surveyed in 2016 by AmCham think that China's IP laws and regulations for patents, copyrights, and trademarks are effective (AmCham 2016a). Similarly, the EU Chamber found that from 2009 to 2016 over 50% of respondent firms considered China's IP laws and regulations to be "adequate" or "excellent" (European Chamber 2016, p. 39). In the 2016 AmCham survey, 91% of respondents found that China's enforcement of IP has improved in the last five years (AmCham 2016a, p. 42). Similarly, USCBC surveys indicate that IP enforcement is currently not viewed by US firms to be as challenging relative to other business issues as it was in prior years (USCBC 2016, p. 2). Further, from 2009 to 2016, the EU Chamber found significant improvement in the perceptions of its members about the IP enforcement environment in China (EU Chamber 2016, p. 40).

Surveys of Chinese firms indicate that they are increasingly satisfied with IP protection levels in China, although are not fully satisfied. The most influential survey of Chinese firms' satisfaction with IP protection in China is the Intellectual Property Social Satisfaction Survey conducted since 2012 by the China Patent Protection Association, China Trademark Association, Chinese Copyright Association, and CCTV Market Research. China's latest multi-year National IP Strategy (2014–2020) includes targets for levels of satisfaction with IP protection in China reported in that survey (see Table 1.1 above). The 2015 survey found that 68.7% of 12,893 respondents were satisfied with the levels of IP protection in China, which was up from 65% in 2013 and 67.5% in 2014 (State Council 2015). This nearly meets the 70% satisfaction rating for 2015 targeted in the National IP Strategy (2014–2020).

[17]For example, 81% of US firms surveyed by the American Chamber of Commerce in China (AmCham) considered IP protection in China in 2004 to be "ineffective" or "totally ineffective" (AmCham 2006, p 28).

Collectively, the aforementioned industry perceptions have two main implications. First, they indicate that, on one hand, China's IP enforcement institutions and practices *as well as* China's IP laws, policies, and regulations may deserve reform. Our analysis throughout this book confirms this point. As such, while the notion circulated by some that China has an extremely "weak" IP protection system is false, it is also misleading when some often more informed analysts only emphasize China's IP enforcement challenges without also highlighting that some of China's IP policies, laws, regulations, and other measures also deserve reform.

Second, on the other hand, the aforementioned industry perceptions indicate that China's IP regime is not always business-unfriendly. In fact, as discussed briefly in some places in this book, parts of China's IP regime are actually even more business-friendly than the IP regimes of some large developed economies. This creates a paradox. Much more could be said about this important dynamic, although we do not explore it in depth here. A recommended source analyzing these and other related issues is Prud'homme (2019), which delineates several inter-related business-friendliness paradoxes in China's IP regime. Prud'homme (2019) also constructs a framework of concepts that help explain these paradoxes: (1) firm-related factors including (i) learning & adaption, (ii) capabilities & resources, and (iii) competition; and (2) the state-related factors including (i) institutional capacity, (ii) international obligations, (iii) geo-economics, (iv) poli-economics, (v) technological paradigms, and (vi) strategic calibration.

1.3 Challenges to Reforming China's IP Regime

In our opinion, China still needs to address six main intertwined IP-related challenges complicating its transition to be a high-income country: (1) Creating a legal appropriability environment that is more conducive to R&D and other innovation investments, patent commercialization, and direct technology transfer and spillovers in industries that will sustain growth (see Chaps. 2, 3, 4, 5, and 7 of this book); (2) Proactively encouraging innovation investments, patent commercialization, and direct technology transfer and spillovers in an economy where firms are often reluctant or unable to do so (see Chaps. 4 and 5 and, more generally, Chap. 3 of this book); (3) Balancing the strategic goal of eroding incumbents' IP-derived barriers to entry with the reality that absorption of external resources from foreign firms alongside dynamic use of internal capabilities is needed for sustainable indigenous innovation (see Chap. 4 and, more generally, Chaps. 2, 3, and 7 of this book); (4) Improving the quality of IP rights in order to limit transaction costs and barriers to entry inhibiting innovation as well as avoid path-dependency and increase the economic value of innovations (see Chap. 3 of this book); (5) Proactively developing valuable IP in promising industries (see Chaps. 3 and 4 of this book); and (6) Ensuring that government resources are managed wisely and devoted to the most productive IP-related initiatives (see all chapters of this book). These challenges are of course joined by others facing China as it seeks to avoid the middle-income trap that are not necessarily related to IP.

The six aforementioned challenges to smart IP reform in China are compounded by a range of political economy factors. These factors can be divided into political economy characteristics that are not unique to China and those that are rather particular to China.

China faces a number of political economy obstacles to reforming its IP regime that are not uncommon in other nations. (i) First, there is some uncertainty about which IP-related policy, law, or institutional mechanisms are optimal for meeting the strategic aims of the state to stimulate sustainable competitiveness and innovation. Addressing this challenge requires in-depth analysis and monitoring and evaluation (M&E). (ii) Second, there are rivalries and other coordination issues between government departments, which may limit the efficiency and effectiveness of IP policy formulation and implementation. Smart policy and legal design and administrative management mechanisms are needed to address these issues. (iii) Third, vested interests may undermine smart IP policymaking. This lock-in can create problematic path dependency. Strict governance oversight is needed to limit the negative consequences of this dynamic.

It could also be argued that China faces several fundamental inter-related factors complicating smart reform of its IP regime that are often, although not necessarily always, unique to its political economy. (i) First, the economic decentralization present in China (which, as noted in Walder (1995), is/was not present in other successful East Asian latecomers) poses challenges to the efficiency with which central-level IP initiatives are effectively diffused and implemented throughout the provincial and local levels in China (Mertha 2005; Dimitrov 2009). This being said, China's economic decentralization can paradoxically aid in IP reform tailored to regional needs. (ii) Second, the structure of China's political/government apparatus can hinder smart policymaking and implementation. For example, the apparatus is very much focused on rewarding tangible yet sometimes overly simplistic IP-related performance targets, in part because more complex targets are difficult to monitor and evaluate (Prud'homme 2012; Prud'homme and Song 2016). The apparatus can also incentivize 'over-experimentation' with IP initiatives, which can waste state resources and create other adverse economic effects. At the same time, however, the structure of China's political/government apparatus can paradoxically aid in swift IP reform. (iii) Third, China's massive size, diverse industrial structures, and uneven cross-regional levels of development complicate timely and harmonized IP reform. In effect, there are differing temporal "crossing over" points where Chinese localities need IP reform to drive economic development (Yu 2009, 2013). These factors are rather difficult to fundamentally alter and, as alluded to, are not entirely negative per se. As such, these factors are mentioned throughout this book only when they pose significant obstacles to smart IP reform.

Some may assume that history, ideology, and culture may also pose unique obstacles to smart reform of China's IP regime. For example, some argue that China's history of being beholden to foreign powers in part of the 1800s and 1900s—a period of time known as the "century of humiliation"—creates an incentive for the nation to institute techno-nationalistic industrial policy, IP policy included (e.g., McGregor 2012). However, in our view, it seems unlikely that any accompanying ideology that comes along with this period of Chinese history will per se lead Chinese policymakers to make irrational IP policy decisions of great significance at present. Over the last decade, China has illustrated a strategic and pragmatic approach to IP reform; even though, often due to some of the previously mentioned challenges, there is room for debate about how optimally the state has governed the IP regime.

Although culture plays a role in China's approach to IP policy, its role is debated. Some literature discusses how Confucian values have ingrained the value of copying others' work as a sign of respect into Chinese culture, and how this complicates IP protection in China (Alford 1995). Others de-emphasize these cultural factors in explaining the current sentiment in China towards IP protection, instead finding that state governance of IP institutions is the main determinant of the Chinese mentality towards IP (e.g., Shi 2008).

In our opinion, the traditional culture of copying in China, however it came about, is currently not as condoned as it once was and it should not pose a significant long-term barrier to IP reform in China. We argue this because, from a theoretical perspective, while societal norms impact the design and administration of institutions (including laws, regulations, and enforcement thereof), formal institutions can also beget norms (e.g., generally see Lee 2015). And from a historical perspective, co-evolution of norms and IP-related institutions in both Western and Eastern societal contexts transformed countries that once had a culture of copying into some of the most innovative nations who respect IP today.

To be sure, as documented throughout this book, China's IP institutions are undeniably changing to more seriously protect IP in response to the needs of both Chinese and foreign stakeholders. Much of the reforms to China's IP environment up until China's accession to the World Trade Organization (WTO) (including the WTO's Trade-Related Aspects of Intellectual Property (TRIPs) Agreement) in 2001 were at the behest of foreign stakeholders to make China a less risky location for investment and technology transfer (Yu 2007; Crookes 2010; Farnell and Crookes 2016). However, post accession to the WTO, many reforms to China's IP environment have been driven by the rise in technological and entrepreneurial capabilities of domestic Chinese firms and a corresponding need to strengthen IP protection to ensure these indigenous firms can survive and grow (e.g., see Yu 2007; Lee 2015). At the same time, foreign firms, universities, PRIs, business associations, and governments will still remain relevant to China's NIS in the foreseeable future and therefore will likely still help shape China's IP regime. We see this shift from primarily exogenous to both exogenous and endogenous drivers of IP reform in China—combined with the resolve and growing administrative capabilities of much of the Chinese government, the aforementioned theoretical and historical perspectives, and other factors detailed in Prud'homme (2019)—as a strong signal that businesses, consumers, and policymakers in China will attach increasing importance to an IP regime that fosters innovation.

1.4 Method and Materials Used for This Book

This book evaluates the risks that China's IP regime poses to innovation. By "risk" we broadly mean potential hazards and costs that China's IP regime presents to firms and other actors (stakeholders) in the country's NIS. We explore the complexities of China's IP regime for innovation at different units of analysis (firms, technologies/industries, provinces and the national level) based on a more up-to-date and granular evaluation than appears available in individual scholarly works to date. Our multidisciplinary research approach integrates diverse materials and methods spanning the fields of law, economics, management, and political science.

Several primary and secondary sources have been used for our research. In attempting to ensure that our research was as up-to-date as possible our analysis is based upon review of China's IP regime inclusive of all major reforms thereto as of April 2019. We conducted a literature review (in both English and Chinese) which includes academic literature, practitioner and news publications, and government reports (in Chinese and English) spanning the aforementioned disciplines. We also reviewed the original text of IP-related laws, regulations, polices and other measures from the central-level and sub-central levels in China over the last decade. Our analysis is also informed by interviews, surveys, and other consultations (e.g., discussions at workshops and roundtables in China and elsewhere) we conducted over the last five years. This research involved many representatives from foreign industry in China (primarily, but not limited to, European and US industry associations and individual firms), Chinese firms, Chinese universities and Chinese PRIs, China-based lawyers, Chinese and foreign academics, and Chinese and foreign government officials.

We also collected statistical data from multiple sources. These sources include patent and patent licensing data from China's State Intellectual Property Office (SIPO) (now called the "China National Intellectual Property Administration" (CNIPA); patent data from the World Intellectual Property Office (WIPO) and other IP offices; and various economic data from China's National Bureau of Statistics (NBS), various other Chinese government agencies, the World Bank, and OECD. We also drew upon a particularly rich collection of data sources in Chinese to perform our analysis of IP enforcement in China, including:

- China IPR Yearbook, issued by SIPO since 2000;
- Annual Report of China IPR Protection Status, edited by SIPO together with other IP administrative authorities;
- Annual Working Reports, issued by Supreme People's Court;
- Annual Report on Judicial Protection of IPR in China Court, issued by the Supreme People's Court;
- China Trademark Strategy Annual Report, issued by SAIC;
- The China Customs IP Protection Status, issued by General Administration of Customs;
- Analysis Report on Judicial Protection Data of Beijing IP Court from 2015 and 2016 (Judicial Protection Data of Beijing IP Court), issued by IP House Judicial

Data Research Center. These two reports cover many aspects of the Beijing IP Court's trials in 2015 and 2016, including information on processing times of various IP civil and administrative cases. They include information on more than 20,000 administrative cases and 3500 civil cases.

- China IPR Index Report, issued by the China IP Index Report Research Team. This annual report establishes an index system to evaluate China's IP production, IP commercialization, potential creativity represented by IP, IP enforcement, comprehensive IP performance, among other indicators in different provinces across China. The first volume was issued in 2009.
- Beijing IP Litigation Report 2016, issued by the China IP Index Report Research Team, covering 780 cases concluded by courts in Beijing from 2013 to 2015 and published on the Supreme People's Court's Chinese IP Decisions website (ipr.court.gov.cn).
- Shanghai IP Litigation Report 2016, issued by the China IP Index Report Research Team, covering 770 cases concluded by courts in the Shanghai area from 2013 to 2015 and published on the Supreme People's Court's Chinese IP Decision website (ipr.court.gov.cn).
- The trials of Patent Cases in Shanghai IP Court (2015–2016), issued by the Shanghai IP Court. This book covers 1011 patent cases accepted and 657 patent cases concluded by the Shanghai IP Court from 2015 to 2016.
- Report about the processing times of patent infringement cases (Processing Time of Patent Infringement Cases Report), issued by the IP House Judicial Data Research Center. This book analyzes the processing time of patent infringement cases in more than 20 Chinese courts. It was issued by the IP House Judicial Data Research Center and Beijing Chaofan IPR Research Center on April 17, 2017 (IP House 2017).[18]
- Report on Litigation Costs and Efficiency Analysis of IP Infringement—an Empirical Study based on Cases in Nanjing Area (Nanjing Report), issue by the Nanjing Railway & Transportation Court. This book collects data about four types of IP first instance cases (patent, trademark, copyright, and unfair competition cases) accepted and completed in the Nanjing Area (by Nanjing Intermediate Court, Nanjing Railway & Transportation Court and other six district courts) during the period from December 20, 2009 to October 19, 2015, totaling 6774 cases among which 1374 are concluded with formal judgments.
- Data Analysis of Trademark Lawsuits in Chinese Courts in 2016 (Trademark Lawsuit Report 2016), issued by IP House in 2017. This analysis is based on the judgments and decisions of trademark cases tried and concluded by Chinese courts from January 1, 2016 to December 31, 2016 collected by www.iphouse.cn. More than 13,000 trademark civil cases of first instance, second instance and retrial; and

[18]Data in the report regards decisions made by three key IP Courts and their precedential courts and 12 other intermediate courts (IC) from Jan 1, 2011 to Dec. 31, 2015. In total, 5983 decisions have been analyzed. Among this sample, 644 decisions were made by three IP Courts, 2910 were made by the precedential courts of the three IP Courts, and 2429 were made by 12 other intermediate courts. However, only 1521 decisions have the exact acceptance date (EAD) and can be used to analyze the time for processing patent infringement disputes.

more than 7000 trademark administrative cases of first instance, second instance and retrial are collected in this book.
- Report on Damages Decisions in IP Civil Cases heard by Changsha Intermediate People's Court (Changsha Report, 2016), issued by Changsha Intermediate Court. This analysis is based on the judgments and decisions of IP Civil cases tried and concluded by Changsha Intermediate People's Court from Oct 21, 2016 to December 31, 2015.[19]
- Judicial Big Data Report of IP Infringement (Judicial Big Data Report), issued by Judicial Big Data Research Institute in July 2017. This book covers IP cases of first instance accepted and concluded by Chinese courts from January 1, 2015 to December 31, 2016.
- The Research Report of Rewarded Damages in IP Infringement Cases (Middlesouth Rewarded Damages Report), issued by IP Center of Middlesouth University of Financial and Political Science in 2014. This book covers 4768 IP cases decided from the initiation of National IP Strategy in June 2008 to the end of 2013.
- Report on Civil Judicial Protection of IPR in Zhejiang Province (2015) (Zhejiang Report), issued by Zhejiang Higher People Court with others in 2016, covering all the IP civil cases concluded by all courts in Zhejiang Province in 2015.
- Other materials on IP enforcement edited by scholars.

When available, we often used data starting from 2006 or 2008 (given, as mentioned, that these are the years when major IP-related strategies were introduced in China). Best efforts were made to collect as up-to-date data as possible (as of 2017, when the data collection process was completed), although sometimes the most recent data available at that time was a few years old.

We employ several forms of analysis in this book. Several chapters draw on statistical analysis. When conducting such analyses, we sometimes compared how China performed on certain statistical indicators relative to other countries. The countries we used for comparison were discussed and agreed upon with the World Bank, and supplemented by a few others. These countries include the US, Germany, and the UK (selected given they are well-known technological forerunners from the West), as well as Japan and South Korea (given they are well-known technological forerunners who share some similarities with China in that they are in East Asia, were latecomers compared to the aforementioned Western counterparts, and adopted aggressive developmental state strategies for catch up).

The other main approach we adopted was thematic analysis of qualitative data (i.e., consultation feedback; literature; and texts of laws, policies, other measures and court cases). This analysis was comprised of several steps.

First, we developed a loose/working system of codes based upon the severity of the language and frequency of its occurrence in the qualitative data sources we reviewed to identify major themes in the data. For example, we used this approach to roughly determine how significant certain legal provisions or institutional practices seemed to dis-incentivize R&D, technology transfer, and spillovers in China. This methodology

[19]In this period, Changsha Intermediate People's Court accepted 3309 cases and completed 431 patent cases, 1210 trademark cases, 846 copyright cases, and 17 unfair competition cases.

is in line with those proposed in Miles and Huberman (1994) and Creswell (2007). Second, in line with Creswell (2007), basic casual chain analysis (i.e., logically being able to link each identified issue to its purported effect at the magnitude reported) was used to connect the themes identified to this book's objective of critically evaluating China's IP regime for innovation.

Third, the aforementioned approach was combined with our collective expertise analyzing the legal, economic, and management/governance implications of Chinese policies, laws, and other state measures. We used the framework developed by the OECD on economic policy effectiveness—i.e., (1) if a policy is too ambiguous, (2) too burdensome, (3) too discriminatory, or (4) too impractical to be implemented effectively to meet its stated goals—to guide our analysis (OECD 1995; APEC & OECD 2005). We sometimes used the same benchmark countries mentioned in the above discussion about our statistical analysis methods as points of comparison. Of course, there is some subjectivity in our analysis as we, as authors, inevitably inject some bias when evaluating an IP regime according to such broad indicators.

Fourth, in line with Creswell (2007) and Miles and Huberman (1994), a consensus was reached among us (the authors) regarding the major themes in, and implications of, our data. This was done in order to limit potential bias in any individual author's analysis.

Collectively, our analytical approach allowed us to evaluate the major risks that China's IP regime appears to pose to innovation. This included separating out criticisms about the Chinese IP regime that appear less well-founded (and therefore likely less impactful on China's innovation and entrepreneurship trajectory) or were otherwise more minor from more significant issues. Accordingly, to be sure, this book is *not* intended to provide an exhaustive analysis of every possible way that China's IP regime could be reformed to be potentially "more foreign business friendly". In fact, various concerns about China's IP environment raised by some stakeholders are intentionally left out of this book. Instead, we only highlight what we believe, based upon the aforementioned analytical approaches, *to be the most important areas of China's IP regime deserving reform to better foster innovation by all actors in China's NIS* (i.e., both domestic and foreign businesses, and the other actors shaping China's national development). This approach was intended to make the analysis manageable, more objective, and easily digestible by busy managers, scholars, and state policymakers.

1.5 Roadmap of the Book

This introductory chapter provided background information on the IP-related challenges that China faces to strategically avoid the middle-income trap, discussed the mixed perceptions about how conducive China's current IP environment is to innovation, and outlined the foremost challenges and underlying political economy factors complicating China's ability to smartly reform its IP regime. The remainder of the book provides an assessment of the major risks that China's IP regime poses to innovation and how businesses and policymakers might respond. The book is structured as follows: the next chapter, Chap. 2, focuses on statutory IP laws; Chap. 3 discusses patenting trends in China and the state's role therein; Chap. 4 discusses trends in technology commercialization, transfer and spillovers in China and the state's role therein; Chap. 5 discusses China's experience with important new/experimental IP-related programs and other measures; Chapter 6 discusses the ability of Chinese state institutions to administer patents effectively and efficiently; and Chap. 7 discusses China's IP enforcement environment. Based on the aforementioned analyses, Chap. 8 sets-forth novel IP risk management frameworks for businesses operating in China. Chap. 9 provides recommendations for reform of China's IP regime that will be of interest to policymakers and others. Chap. 10 concludes.

References

Acemoglu, D., P. Aghion, and F. Zilibotti. 2006. Distance to frontier, selection, and economic growth. *Journal of the European Economic Association* 4: 37–74.

Ahn, S., B.H. Hall, and K. Lee. 2014. Introduction. In *Intellectual property for economic development*, ed. S. Ahn, B.H. Hall, and K. Lee, 1–10. Northhampton, Mass: Edward Elgar and Korean Development Institute.

Allred, B., and W. Park. 2007. Patent rights and innovation activity: Evidence from national and firm-level data. *Journal of International Business Studies* 38: 878–900.

Alford, W. 1995. *To steal a book is an elegant offense: Intellectual property Law in Chinese civilization*. Stanford: Stanford University Press.

AmCham. 2006. American corporate experience in a Changing China—insights from AmCham Business Climate Surveys. 1999–2005.

AmCham. 2016a. American chamber of commerce in China Business Climate Survey 2016, available at https://www.amchamchina.org/policy-advocacy/business-climate-survey/2016-business-climate-survey.

AmCham. 2016b. AmCham China releases 2016 business climate survey, available at https://www.amchamchina.org/about/press-center/amcham-statement/amcham-china-releases-2016-business-climate-survey.

APEC and OECD. 2005. Integrated checklist on regulatory reform. OECD publications, available at https://www.oecd.org/regreform/34989455.pdf.

Arrow, K. 1962. Economic welfare and the allocation of resources for invention, in *The rate and direction of inventive activity, economic and social factors*, ed. R. Nelson (Ed.). Princeton, NJ.

Baker, D., A. Jayadev., and J. Stiglitz. 2017. Innovation, intellectual property, and development: A better set of approaches for the 21st Century. AccessIBSA, available at http://cepr.net/images/stories/reports/baker-jayadev-stiglitz-innovation-ip-development-2017-07.pdf.

Boldrin, M., and D. Levine. 2005. *Against intellectual monopoly*, 1st ed. Cambridge, UK: Cambridge University Press.

Brander, J., V. Cui, and I. Vertinsky. 2017. China and intellectual property rights: A challenge to the rule of law. *Journal of International Business Studies* 48: 908–921.

Chan, L., and T. Daim. 2011. Technology transfer in China: Literature review and policy implications. *Journal of Science and Technology Policy in China* 2: 122–145.

Cohen, M. 2015. Testimony in hearing on the foreign investment climate in China: Present challenges and potential for reform. US-China Economic Security and Review Commission, available at https://www.uscc.gov/sites/default/files/transcripts/January282015HearingTranscript.pdf.

Cohen, M. 2016a. Slouching towards innovation—a survey of the surveys on China's IP environment. China IPR, available at https://chinaipr.com/2016/01/25/slouching-towards-innovation-a-survey-of-the-surveys-on-chinas-ip-environment/.

Creswell, J.W. 2007. *Qualitative inquiry and research method: Choosing among five approaches*. Thousand Oaks, CA: Sage Publications.

Crookes, P.I. 2010. *Intellectual property regime evolution in China and India: Technological, political, and social drivers of change*. Leiden, Netherlands: Brill.

Dimitrov, M.K. 2009. *Piracy and the state: The politics of intellectual property rights in China*. Cambridge, UK: Cambridge University Press.

Drahos, P. 2001. BITS and BIPS: Bilateralism in intellectual property. *Journal of World Intellectual Property* 4: 791–808.

Dinwoodie, G. 2006. The international intellectual property law system: new actors, new institutions, new sources. *Marquette Intellectual Property Law Review* 10: 205–214.

Encaoua, D., D. Guellec, and C. Martínez. 2006. Patent systems for encouraging innovation: Lessons from economic analysis. *Research Policy* 35: 1423–1440.

European Chamber. 2016. European Union chamber of commerce in China business confidence survey 2016, available at http://www.europeanchamber.com.cn/en/publications-archive?page=1&q=business+confidence+survey.

Fagerberg, J., Srholec, M., and B. Verspagen. 2010. Innovation and economic development, in *Handbook of the economics of innovation*, ed. B. H. Hall, and N. Rosenberg, vol. 2, 834–72. North Holland, Amsterdam: Elsevier.

Falvey, R., and N. Foster. 2006. The role of intellectual property rights in technology transfer and economic growth: Theory and evidence. UNIDO Publication. Available from http://www.unido.org/fileadmin/import/60030_05_IPR_rights_in_technology_transfer.pdf.

Farnell, J., and P. Crookes. 2016. *The politics of EU-China economic relations: An uneasy partnership*. London, UK: Palgrave Macmillan.

Fink, C., and K. Maskus. 2005. *Intellectual property and development: Lessons from recent economic research*. Washington, D.C.: World Bank.

Freeman, C. 1987. Technology policy and economic performance: Lessons from Japan. London: Pinter Publishers.

Gans, J., and S. Stern. 2010. Is there a market for ideas? *Industrial and Corporate Change* 19: 805–837.

Ginarte, J., and W.G. Park. 1997. Determinants of patent rights: A cross-national study. *Research Policy* 26: 283–301.

Hall, B.H. 2014. Does patent protection help or hinder technology transfer? In *Intellectual property for economic development*, ed. S. Ahn, B.H. Hall, and K. Lee, 11–32. Mass.: Edward Elgar and Korean Development Institute, Northhampton.

Huang, C. 2017. Recent development of the intellectual property rights system in China and challenges ahead. *Management and Organization Review* 13: 39–48.

Jaffe, A., and J. Lerner. 2004. *Innovation and its discontents: How our broken patent system is endangering innovation and progress, and what to do about it*. Princeton, New Jersey: Princeton University Press.

Kharas, H., and H. Kohli. 2011. What is the middle-income trap, why do countries fall into it, and how it can be avoided? *Global Journal of Emerging Markets* 3: 281–289.

Kim, L. 1997. *Imitation to innovation: The dynamics of Korea's technology learning*. Cambridge, Mass: Harvard Business School Press.

Kim, Y.K., K. Lee, W.G. Park, and K. Choo. 2012. Appropriate intellectual property protection and economic growth in countries at different levels of development. *Research Policy* 41: 358–375.

Kumar, N. 2003. Intellectual property rights, technology and economic development: Experiences of Asian countries. *Economic and Political Weekly* 38: 209–226.

Lall, S. 2003. Indicators of the relative importance of IPRs in developing countries. *Research Policy* 32: 1657–1680.

Lee, N. 2015. Intellectual property law in China—from legal transplant to governance. In *Governance of intellectual property rights in China and Europe*, eds. N. Lee, N. Bruun, and M. Li, 5–19. Cheltenham, UK: Edward Elgar.
Lee, K. 2013a. *Schumpeterian analysis of economic catch-up: Knowledge, path-creation, and the middle-income trap*. Cambridge, UK: Cambridge University Press.
Lee, K. 2013b. Capability failure and industrial policy to move beyond the middle-income trap: From trade-based to technology-based specialization. In *The industrial policy revolution I: The role of government beyond ideology*, ed. J. Stiglitz and J.Y. Lin, 244–272. New York: Palgrave Macmillan.
Lee, K., and J. Mathews. 2010. From the Washington consensus to the best consensus for world development. *Asian-Pacific Economic Literature* 24: 86–103.
Linton, K., A. Hammer, et al. 2010. China: Intellectual property infringement, indigenous innovation policies, and frameworks for measuring the effects on the US economy. USITC Publication 4199.
Liu, F.C., D. Simon, Y.Y. Sun, and C. Cong. 2011. China's innovation policies: Evolution, institutional structure, and trajectory. *Research Policy* 40: 917–931.
Lopez, A. 2009. Innovation and appropriability, empirical evidence and research agenda. in *The economics of intellectual property*. Geneva: WIPO. Available from http://www.wipo.int/edocs/pubdocs/en/economics/1012/wipo_pub_1012.pdf.
Lundvall, B.A. 1992. National systems of innovation: Towards a theory of innovation and interactive learning. London: Pinter Press.
Machlup, F. 1958. An economic review of the patent regime, study on the subcommittee on patents. Trademarks, and Copyrights of the Committee on the Judiciary, US Senate, 85th Congress. Washington D.C., Government Printing Office, Access on 15 June 2015 from https://mises.org/sites/default/files/AnEconomicReviewofthePatentRegime_Vol_3_3.pdf.
Maskus, K. 2000. *Intellectual property rights in the global economy*. Washington, D.C.: Institute for International Economics.
Maskus, K., and M. Penubarti. 1995. How trade-related are intellectual property rights? *Journal of International Economics* 39: 227–248.
Mazzoleni, R., and R. Nelson. 1998. The benefits and costs of strong patent protection: a contribution to the current debate. *Research Policy* 27: 273–284.
Mertha, A. 2005. *The politics of piracy*. Ithaca, NY: Cornell University Press.
McGregor, J. 2012. *No ancient wisdom, no followers: The challenges of Chinese authoritarian capitalism*. Westport, CT: Prospecta Press.
Miles, M.M., and A.M. Huberman. 1994. *Qualitative data analysis*. Thousand Oaks, CA: Sage Publications.
Nelson, R (ed.). 1993. National innovation systems: A comparative analysis. UK: Oxford University Press.
OECD. 1995. Recommendation of the Council of the OECD on improving the quality of government regulation, including the OECD reference checklist for regulatory decision-making and background note. OECD, available at http://www.oecd.org/officialdocuments/publicdisplaydocumentpdf/?cote=OCDE/GD(95)95&doclanguage=en.
Odagiri, H., A. Goto, A. Sunami, and R. Nelson. 2010. Introduction. In *Intellectual property rights, development, and catch-up*, ed. H. Odagiri, A. Goto, A. Sunami, and R. Nelson, 1–28. Oxford, UK: Oxford University Press.
Odagiri, H., Goto, A., and A. Sunami. (2010b). IPR and the catch-up process in Japan. in *Introduction*, H. Odagiri A. Goto, A. Sunami, and R. Nelson (2010). H. Odagiri, A. Goto, A. Sunami, and R.Nelson (Eds.), *Intellectual property rights, development, and catch-up*, 95–132. Oxford, UK: Oxford University Press.
OECD. 1992. Oslo Manual: The measurement of scientific and technological activities, proposed guidelines for collecting and interpreting technological innovation data. OECD, available at http://www.oecd.org/sti/inno/2367580.pdf.
Oddi, S. 1996. TRIPS—natural rights and a polite form of economic imperialism Vanderbilt. *Journal of Transnational Law* 29: 415–470.

Park, W. 2008. International patent protection 1960–2005. *Research Policy* 37: 761–766.
Peng, M., D. Ahlstrom, S. Carraher, and W. Shi. 2017a. History and the debate over intellectual property. *Management and Organization Review* 13: 15–38.
Peng, M., D. Ahlstrom, S. Carraher, and W. Shi. 2017b. An institution-based view of global IPR history. *Journal of International Business Studies* 48: 893–907.
Penrose, E. 1951. *The economics of the international patent system*. Baltimore, MD: Johns Hopkins University Press.
Prud'homme, D. 2012. *Dulling the cutting edge: How patent-related policies and practices hamper innovation in China*. Beijing: European Chamber.
Prud'homme, D. 2017. Utility model patent "strength" and technological development: Experiences of China and other East Asian latecomers. *China Economic Review* 42: 50–73.
Prud'homme, D., and H. Song. 2016. Introduction. in *Economic Impacts of Intellectual Property-Conditioned Government Incentives*, ed. D. Prud'homme, and H. Song, H. 1–12. Springer.
Prud'homme, D. 2019. Re-conceptualizing intellectual property regimes in international business research: Foreign-friendliness paradoxes facing MNCs in China. *Journal of World Business*.
Prud'homme, D., and M. von Zedtwitz. 2018. The changing face of innovation in China. *MIT Sloan Management Review* 59: 24–32.
Prud'homme, D., M. von Zedtwitz, J. Thraen., and M. Bader. 2018. Forced technology transfer policies: Workings in China and strategic implications. *Technological Forecasting and Social Change* 134: 150–168.
Raustiala, K., and C. Sprigman. 2013. Fake it till you make it: The good news about China's knockoff economy. *Foreign Affairs* 92: 25–30.
Reichman, J. 2009. Intellectual property in the twenty-first century: Will the developing countries lead or follow? *Houston Law Review* 46: 1115–1185.
Schumpeter, J. 1912. The theory of economic development. Tenth printing 2004. New Jersey: Transaction Publishers.
Schumpeter, J. 1942. *Capitalism, socialism, and democracy*. New York: Harper & Brothers.
Shao, K., and X. Feng (eds.). 2014. *Innovation and intellectual property in China: Challenges, strategies and implementations*. UK: Edward Elgar.
Shi, W. 2008. The paradox of confucian determinism: Tracking the root causes of intellectual property rights problem in China. *The John Marshall Review of Intellectual Property* 7: 454–468.
Song, H. 2013. *Indigenous innovation capability-building and the development of intellectual property rights (in Chinese)*. Beijing: Chinese Academy of Sciences Intellectual Property Rights Press.
State Council. 2006. National Medium- and Long-Term Science and Technology Development Plan (2006–2020) (in Chinese).
State Council of PRC. National Intellectual Property Strategy (2014–2020) (in Chinese).
State Council. 2015. 2015 年知识产权保护满意度总体平稳 (Overall satisfaction with IP protection in 2015 in stable) (in Chinese), available at http://www.gov.cn/xinwen/2016-04/27/content_5068282.htm.
Suttmeier, R, and X. Yao. 2011. China's IP transition: rethinking intellectual property rights in a rising China. National Bureau of Asian Research, available at http://nbr.org/publications/element.aspx?id=520.
USCBC. 2016. USCBC 2016 Membership Survey: The business environment in China, available at https://www.uschina.org/sites/default/files/USCBC2016AnnualMemberSurveyENG_1.pdf.
US Chamber. 2017. Made in China 2025: Global ambitions built on local protections. United States Chamber of Commerce, available at https://www.uschamber.com/sites/default/files/final_made_in_china_2025_report_full.pdf.
USTR. 2018. Findings of the investigation into China's acts, policies, and practices related to technology transfer, intellectual property, and innovation under Section 301 of the Trade Act of 1974. Office of the United States Trade Representative, available at https://ustr.gov/sites/default/files/Section301FINAL.PDF.
Walder, A. 1995. Local governments as industrial firms: an organizational analysis of China's transitional economy. *The American Journal of Sociology* 101: 263–301.

Wild, J. 2010. There is more IP litigation in China than anywhere else on earth. Intellectual Assessment Management, available at http://www.iam-media.com/blog/detail.aspx?g=3a9c9c06-dd4f-4adc-8e2f-5a6eadc847c1.

Wong, D. and A. C. Koty. 2019. The US-China trade war: A timeline. China Briefing, available at https://www.china-briefing.com/news/the-us-china-trade-war-a-timeline/.

World Bank. 2001. Intellectual property: Balancing incentives with competitive access. In *Global economic perspectives*. World Bank, Washington D.C., 129–150, available at http://documents.worldbank.org/curated/en/285571468337817024/310436360_20050012013328/additional/multi0page.pdf.

Yu, P. 2007. Intellectual property, economic development, and the China Puzzle. In *Intellectual property, trade and development: Strategies to optimize economic development in a TRIPs plus area*, ed. D. Gervais, 173–220. Oxford: Oxford University Press.

Yu, P. 2009. Global intellectual property order and its undetermined future. *WIPO Journal* 1: 1–15.

Yu, P. 2013. Five oft-repeated questions about China's rise as a patent power. *Cardozo Law Review De Novo* 78: 81–88.

Xiao, Y., A. Tylecote, and J. Liu. 2013. Why not greater catch-up by Chinese firms? *The impact of IPR, corporate governance and technology intensity on late-comer strategies', Research Policy* 42: 749–764.

Xinhua, 2016. China releases guideline on protection of property rights. Available at http://english.gov.cn/news/top_news/2016/11/28/content_281475502537235.htm.

Chapter 2
Statutory IP Laws

2.1 Evolution of China's Core IP Laws and Regulations

China has established a relatively complete legal infrastructure for IP protection over the past 30 years. During this time, China's IP laws and regulations have become increasingly conducive to innovation rather than mere imitation. Many of these aspects of China's IP regime are currently broadly in line with international standards. However, there are some important exceptions to this trend discussed in this chapter.

Table 2.1 provides an overview of the evolution of China's core IP laws and main implementing regulations, as well as some other important IP-related laws to date. These measures cover various types of IP including patents (invention patents, utility models, and registered designs), trademarks, copyrights, trade secrets, integrated circuits, plant varieties, geographical indications, amongst other areas of IP protection. The table illustrates the incredible number of reforms that have already been made to China's legal framework for IP. Even at the time of writing this book, several major revisions to China's IP laws were just completed or underway: the E-commerce Law was promulgated in 2018, the Anti-Unfair Competition Law was amended in 2018 and again in 2019, the Trademark Law was amended in 2019, and several laws were undergoing revisions, including but not limited to the Patent Law and Copyright Law.

As mentioned in Chap. 1, many of China's core IP laws were adopted or revised in order to meet obligations in key international treaties, including but not limited to the WTO's TRIPs Agreement to which China acceded in 2001. However, post accession to the WTO, many reforms to China's IP environment have been driven by the rise in technological and entrepreneurial capabilities of Chinese firms and a corresponding need to strengthen IP protection (both laws and enforcement) to ensure these indigenous firms can survive and grow (e.g., Yu 2007; Lee 2015). At

The original version of the book was revised: Author's belated correction has been incorporated. The correction to the book is available at https://doi.org/10.1007/978-3-030-10404-7_11

D. Prud'homme and T. Zhang, *China's Intellectual Property Regime for Innovation*, https://doi.org/10.1007/978-3-030-10404-7_2

Table 2.1 China's core IP laws and implementing regulations

Type of IP	Laws	Implementing regulations	Governing authorities
Invention, utility model, and design patents	Patent Law of the PRC (adopted in 1984; revised in 1992, 2002, 2008)	Implementing Rules of the Patent Law of the PRC (adopted in 1985, revised in 1992, 2001, 2002, 2010); Regulation on the Administration of National Standards Involving Patents (2014) issued by SAC and SIPO	CNIPA (SAMR) and local AMR since 2018/SIPO, SAC, and local IPOs before 2019
Trademarks, service marks	Trademark Law of the PRC (adopted in 1982; revised in 1993, 2001, 2013, 2019)	Implementing Regulations of the Trademark Law of the PRC (adopted in 1982, revised in 1988, 1993, 1995, 1999, 2012, 2014)	CNIPA (SAMR) and local AMR since 2018/SAIC and local AICs before 2019
Copyrights	Copyright Law of the PRC (adopted in 1990, revised in 2001, 2010)	Implementing Regulations of the Copyright Law of the PRC (adopted in 1991, revised in 2002, 2011, 2013); Regulations on Computers Software Protection (adopted in 1991, revised in 2001); Regulations on Protection of the Right of Communication through Information Network (adopted in 2006, revised in 2013); Regulations on Copyright Collective Administration (adopted in 2004)	National Copyright Administration (NCA)
Trade secrets and anti-competitive behavior	Anti-Unfair Competition Law of the PRC (adopted in 1993)	–	CNIPA (SAMR) and local AMR since 2018/SAIC and local AICs before 2019

(continued)

Table 2.1 (continued)

Type of IP	Laws	Implementing regulations	Governing authorities
Integrated circuits	Regulations on the Protection of Layout-Designs of Integrated Circuits (adopted in 2001)	Implementing Rule of Regulations on the Protection of Layout-Designs of Integrated Circuits (adopted in 2001)	CNIPA (SAMR) since 2018/SIPO before 2019
Geographical Indications (GIs)	Trademark Law of the PRC (adopted in 1982, revised in 1993, 2001, 2013)	The Measures for the Registration and Administration of Collective Marks and Certification Marks (adopted in 2003); Regulations of Protection on GI Products (adopted in 2005); Methods of Management for GIs of Agricultural Products (adopted in 1997, revised in 2007)	Ministry of Agriculture and Rural Affairs (MoARA) and CNIPA (under SAMR) since 2018/MoA, SAIC, AQSIQ, and CFDA before 2019
New plant varieties	Regulations on the Protection of New Plant Variety Protection (adopted in 1997, revised in 2013); Seed Law of the PRC (adopted in 2000, revised in 2004, 2013, 2015)	Implementing Regulations on the Protection of New Plant Varieties (Agricultural section adopted in 1999, revised in 2007, 2011, and 2014) (forestry section adopted in 1999); Rules for Examination of New Plant Variety Rights for Forestry (adopted in 2014)	MoARA since 2018/MoA before 2019; State Administration of Forestry and Grasslands (SAFG) since 2018/SFA before 2019
Various IPRs	–	Regulations for Intellectual Property Customs Protection (adopted in 1995; Revised in 2003 and 2013)	General Administration of Custom (GAC) and local Customs
Various IPRs	Law on Scientific and Technological Progress of the PRC (adopted in 1993, revised in 2007)	Regulations of regional levels	Ministry of Science and Technology of the PRC (MoST)

(continued)

Table 2.1 (continued)

Type of IP	Laws	Implementing regulations	Governing authorities
Various IPRs	Law on Promotion of Transformation of Scientific and Technological Achievement of the PRC (adopted in 1996, revised in 2015)	Regulations of regional levels	MoST and others
Various IPRs	Anti-Monopoly Law of the PRC (adopted in 2008)	Provisions on the Prohibition of the Abuse of IPRs to Eliminate or Restrain Competition (adopted in 2015); Guidelines on General Conditions and Procedures for the Exemption of Monopoly Agreements (adopted in 2016)	SAMR
Various IPRs	The General Principles of Civil Law (adopted in 1986); The General Principles of Civil Code (adopted in 2016); Contract Law (adopted in 1999); Property Law (adopted in 2007); Administrative Licensing Law (adopted in 2003); various other laws and rules (e.g., on technology import and export, technical standards involving IPR, trade fairs, data privacy, regulatory data protection, domain names, Internet security, e-commerce, etc.)		

Source Review of Chinese laws and regulations
Note "PRC" is the full official name of mainland China (the People's Republic of China); SAMR was established near the end of 2018. However, SAIC, AQSIQ, and CFDA are still performing their previously-assigned duties at the time we wrote this book

the same time, foreign firms, governments, and other actors still help shape China's IP regime.

China's core IP laws, their implementing regulations, and supporting judicial interpretations establish IPR protection in China. They establish rules defining types of IP rights available in China, the substantive and procedural requirements to prosecute these rights, the exclusive power and limitations of the rights, the way to determine the ownership of the rights, and the rules to enforce the rights via judicial or administrative channels. Different state agencies at the central, provincial, and local levels have been set up according to these laws to oversee their administration (see Chaps. 6 and 7).

Meanwhile, various laws that govern IP rights more generally have also been adopted and revised in China to better support a knowledge-based economy. These laws include, for example, the Law on Scientific and Technological Progress, Law on Promotion of Transformation of Scientific and Technological Achievement, and Anti-Monopoly Law.

In 2018, a significant change took place to the governance of enforcement of these IP laws and regulations: the launch of a new government agency, the State Administration for Market Regulation (SAMR). SAMR was launched on April 10th 2018 to take over various IP administrative enforcement affairs which used to be separately governed by SIPO, the State Administration for Industry & Commerce (SAIC), General Administration of Quality Supervision, Inspection and Quarantine (AQSIQ), the China Food and Drug Administration (CFDA), and their local bureaus.

SAIC, AQSIQ, and CFDA will be gradually absorbed into SAMR. Also, SIPO—with the new name "China National IP Administration" (CNIPA)—will be an affiliate of SAMR. Meanwhile, the functions of the three previous antitrust agencies—i.e. merger review under the Anti-monopoly Bureau from Ministry of Commerce (MOFCOM), price-related antitrust investigations under the National Development and Reform Commission (NDRC), and non-price related investigations under the State Administration for Industry and Commerce (SAIC)—have also been consolidated under SAMR. The Standardization Administration of the PRC (SAC), which helps govern standards involving IP, will also be consolidated under SAMR.

2.2 IP Laws Still Deserving Reform

Despite the many changes made to China's IP laws and implementing regulations to date, there are certain legal provisions that we, many firms, and academics believe can be reformed in order to better foster innovation and entrepreneurship in China. This chapter briefly outlines these areas of the law. It is divided into laws we believe should be reformed as a matter of first priority to better enable innovation, and laws which could be reformed as a matter of second priority. Several important IP policies, regulations, and other measures are not mentioned in this chapter because they do not constitute statutory laws; however, many of these also deserve reform and therefore are mentioned in the next chapters of this book.

2.2.1 *First Priority Challenges for Innovation*

2.2.1.1 Patent Law

Since 2012 SIPO has released several draft revisions to China's Patent Law (Luginbuehl and Ganea 2014). Revisions proposed in 2015 garnered significant attention. A non-exhaustive list of key proposed revisions in 2015 includes: allowing protection for partial designs, and extending protection for designs to 15 years in line with Hague Convention obligations; development of a patent information service where patentees can identify patents they are willing to license; and other articles related to better promoting commercialization of patents via provisions to facilitate commercialization practices of universities, provisions governing licensing of patents, including on fair, reasonable and non-discriminatory (FRAND) terms, and usage of patent pledges. A range of provisions meant to improve enforceability of patents are discussed, including expanding judicial power regarding claims and evidence to determine the amount of compensation where the infringer does not provide information or provides false books and information; expanding enforcement powers afforded to administrative officials to confiscate infringement-related accounting documents among other materials and themselves impose fines for infringement (i.e. where illegal turnover $\geq$ 50,000 RMB, a fine of more than the value of the illegal turnover and less than five times the value of the turnover, and where no illegal turnover or illegal turnover < 50,000 RMB, a fine of up to 250,000 RMB); increasing compensation up to 3 million RMB for intentional infringement of patent rights; joint liability provisions for contributory infringers, "inducing" infringers, and Internet Service Providers (ISPs) engaging in indirect infringement; punitive damages for patent "counterfeiting" (i.e. passing-off) in line with the aforementioned thresholds; and expanded police power to prosecute and pursue criminal prosecution against infringement and passing-off. Other provisions aim to improve oversight of patent attorneys. Additionally, the draft includes several incremental efforts to improve patent quality, including through reform of Patent Re-Examination Board (PRB) practices to encourage the board to be more active in assessing quality of patents, and minor reforms to requirements relating to utility models.

The proposed revisions to the draft law in 2015 have been greeted with mixed sentiments from stakeholders. A number of the provisions are well received by stakeholders from industry, universities, PRIs, and academia. Such provisions include but are not limited to the extended protection for designs, increase of infringement damages, indirect infringement provisions, and mechanisms to promote patent commercialization (Yi 2017). However, there are several controversial provisions in the law that may undermine investment in innovation in China.

The most significant concern with the 2015 draft patent law is that it provides provincial/local administrative IP enforcement authorities expanded power to determine intentional patent infringement and issue binding orders in patent infringement disputes, including monetary fines and confiscation. Industry is concerned that this expansion runs counter to the private right nature of the patent system and international practice that emphasizes formal judicial protection of patent rights (Lee and Li 2016). More specifically, this expansion of power of the subnational IP enforcement authorities, which is otherwise restricted to patent passing-off in the current law, is feared because many local administrative enforcement authorities still suffer from a lack of technical knowledge about patents, and expanding their powers could increase the costs of flawed judgements in the form of misappropriation, direct costs, and/or transactions costs in appealing legal decisions.

More generally, the recent trend to expand administrative enforcement power in various IP disputes has been criticized by many observers (e.g., Zhang 2012, 2013; Qin and Ma 2015). This being said, currently many foreign and domestic firms benefit from at least a basic degree of administrative IP enforcement in China, and actually prefer it to judicial enforcement (discussed further in Chap. 7).

Another significant concern regards a proposed provision (Article 85) in the 2015 draft Patent Law establishing that if a patentee participating in the formulation of a compulsory national standard fails to disclose its standard essential patents (SEPs) related to the standard, it will de facto be considered to license its SEP to the standard implementer. Also, it is specified that the SEP royalty should be decided by the SEP owner and standard implementer, but if this negotiation fails SIPO may be asked to make a decision about the royalty rate. Although intended to prevent the hold-up of implementation of technical standards, this article is riddled with ambiguous language, which creates significant uncertainty and therefore may hamper patent commercialization and, in effect, innovation, to some extent (Zhang et al. 2017). Moreover, it is arguable that the provision may violate the 'case by case' doctrine in the TRIPs Agreement (Zhang 2016).

Additionally, the article in the 2015 draft Patent Law introducing joint liability provisions for ISPs might cause uncertainty for firms because it directly introduces a "notice and take down" rule from the Copyright Law without considering the difficulty of determining the technical feature of patents when investigating suspected products. Lacking a corresponding "counter notice and replacement" rule (which is present in the Copyright Law), the application of the proposed rule in the draft Patent Law may render the "notice and remove" rule a de facto preliminary injunction on Internet business platforms. This would constitute a burdensome provision for online merchants, significantly increasing their costs of doing business in China (Wang 2016).

As this book was being finalized, the State Council approved a new draft amendment to the patent law on December 5th 2018 (State Council 2018). This amendment still needs to be approved by the National People's Congress (NPC) in order to become law and it is possible that the NPC could make further revisions to the draft law beforehand. When passed by the NPC, the amendment will constitute the fourth substantive revision to China's patent law. Responding to criticism from stakeholders, the 2018 draft contains some of provisions in the draft revision of 2015 while removing some, but not all, of the controversial ones mentioned above.

Main amendments to the current Patent Law in the 2018 draft include the following aspects:

(1) Improve the patent granting system

The new draft proposes to extend the term of patent right for design rights from 10 to 15 years to meet the need for China to accede to the Hague Agreement on the protection for designs; to establish a domestic priority system for patent application for designs according to which any applicant who files a patent application for a design of the same subject matter within six months from the date of filing his first patent application for the design in China may enjoy the priority of the first-filed application for design; and to optimize the priority claiming procedure to relax the time limit for the patent applicant to submit a copy of the first patent application documents.

(2) Strengthen the protection of legitimate rights and interests of patentees

The new draft introduces a system for extending the term of patents on innovative pharmaceutical inventions, whereby the State Council may decide to extend the term of such patent rights to compensate for the time spent during the administrative review and approval of listing innovative drugs if an application is made to list the innovative drug in China and abroad simultaneously. The extension period shall not exceed five years and the total remaining effective term of patent after the listing of the innovative drug shall not exceed fourteen years.

The new draft proposes to extend the statute of limitations concerning the patent infringement from two years to three years and to increase the compensation for patent infringements. Regarding the latter provision, for intentional patent infringement where the circumstances are serious the amount of compensation may be determined to be one to five times the amount calculated according to the loss suffered by the right holder, the benefit obtained by the infringer or the patent license fee. When the amount of compensation is difficult to calculate, the statutory compensation that the court may determine at its discretion increases from between RMB 10,000 and 1,000,000 (as stipulated in the current Patent Law) to between RMB 100,000 and 5,000,000. The new draft also proposals to improve rules on burden of proof. For example, in order to determine the amount of compensation, where the patentee has made best efforts to provide evidence yet the accounting books and materials related to the infringement are primarily controlled by the infringer, the people's courts may order the infringer to provide the books and materials related to the infringement. Where the infringer does not provide this information or provides false information, the people's court may determine the amount of compensation with reference to the claim of, and the evidence provided by, the patentee.

Administrative enforcement of patent rights is also one focus of the new draft. In the new draft, patent administrative authorities have power to investigate patent infringement activities and take measures such as interviewing involved parties, inspecting suspicious areas and products, duplicating relevant materials and so on. The patent administrative authorities under the State Council may also, at the request of the patentee or interested parties, handle patent infringement disputes that have significant nationwide impact; the local patent administrative authorities, when handling patent infringement disputes at the request of the patentee or interested party, may combine cases in which the same patent right is infringed in the administrative jurisdiction. Patent administrative authorities under a higher-level people's government can also be requested to handle cases involving infringement of the same patent right across jurisdictions.

Circumstances under which joint liability for ISPs for internet infringement is determined have been further clarified in the new draft. A patentee or interested party may notify the ISP to take necessary steps to remove website link(s) to the infringing product according to the judgment, ruling, mediation issued by the people's court or the order made by the patent administrative authorities. Where the ISP fails to take necessary measures in a timely manner, that ISP is jointly liable for direct or indirect infringement.

(3) Promote the utilization of patents

Proposals have been made in the 2018 draft to improve the incentive mechanism for inventors, designers and the patent granting system, strengthen public services for patents, provide more convenience for the acquisition and implementation of patent rights, stimulate a desire to innovate, and promote invention-creation. Provisions clarify an entity's right to dispose of service inventions and its right to the application and patent according to law; to strengthen patent commercialization services of the patent administrative department under the State Council and local people's governments (i.e., to improve the patent information public services system, provide basic data on patent information, and promote the dissemination and utilization of patent information as well as the implementation and application of patents). Other provisions establish a patent open licensing system according to which the patentee may declare in a written statement to the patent administrative department under the State Council that he/she is willing to permit anyone to implement his/her patent; under this system, the patentee should specify the payment method and license fees, and the patent administrative department under the State Council should make an announcement and implement an open license, and anyone interested in an open-licensed patent may obtain a license after he notifies the patentee in written statement and pays the license fee in accordance with the announced payment method and rate. Meanwhile, according to the 2018 draft patent law, the principles of honesty during patent prosecution and commercialization should be followed and patentees should not abuse patent rights to damage public interests, damage the legitimate rights and interests of others, or to excessively exclude or restrict competition.

On one hand, several parts of the 2018 draft amendment may better enable innovation compared to the 2015 draft amendment. First, the 2015 provision on compulsory licensing of SEPs has been abandoned by the State Council in the 2018 draft, which is a positive development. Second, the power of administrative authorities to impose fines and confiscate suspected goods in patent infringement disputes has been abandoned in the 2018 draft. Third, the controversial introduction of the "notice and take down" rule from the Copyright Law into the 2015 draft has been clarified as involving submission of effective decisions, ruling, conciliation and order from courts or administrative agents. Fourth, to harmonize the rules in various IP laws, the statute of limitations of patent infringement has been extended from two years to three years, which offers a better position to patentees to seek relief, including damages, from the courts. Fifth, the addition of a domestic priority system for design patent applications along with provisions for optimizing the priority claiming procedure might help stimulate innovation in the design industry. Further, the system for extending the patent terms for innovative pharmaceutical inventions, if indeed verified to be truly innovative, could also facilitate innovation in the drug industry.

On the other hand, several changes to the 2018 draft amendment vis-à-vis the 2015 amendment may only marginally, or not at all, better enable innovation. First, the provision granting additional powers to subnational IP administrative enforcement bodies still exists in Article 69 and 70 of 2018 draft, although (as mentioned above) explicit mention of the power to impose fines and confiscate suspected goods in patent infringement disputes has been removed. Second, ambiguity exists about how the "notice and take down" rule in the 2018 draft law should be applied. This ambiguity exists despite the helpful specification in the 2018 draft that patentees should submit valid judicial decisions or administrative decisions to the ISP when asking for a "take down". Given the time required to receive an effective decision, the new requirement to submit valid decisions before requesting taking down could itself become a notable hurdle for the efficient enforcement of patent rights. Third, the 2018 draft's exclusion of the provision in the 2015 draft allowing partial designs to be patented may somewhat lessen enthusiasm for innovation in design-intensive industries. Fourth, several articles in the 2018 draft are still vague about various aspects of the patent system, including the proposed discretionary privileges of an entity to dispose its service inventions, the open patent licensing system, and patent misuse (Zhang 2019a, b).

While other areas of the latest draft Patent Law potentially deserving rethinking, none appear to as significantly challenge the conduciveness of China's environment for innovation as the aforementioned issues.

2.2.1.2 Anti-unfair Competition Law

The main governing rule of trade secrets protection is Article (interchangeable "Art." hereafter) 10 of China's Anti-Unfair Competition Law. Similar to the law in many other jurisdictions around the world, the provision lays down the definition of trade secrets and punishable activities that infringe trade secrets. If these infringement activities are serious enough, criminal punishment can be imposed according to Art. 219 of China's Criminal Code.

There are a number of ambiguities in China's trade secret regime that could be corrected with procedural and evidential rules flanking the Anti-Unfair Competition Law (Kong 2016). One major issue to be dealt with is the so-called second disclosure (i.e., unwanted disclosure after the initial infringement) of trade secrets during litigation (Higher People Court of Jiangsu Province and Liu 2018). There is no clear rule explaining the scope of disclosure of information necessary for trade secrets during litigation cases. This hinders the effective enforcement of trade secrets.

Another longstanding concern for trade secret right holders in China involves how to acquire evidence from alleged infringers. Without such evidence, which is normally only in the hands of alleged infringers, it is impossible to prove damages.

China's Anti-Unfair Competition Law was promulgated 25 years ago in an age where the Internet and a number of technologies and practices commonly used in business today were not ubiquitous. Many Chinese courts, therefore, frequently cite the general principle (Art.2) of the original law as the foundation of their rulings. However, new types of unfair competition activities not clearly captured within that principle have emerged since the law was first introduced. This dynamic leads to uncertainty in the application of the Anti-Unfair Competition Law in China.

This situation has to some extent, but not fully, been addressed by a few revised articles in the newly amended Anti-Unfair Competition Law which became effective on January 1st 2018. These include: (i) the Internet unfair competition clause (Article 12) which prohibits a competitor from using technical means in an Internet platform to interfere with the choice of service users and the business of other operators; (ii) prohibiting the use of various market identities such as package, trade dress, trade name, logo, penname, domain names and so on to confuse the consumer (Article 6); and (iii) expanding the scope of commercial bribery to cover third parties that may also affect online transactions in a covert way (Article 7).

According to the Anti-Unfair Competition Law before 2018, the cap on statutory damages against unfair competition in China was only 1 million RMB, which is much lower than those afforded in China's Trademark Law (3 million RMB). Given that almost all the courts in China apply statutory damages in unfair competition cases even though unfair competition activities sometimes cause more significant damages to firms, the cap on statutory damages for unfair competition cases in China has been increased to 3 million RMB by the newly amended Anti-Unfair Competition Law in 2018 to better discourage unfair competition activities. This is a positive development that should better deter trade secret misappropriation. However, the positive effect of this legislative effort might be significantly lessened if judicial branches still prefer low statutory damages in the actual enforcement stage.

Another problematic issue involves the enforcement mechanisms for the Anti-Unfair Competition Law. Many state agencies in China are still involved in enforcing laws against unfair competition activities in various industries (Article 4). This leads to different standards in China for enforcing unfair competition matters. Meanwhile, there is no stipulation on the administrative responsibility of certain stakeholders and witnesses (Article 28), which makes the investigation of cases difficult. (AIC of Jinan City 2018). This is a significant challenge that increases transaction costs incurred by firms in China trying to enforce their rights. Further discussion on related IP enforcement issues can be found in Chap. 7.

As this book was in the final stages of proofing, on April 23rd 2019 the NPC passed several revisions to the Anti-Unfair Competition Law (effectively immediately) that improve China's regime for trade secret protection. (The speed with which these changes were made appears to at least partially be in response to continued pressure from the US and other nations for IP reform in China.) First, the revised law stipulates that not only "business operators" but also individual legal persons and unincorporated units can be held liable for trade secret infringement. Second, the new law provides slightly more detail about what can be considered a trade secret. Third, the revised law includes new types of trade secret misappropriation: (i) "hacking" to acquire trade secrets and (ii) "abetting, inducing, or assisting in" the breach of confidentiality related to trade secrets. Fourth, the revised law raises the ceiling on damages available in trade secret infringement cases. In instances of "malicious" trade secret infringement, punitive damages are now available up to five times the amount of the illegal gains of the infringers or the real loss of the right holder. Further, the cap on statutory damages in civil cases and administrative penalties involving trade secret infringement have been increased from 3 million RMB to 5 million RMB. Sixth, the revised law reverses the burden of proof in civil trade secret litigation. Rather than the onus to prove infringement primarily falling on the plaintiff, it is now up to the defendant to prove that no infringement was committed if the plaintiff is able to show at least prima facie evidence that measures were taken to protect the secrecy of the information in dispute, shows that the alleged infringer had access to the trade secret in dispute, and demonstrates substantial similarity between the trade secret in dispute and the allegedly infringing information. Collectively, these amendments somewhat address some of the challenges to optimal trade secret enforcement previously mentioned, for example regarding difficulties acquiring evidence from infringers and overly narrow definitions of types of trade secret infringements, and otherwise help improve China's trade secret regime. However, some of aforementioned concerns (regarding secondary disclosure, different enforcement standards across government agencies, different enforcement standards in practice, and perhaps some newly emerging types of trade secret misappropriation not covered in the law) still do not appear fully addressed in the revisions.

2.2.1.3 Upov '91

China is currently a member of the International Union for the Protection of New Varieties of Plants (UPOV) 1978 Convention (UPOV '78); however, it has yet to accede to the UPOV 1991 Convention (UPOV '91). The UPOV '91 agreement provides far more appropriability and, in some ways, higher standards for plant varieties protection (PVP) than UPOV '78. It does this by providing (i) a much wider scope of protectable plant specifies and genera; (ii) a longer minimum duration of protection for PVP; (iii) limiting the so-called "breeder's exemption"; (iv) extended scope of PVP-related activities, for example stocking of protected breeding material; and (v) restricting (although there is some room for flexibility) farmers from reusing harvested plant varieties (the "farm-saved seed/farmers' privilege provisions). Our consultations with foreign plant breeders' associations and individual breeders, and some large Chinese firms, indicate that China's lack of accession to UPOV '91 limits their willingness to invest in transfer and development of cutting-edge plant varieties in China. This finding is broadly corroborated by the limited empirical scholarly literature on the subject, for example Srinivasan (2004) who finds that accession to newer PVP laws may create an appropriability environment more conducive to innovation. In effect, China's lack of accession to UPOV '91 (or at least core components thereof) may limit innovation and potential spillovers in a variety of sectors that are potentially important for economic growth in China, including agriculture, new energy, and biotechnology.

China's MoA (as of 2018, "MoARA") governs the majority of PVP in China and SFA (as of 2018, "SAFG") governs PVP on trees, vines, and several other types of plants. In 2017, MoA and SFA completed a major year-long study on the potential impacts of accession to UPOV '91 on the agriculture and forestry sectors in China (MoA & SFA 2017). Several findings from MoA & SFA (2017) were reached: First, it was agreed that accession to UPOV '91 will likely increase trade and breeding innovation in China, and that, in turn, this would contribute to economic development in China. Second, however, it was said that China is not in a position to fully accede to UPOV '91 in the immediate future for several reasons. These reasons include: (i) lack of clarity in the definition of "essentially derived varieties" (EDV) in UPOV '91, which makes it difficult to institutionalize in China; (ii) concern that despite including exceptions for royalty payments, UPOV '91 may still harm small farmers and small businesses in China; (iii) limited awareness among many entities in China about the full scope of impacts of UPOV '91, which make these entities reluctant to support the agreement; and (iv) concern about the institutional costs that Chinese state agencies will incur as a result of China's accession to UPOV '91 (e.g., in terms of processing new PVP applications for multiple species, instituting the ambiguous concept of EDV, etc.).

Third, despite the reluctance of MoA and SFA to recommend full-on accession to UPOV '91 in the near term, they did provide suggestions for a way forward towards UPOV '91 accession. They suggested that (i) in the near-term China will seriously explore expanding their UPOV commitments—for example, by adopting UPOV '78 plus-style provisions/piloting important aspects of UPOV '91 (e.g., instituting EDV for certain types of plant varieties) in order to see how the system works in practice. They also suggested that (ii) China will continue exploring several ways to strengthen its PVP system under the framework via further international cooperation initiatives.

Overall, as a result of the aforementioned research, MoA and SFA expressed an intention to formulate a long-term plan to gradually satisfy key requirements of UPOV '91. It would seem that MoA's and SFA's piloting aspects of UPOV '91 would send a signal to plant breeders worldwide that China is serious about encouraging development of innovative varieties of plants and industries reliant on such innovations.

2.2.1.4 Law on Scientific & Technological Progress

The Law on Scientific and Technological Progress (LSTP), which was last amended in 2007, is intended to help develop science and technology (S&T) in China via governing S&T inputs, public institutions carrying out R&D, incentives for S&T, and certain reward systems for innovation. Our consultations suggest that Article 20 and 21 in the law may be hampering the willingness of foreign firms to participate in state-funded research in China, and thereby contribute potentially valuable innovations and spillover opportunities for domestic Chinese entities. The provisions include broad allowances for the Chinese government to claim ownership of publicly-funded research if it is in the "public interest, national security interest, or national interests", and require that if ownership of IP resulting from government-funded research is to be transferred to foreign entities or is to be exclusively licensed to foreign entities then the government should first approve such a transaction.[1] By way of comparison, the US has "march-in rights" in its equivalent of the LSTP, the Bayh-Doyle Act, which allow the state to govern licensing of inventions resulting from state-funded research. However, firms we talked with reported that, given the wide discretion afforded to the Chinese state in the LSTP, the Chinese state is more likely to exercise march-in rights. To date, no federal US agency has ever exercised march-in rights under the Bayh-Doyle Act (Thomas 2016).

There are some other areas of the LSTP that could be improved to better promote patent commercialization in China, which are discussed in Chap. 4 of this book. That chapter also discusses some aspects of the Law on the Promotion of the Transformation of Scientific and Technological Achievements (LPTSTA), which is a subordinate law to the LSTP and could be reformed to better promote patent commercialization in China.

2.2.2 *Second Priority Challenges for Innovation*

2.2.2.1 Trademark Law

China's Trademark Law has experienced three revisions since 1982. The last revision in 2014 introduces, amongst other changes, sound mark protection, streamlines the application process for trademarks, provides greater protection to well-known marks, revises the fair use and prior use defense doctrines, adds a likelihood of confusion analysis for infringement of similar marks or goods, and imposes harsher penalties on infringers. It also highlights the importance of cracking down on bad faith trademark filing and infringement activities by adding a new section in Art.7 of the law stipulating that "The registration and use of a trademark [in China] must be in good faith". The 2014 amendment to the trademark law further prohibits trademark agents from registering a mark if they know, or should know, that their client is seeking to register the mark in bad faith (Art.19).

Despite these largely positive revisions, there are still some aspects of China's trademark law that create an uncertain legal environment for firms, which raises their

[1] Article 15 of the Interim Provisions on the Administration of IPR of Major National S&T Projects provides some clarity on circumstances under which Article 20 and 21 of the LSTP will be applied, although further clarity could still be provided.

costs of innovating. The law requires clarifications in statute or judicial interpretations regarding the following major issues:

(i) The scope of the likelihood of confusion analysis for determining trademark infringement is vague. Due to differing understandings about the concept of likelihood of confusion, many inconsistent decisions have been made by Chinese courts in recent years. For example, in original equipment manufacturer (OEM) cases where the suspected goods unauthorizedly bear the same mark (i.e., typical double-identity cases/cases involving identical marks and identical goods) and are only sold abroad, some Chinese courts rule in favor of the manufactures and exporters based on the fact that no goods are sold in the domestic Chinese market and therefore no "confusion" can occur in China. Other courts rule in favor of the trademark right holder and grant injunctions without damages or with low damages. These conflicting approaches to applying the trademark law create great legal uncertainty in the Chinese market.
(ii) The good faith principle is not actively applied in cases in China and therefore does not sufficiently dis-incentivize bad faith activities. Some trademark applicants prosecute significant numbers of trademarks only with an intent to racketeer other market players by taking advantage of the notice-and-take down rule of many e-commerce platforms (Liu et al. 2017). Meanwhile, certain bad faith activities are not punished by the court under the good faith principle. These activities include registering a well-known foreign trademark or the name of a celebrity under the shield of first-to-file doctrine, or relying on dominant market position to quickly spread the use of third parties' prior registered trademarks.
(iii) Courts sometimes misuse certain judicial guidance such as the co-existence of trademark doctrine or market structure doctrine according to which likelihood of confusion analysis they believe should lend the most weight to a competitor's market share at the time of litigation. This weakens the faith factor at the time of trademark application. This dynamic is exhibited in the Boss v. Bosssunwen case (Zhang and Zhang 2017).

As this book was in the final stages of proofing, on April 23rd 2019 the NPC passed several revisions to the Trademark Law (effective on November 1st 2019) that improve China's trademark regime. First, the revised law raises the ceiling on damages available in trademark infringement cases. In instances of "malicious" trademark infringement, the revised law allows imposition of punitive damages up to five times the amount of the illegal gain of the infringers or the real loss to the right holder. Further, the revised law raises the cap of statutory damages possible in civil cases from 3 million RMB to 5 million RMB. Second, the revised law stipulates that goods with counterfeit registered-trademarks and tools primarily used to manufacture these goods should be destroyed without any compensation. Third, the revised law introduces new provisions meant to deter bad faith trademark filings and litigation. The law allows the China Trademark Office to reject bad faith trademark filings when it is apparent that there is no intention to actually use such trademarks. Further, the law allows the responsible authorities to punish, with warnings and/or administrative fines, bad faith trademark applicants; and the law allows courts to punish bad faith trademark litigation. These new revisions can help create an environment more conducive to innovation and entrepreneurship. However, the legal standards in China for determining confusion, bad faith, and trademark use remain vague, and therefore if clarified could better facilitate innovation and entrepreneurship.

2.2.2.2 Copyrights

China's Copyright Law is now undergoing its third amendment. More than ten drafts have been created to date, some of which were published for public comments.

Limitations on the scope of copyright protection in China is a significant concern for innovative firms in many industries. According to the present law, performers do not have the right to collect remuneration for the renting and use of their "audiovisual works". Record producers cannot claim remuneration if a phonogram they own is broadcasted or publicly performed. And "photographic works" can only be protected for 50 years starting from the date of first publication, which is a shorter duration than that allowed for other types of works (whose protection period is normally the lifetime of the author plus 50 years). Further, works of applied art are not clearly recognized as one specific type of work protected by copyright.

There are notable legal uncertainties surrounding the commercialization or exploitation of copyrights in China, which raises their costs of innovating. For example, there are many "orphan works" in today's Internet-intensive economy, but there are no rules in China about how to acquire licenses for these works, exploit them and deposit remuneration for these rights. There is a closed list of twelve types of behaviors in the present provision governing fair use of copyrights (Art. 22 of the Copyright Law) which is not flexible enough to cover all relevant types of what should be considered fair use. Also, copyright users seldom pay remuneration according to provisions on mandatory licensing and it is impossible for copyright holders to benefit from a mandatory copyright licensing system without a more effective and efficient copyright collective management system (to collect royalties for copyright licenses) and a more developed regime for copyright agents.

China's copyright enforcement mechanisms are also less than optimal. For example, the cap of statutory damages for copyright infringement is only RMB 500,000, which is much lower than that for infringement in the Patent Law and Trademark Law. These low damages often cannot even cover the litigation cost incurred by copyright holders trying to adjudicate their rights in China. This limitation and the difficulty of proving copyright infringement dis-incentivizes enforcement of copyrights in China, which in turn can dis-incentivize various innovative activities in China.

2.2.2.3 Geographical Indications

The Chinese state has started to protect GIs since China acceded to the Paris Convention on the Protection of Industrial Property in March 1985. In December 1994,

SAIC issued, and revised in 2003, the Measures for the Registration and Administration of Collective Marks and Certification Marks which allowed GIs to be protected as certification marks in China.[2]

Before the establishment of the SAMR in April 2018, at the administrative level, SAIC/TMO, AQSIQ, MoA, and SFA all had the power to protect and register GIs. These agencies supervised and protected different GIs/different aspects of GIs. SAIC and TMO protected GIs as trademark rights; AQSIQ certified the quality of production process and related production standards when registering GIs; MoA focused on GI protection of most agricultural products; and SFA focused on the GI protection of forestry products.

Over time, various revisions have been made by different agencies to China's regime for GI protection. In August 1999, AQSIQ issued the Regulations on the Protection of Appellations of Origin Products and started to receive and approve registrations of GIs. In 2005, AQSIQ issued new Regulations on the Protection of GI Products and abolished the previous regulation. In 2016, AQSIQ issued the Measures on the Protection of Foreign GI Products to ensure that foreign GIs and domestic GIs receive equal protection in China. However, the number of GIs registered at AQSIQ is much lower than that at TMO. In December 2007, MoA issued the Administrative Measures of GIs of Agricultural Products and expanded its authority to govern the certification of GIs; it was later responsible for the registration of GIs of agricultural products. Following MoA's expansion of administrative power, SFA also drafted a similar regulation but it is not yet in effect.

The overlapping GIs administrative system in China caused significant confusion among businesses and other actors in China's NIS. Few firms can understand the differences among the disparate GI registration or certification systems in China, and different parties or even competitors registered identical GIs with different administration systems (Li 2017). The currently fragmented system of administering GIs in China is still in place at present while CNIPA and SAMR are being set-up. However, the system is slated to become more efficient, with GI registration better coordinated under CNIPA and SAMR – although still not fully streamlined. This issue is revisited in Chaps. 6 and 7.

2.2.2.4 Integrated Circuits

China's Regulations on the Protection of Layout-Designs of Integrated Circuits (RPLDIT) and its implementing rules incorporate all the main provisions from relevant international treaties, especially the Treaty on Intellectual Property in Respect of Integrated Circuits (IPIC Treaty). The TRIPS Agreement adopts the provisions in the IPIC Treaty subject to minor modifications, and therefore China's integrated circuits legislation in effect meets the requirement of TRIPs Agreement (Guo 2005).

[2]Article 16 of the present China Trademark Law (2014) defines GIs as "the signs that signify the place of origin of the goods in respect of which the signs are used, their specific quality, reputation or other features as mainly decided by the natural or cultural factors of the regions".

At the end of 2015, there were 10,861 registered layout-designs published in China. In sharp contrast to the litigation explosion witnessed for other IP rights in China, only very limited numbers of cases involving integrated circuits (less than ten cases before 2016) have been argued before courts since the promulgation of RPLDIT in 2001 (Zhu 2016). Without a corresponding judicial interpretation, development of the integrated circuits protection regime in China has been quite slow.

In our opinion and according to the stakeholders we spoke with, one shortcoming of China's regime for integrated circuits is its lack of clarity about disclosure procedures. Present rules request that applicants submit written documents, models and an e-copy (a CD) of the applied integrated circuits but do not specify which of these information sources determines the protection scope of integrated circuits. These provisions lead to some confusion in practice. As such, provisions could be added to clarify that the scope of protection of registered layout-designs should be determined solely by a written document submitted to SIPO (CNIPA). Further, it could be specified that the accompanying integrated circuits model or the e-version of the submitted written document (see Regulation 18; Implementing Rule 14 and 16) cannot be used as the "claim-like" item especially when they are inconsistent with the written document for layout-designs submitted to SIPO (CNIPA).

Another concern regarding the integrated circuits legal regime in China involves the initiation of the invalidation procedure. At present, only SIPO's Patent Reexamination Board (PRB) has the authority to initiate this procedure. This *ex officio* invalidation procedure limits the ability of the public to correct improper registration of low quality integrated circuits. Provisions could be added to the law to involve active participation of the public in this process, for example to allow the procedure to be initiated by third parties.

2.3 Regulations and Other Measures

In addition to the aforementioned statutory laws, several regulations and other IP-related measures below the level of statutory law deserve reform in order to better foster innovation in China. These measures are discussed in subsequent chapters of this book.

2.4 Summary

China has established a relatively complete legal infrastructure for IP protection over the past 30 years. During this time, China's IP laws and regulations have become increasingly conducive to innovation rather than mere imitation. Many of these aspects of China's IP regime are currently broadly in line with international standards.

However, some aspects of Chinese IP law contribute to an appropriability environment that is below optional for enabling innovation. Potentially problematic provisions in the 2018 draft Patent Law include the expansion of power for provincial/local administrative authorities to determine patent infringement and the removal of protection for partial designs present in the 2015 draft of the law. Also, the draft law is still vague about the proposed discretionary privilege of an entity to dispose of its service inventions, the approach to ISP liability, the open patent licensing system, and patent misuse.

Despite being revised in April 2019 in a number of helpful ways, there are still sub-optimal aspects of the Anti-Unfair Competition Law, which governs trade secrets and other types of unfair competition. These include lack of procedures to prevent second disclosure in litigation. The law also lacks a clear definition of "unfair competition activities", so even though the most recently revised version of the law includes a list of unfair competition activities it still does not effectively govern all potentially relevant behaviors. Meanwhile, enforcement provisions in the law, which involve different enforcement agents and administrative liabilities, are still problematic, which creates challenges in administrative enforcement of trade secrets and other types of unfair competition.

Several other Chinese IP laws offer sub-optimal appropriability for innovation and entrepreneurship. China's legal framework for plant variety protection is sub-optimal as China has not yet acceded to UPOV '91. The Law on Scientific & Technological Progress includes ambiguous provisions on situations where the state may restrict licensing of IP derived from state-funded research. In April 2019, the Trademark Law was revised to help punish serious trademark infringements and malicious/bad faith trademark registration and litigation; however, the exact standards to determine confusion, bad faith, and trademark use remain vague. Potentially sub-optimal provisions in Copyright Law include a low cap on statutory damages, limited rights for performers and record producers to collect remuneration, an unbalanced mandatory licensing system, rigid fair-use system, and lack of an effective way to exploit "orphan works". A complex web of state administration for different aspects of GIs still undermines efficient and effective protection of the rights at present, although is slated to be somewhat better streamlined after the establishment of SAMR. Potentially sub-optimal provisions in China's integrated circuits legislation include ambiguous rules on the scope of protection of integrated circuits and the ex officio invalidation procedure for the rights.

In response to these challenges, several of the aforementioned IP laws should be revised. These revisions should make the laws more optimal by increasing damages for IP infringement, expanding appropriability afforded by several of the laws, and clarifying or removing ambiguous provisions in some laws.

References

AIC of Jinan City. 2018. 贯彻新《反不正当竞争法》工作中存在的问题及对策建议 (Problems and countermeasures in implementing the new anti-unfair competition law) (in Chinese). *Journal of Business Administration*, available at http://wemedia.ifeng.com/53022039/wemedia.shtml.

Guo, H. 2005. 中国集成电路布图设计权保护评述 (Comment on the protection of layout design of integrated circuit in China) (in Chinese). *Intellectual Property* 1: 9–14.

Higher People Court of Jiangsu Province., and Y.Z. Liu. 2018. 知识产权诉讼中防范商业秘密泄露问题研究(Study on the prevention of trade secret disclosure in intellectual property litigation) (in Chinese). *Law Application* 5:107–113.

Kong, X. 2016. 商业秘密: 保护难是个突出问题 (Trade secret: The difficulty to protect is a significant problem) (in Chinese). *China Intellectual Property* 11.

Lee, N. 2015. Intellectual property law in China—From legal transplant to governance. In *Governance of intellectual property rights in China and Europe*, ed. N. Lee, N. Bruun, and M. Li, 5–19. Cheltenham, UK: Edward Elgar.

Lee and Li. 2016. Highlights of the draft amendment of China's patent law, available at https://www.lexology.com/library/detail.aspx?g=0a0c8df9-6bb7-4dda-a3bb-f1dc151a896f.

Li, S. 2017. 最高人民法院多元化纠纷解决机制改革意见和特邀调解规定的理解和适用 (Understanding and application of Supreme People's Court's Opinion of ADR Mechanism Reform and Rule of Special Invited Mediation) (in Chinese). People's Court Press.

Liu, Xiaochun, Taolue Zhang, and Hongying Zhu. 2017. 借电商平台、行商标挟持: 无显著性商标恶意投诉现状与治理研究报告 (Trademark holdup via e-commerce platform: Report on the status and regulation of malicious complaints on e-commerce platform by using non-distinctiveness trademark) (in Chinese), available at https://mp.weixin.qq.com/s?__biz=MzIxNDYzNTE3Ng%3D%3D&idx=1&mid=2247483845&sn=fc4466d807eb231c51d6e349f23635eb.

Luginbuehl, S., and P. Ganea. 2014. *Patent law in Greater China*. Cheltenham, UK: Edward Elgar.

MoA & SFA. 2017. Study on UPOV '91's potential impact on the development of agriculture and forestry in China. Unpublished report by China's Ministry of Agriculture and China's State Forestry Administration under the framework for the EU-China IP Key project.

Qin, Q., and Z.G. Ma. 2015. 论我国《专利法》修改草案(征求意见稿)中专利侵权行政执法的"得"与"失" (Comment on the pros and cons of the patent administrative enforcement provisions in the draft revision of China's patent law) (Papers of China IP Forum 2015) (in Chinese), available at http://kns.cnki.net.

Srinivasan, C.S. 2004. Plant variety protection, innovation, and transferability: Some empirical evidence. *Review of Agricultural Economics* 26: 445–471.

State Council. 2018. 关于《中华人民共和国专利法修正案(草案)》的说明 (Explanation about the draft amendment of the patent law of PRC), available at http://www.npc.gov.cn/COBRS_LFYJNEW/user/UserIndex.jsp?ID=13137851#.

Thomas, J. 2016. March-in rights under the Bayh-Dole Act. Congressional Research Service Paper 7-5700, available at https://fas.org/sgp/crs/misc/R44597.pdf.

Wang, Q. 2016. 论"通知与移除"规则对专利领域的适用性—兼评《专利法修订草案(送审稿)》第63条第2款 (Applicability of the notice and removal rule to the patent law—Also comment on article 63 (2) of the draft revision) (in Chinese). *Intellectual Property* 3: 20–32.

Yi, J.M. 2017. 专利法的转型:从二元结构到三元结构—评《专利法修订草案(送审稿)》第8章及修改条文建议 (The transformation of patent law: From dualistic structure to triadic structure—Comments on chapter VIII of the revised draft of the patent law (Draft submitted) and amendments proposals) (in Chinese). *Fa Xue Za Zhi* 7: 41–51.

Yu, P. 2007. Intellectual property, economic development, and the China puzzle. In *Intellectual property, trade and development: Strategies to optimize economic development in a TRIPs plus area*, ed. D. Gervais, 173–220. Oxford: Oxford University Press.

Zhang, W. 2012. 三大知识产权法修改接近尾声, 行政权次次扩张被批越俎代庖 (The revision of three IP laws is close to the end; repeated expansion of administrative power is criticized) (in Chinese), https://www.chinacourt.org/article/detail/2012/12/id/799875.shtml.
Zhang, T. 2013. 有关专利法第四次修订的几点意见 (Comment on the fourth amendment of the patent law of PRC) (in Chinese), http://blog.sina.com.cn/s/blog_4d7d20930101a2xf.html.
Zhang, W.J. 2016. Implied license or statutory license? On the provision of SEPs disclosure in the draft amendments to the patent law. *Journal of Tongji University (Social Science Section)* 103–116.
Zhang, W.J., and T. Zhang. 2017. "市场格局论"之辨析 (Review of market structure test in trademark disputes) (in Chinese). *Electronics Intellectual Property* 1–2:121–128, 3:80–90.
Zhang, T., D. Prud'homme., and O. Lutze. 2017. China's new patent commercialization strategy. *Journal of Intellectual Property Law & Practice* 12: 474–488.
Zhang, W.J. 2019a. 聚焦《专利法(修正案草案)》: 滥用专利权条款解析以及修改建议 (Focusing on the draft amendment of patent law: Analyzing the patent right misuse provision and proposed revision), available at https://mp.weixin.qq.com/s/YOgmcVRRRhZQxKESmMazrg.
Zhang, W.J. 2019b. 聚焦《专利法(修正案草案)》: 仅出于自愿的开放许可会带来促进技术转化的效果吗? (Focusing on the draft amendment of patent law: Can open licensing alone based on willingness stimulate the commercialization of technologies), available at https://mp.weixin.qq.com/s/QnplEAZY2NVLtGs19Lj1bw.
Zhu, J. 2016. 对集成电路布图设计专有权司法保护有关问题的思考 (Comment on the problems of judicial protection of layout design of integrated circuit) (in Chinese). *Intellectual Property* 9: 38–44.

Chapter 3
Chinese Patenting Trends and the Role of the State

Patenting figures are commonly used as a proxy of technological-knowledge creation (Griliches 1990; Nagaoka et al. 2010). However, while patent applications are indicators of invention, they are not necessarily good indicators of innovation; and not all inventions are patentable in the first place. Further, patents are only one of several methods for firms to effectively appropriate economic returns from their technological investments, and sometimes are not the most effective tools for doing so (e.g., Teece 1986; Cohen et al. 2000). With this in mind, this chapter looks at trends in Chinese patent quantity as well as Chinese patent "quality", which is one way to measure the extent to which patents reflect innovation. The role of the Chinese state in influencing patent quantity and quality is also explored.

This chapter does not assess the value of "strategic patenting" in China at length; however, it does briefly mention how such patenting should be considered in the context of China's attempts to catch up with forerunners.[1] Strategic patenting is controversial because, on one hand, it can sometimes undermine the willingness of firms to invest in innovation. On the other hand, strategic patents may serve as economically valuable intangible assets to firms.

3.1 Chinese Patenting Trends: An Overview

3.1.1 Domestic Filings

Over the last decade, the number of applications for all three types of patents available in China (invention patents, utility models, and designs) has risen substantially (see Fig. 3.1). In fact, as of 2011, China became the world's foremost filer of domestic patent applications (Lee 2011), with SIPO accounting for 87.7% of all patents filed

[1] Strategic patenting can take a variety of forms, for example in terms of patent "bullying", "foils", cross-licensing, and "blocking" (e.g., Graham and Sichelman 2008; Sichelman and Graham 2010).

D. Prud'homme and T. Zhang, *China's Intellectual Property Regime for Innovation*, https://doi.org/10.1007/978-3-030-10404-7_3

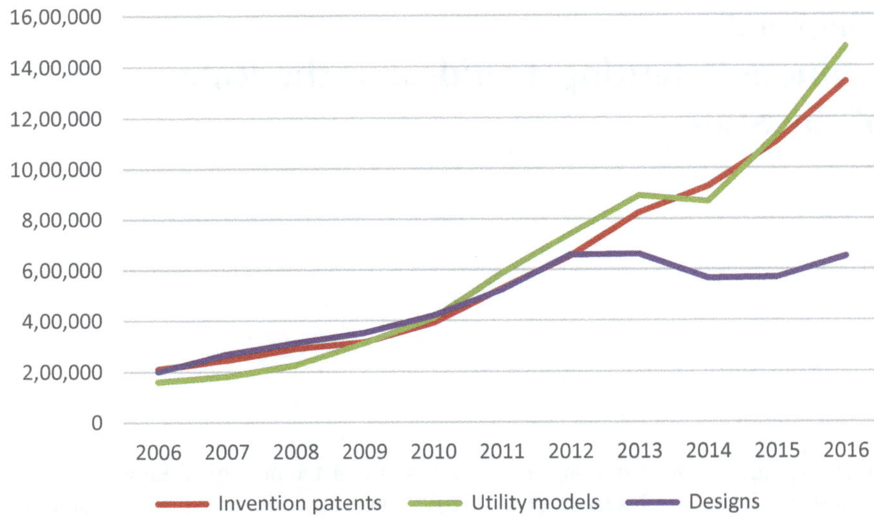

Fig. 3.1 Patent applications in China (2006–2016). *Source* SIPO statistics

in upper middle-income countries around the world in 2015 (WIPO 2016, p. 22). Applications for utility models and invention patents in particular have skyrocketed, with utility models outpacing invention patents in recent years. The implications of this trend are discussed in the section below on patent quality. At the same time, it should be noted that there was a decline then leveling off of design patenting. The reasons for this trend in designs are not fully clear, although it may reflect state initiatives to steer the economy more towards technological inventions.

Much of the invention patenting surge from Chinese entities has historically been concentrated in the information and communications technology (ICT) sector. Eberhardt et al. (2011) look at Chinese entities' invention patenting at SIPO (and the USPTO) using data from 1996–2006 and concludes that a significant portion of China's invention patenting surge has been concentrated in the ICT sector. Eberhardt et al. (2017) also reach similar conclusions. Zheng and Lan (2009) reach broadly similar conclusions, at least for a sample of top 500 firms in China, which is not particularly surprising given the high propensity to patent in ICT industries (Hall and Ziedonis 2001).

A significant amount of patenting is also occurring in other industries in China. Hu et al. (2016, pp. 111–112), using data from 2007–2011, find a drop in the proportion of both invention patents and utility models in the telecommunications equipment and computers industries (key ICT industries) in China and greater similarity in the propensity to patent across several industries. Data from the National Bureau of Statistics of China indicates a rather widely dispersed propensity to invention patent and utility model patent across a range of fields (see Fig. 3.2). With the exception of personal use items, all the major areas of technology have experienced strong growth

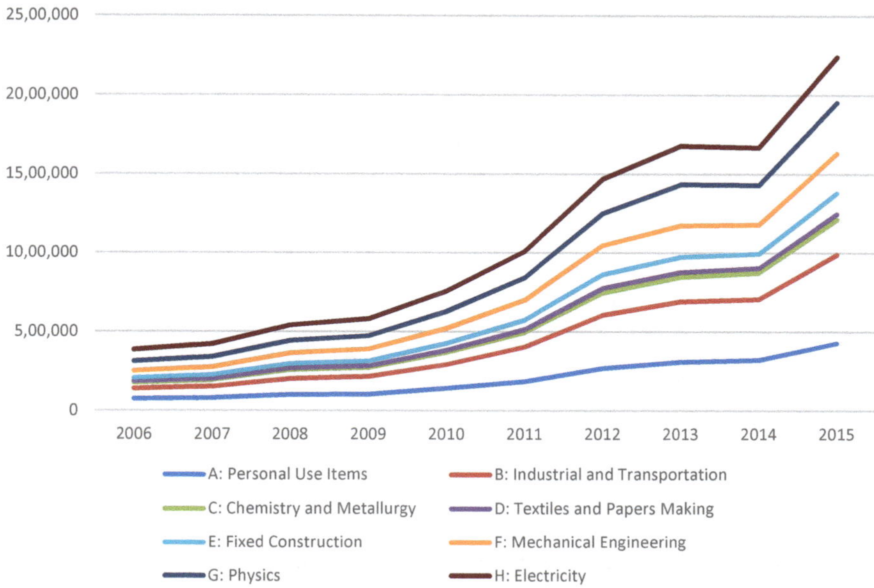

Fig. 3.2 Invention patent and utility model applications in China (2006–2015), by technology area. *Source* China's National Bureau of Statistics. Refers to invention patents and utility model applications "accepted", yet distinguished in the database from those granted. Letter refers to corresponding international patent classification (IPC) code. For details about which technologies are covered in each IPC see http://www.wipo.int/classifications/ipc/en

in the last decade, with patenting in the areas of electricity, physics, and mechanical engineering leading the way.

3.1.2 Grants

Figure 3.3 depicts the number of patents granted in China over the last decade. It shows that grants of invention patents have increased over the years, although have remained relatively stable in recent years. There has been a dramatic rise in grants of designs up until 2015, followed by a sharp drop in 2016. This at least partially reflects the decline in design patenting mentioned earlier. A concerning trend also emerges in the data: the grants of utility models in China have skyrocketed since 2015. The implications of this trend are discussed in the below section on patent quality.

Table 3.1 illustrates that China has met, and often times exceeded, the intellectual property filing targets set in the National IP Strategy (2014–2020) (which focus on patents and copyrights) for 2015. This generally indicates that the country is building some form of technological capabilities. However, Table 3.1 also illustrates that China has fallen somewhat short on a state-set target for a core indicator of patent

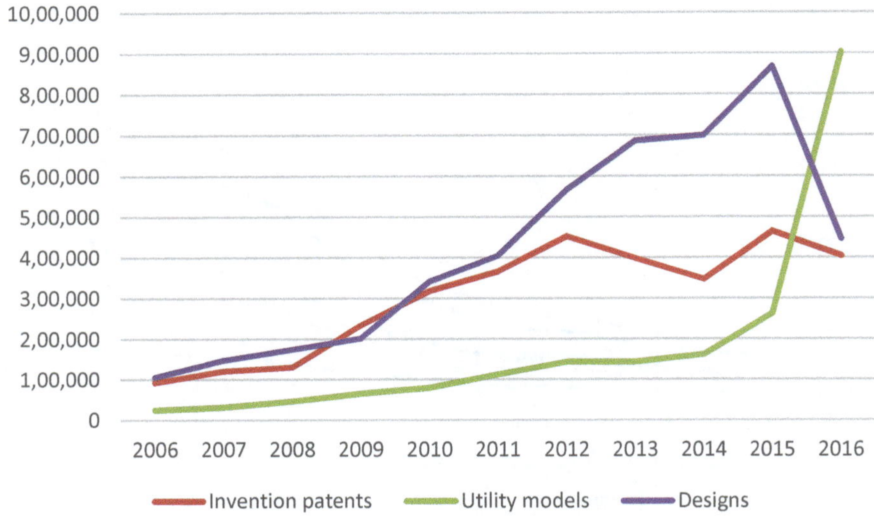

Fig. 3.3 Patents granted in China (2006–2016). *Source* SIPO statistics

Table 3.1 Progress on patenting targets from China's National IP Strategy (2014–2020)

Targets	2015—target	2015—actual
Invention patents per every 10,000 people (number)	6	6.3
Number of patent applications submitted via the PCT (in 10,000s)	3.0	3.1
Average maintenance period of domestic invention patents (in years)	6.4	6.0
Number of registered copyrights of works (in 10,000s)	90	134.8
Number of registered copyrights on computer software (in 10,000s)	17.2	29.2

Sources National Statistical Monitoring Report on Scientific and Technological Progress (2015), WIPO statistics, Report on the Development of China's IP rights in 2015, Bulletin on National Copyright Registration in 2015

quality (average maintenance time of domestic invention patents). Trends in patent quality are discussed further in the next part of this chapter.

Analysis of the regional distribution of patenting in China shows that technological and design capabilities are concentrated in a few locations in Eastern China. As shown in Table 3.2, Guangdong, Beijing, Jiangsu, Zhejiang, and Shanghai are home to the most invention patents granted in China. This reflects the large populations of these regions and their strong technological capabilities. Zhejiang, Guangdong, Jiangsu, Shandong, Shanghai, and Beijing are the source of the most utility models granted, reflecting the large populations of these areas and their abilities in making incremental improvements on existing inventions. Jiangsu, Guangdong, and Zhejiang account for 66% of all design patents granted in China, suggesting that firms in these areas are highly specialized in product design—likely owing to years of manufacturing design-intensive products.

While reflecting capabilities that can be used to drive economic growth in much of Eastern China, these figures also reflect that Central, Western, and to some extent Northern China have a notable distance to close in order to catch up with Eastern China. Despite the fast pace of industrialization nationwide, productivity (measured by GDP output/labor force) in Eastern China is nearly twice that of Central China and three times that of Western China (World Bank 2013, p. 168). This gap appears to be reflected in the regional patenting trends of Chinese firms. These trends affirm the need for Chinese state policy to improve the technological and/or design capabilities of firms situated outside Eastern China while also highlighting that a differentiated development strategy is likely needed to build on pre-existing endowments in these regions.

The increases in patenting in China are correlated with a significant positive impact on firm productivity, which can contribute to economic growth. Various studies have found that growth in utility model patenting in China is correlated with increases in labor productivity (Liu 2002; Sui et al. 2005; Huang and Yu 2007; Li 2012a). Zhao and Liu (2011) find that growth in utility model patenting in China had a significant positive impact on total factor productivity (TFP) from 1988 to 1998, and from 1999 to 2009 growth of both invention patents and utility models had significant positive impacts on TFP. Fang et al. (2016) show that an increase in the patent stock from 1998 to 2007 in Chinese firms—even if the patents had relatively low inventiveness, as utility models do—was correlated with an increase in the firms' TFP.

However, utility models may not be as useful in contributing to productivity in China as they once were at earlier stages in the country's technological development process. Hu et al. (2016) show that the correlation between filing utility models in China and labor productivity gains has become weaker over time, while Zhao and Liu (2011) find that from 1999 to 2009 growth of invention patents had a stronger positive impact on TFP in China than the growth in utility models. This evidence suggests a diminishing marginal productivity to utility models in China. Therefore, while utility models may theoretically provide some type of strategic benefit to Chinese firms, this may no longer be translating into tangible improvements in productivity which can benefit the Chinese economy. This issue is further discussed in the below discussion on patent quality in China.

Further, although firms in China generally experience increases in productivity when they patent, Chinese state-owned enterprises (SOEs) are not as efficient at generating productive innovations as private Chinese firms. On one hand, increases in the patent stock in China between the late 1990s and 2007 has contributed to productivity increases in both private Chinese firms and Chinese SOEs (Fang et al.

Table 3.2 Patent grants in China, by province (2006–2015)

Province	Annual avg. # invention patents granted	% of total inventions granted in China (%)	Growth rate % inventions granted (%)	Annual avg. # utility models granted	% of total utility models granted in China (%)	Growth rate % utility models granted (%)	Annual avg. # designs granted	% of total designs granted in China	Growth rate % of designs granted (%)
Anhui	2900	2	56	18,067	3	59	6463	2	57
Beijing	15,284	15	30	22,523	5	29	5565	2	30
Chongqing	1635	2	41	10,074	2	38	4541	2	26
Fujian	2064	2	44	13,681	3	38	9013	3	27
Gansu	533	1	29	1921	0	29	490	0	33
Guangdong	15,737	16	38	53,346	13	25	58,342	21	21
Guangxi	1021	1	46	3206	1	29	1203	0	23
Guizhou	613	1	27	2821	1	28	1821	1	50
Hainan	243	0	47	457	0	32	216	0	27
Hebei	1486	1	31	8856	2	26	2657	1	31
Heilongjiang	1808	2	28	6920	2	21	2545	1	53
Henan	2237	2	36	14,419	3	32	4456	2	25
Hubei	3083	3	30	12,580	3	29	3716	1	37
Hunan	2686	3	33	9679	2	29	4590	2	25
Inner Mongolia	363	0	29	1722	0	25	570	0	17
Jiangsu	12,154	10	45	57,007	12	39	84,044	25	48

(continued)

Table 3.2 (continued)

Province	Annual avg. # invention patents granted	% of total inventions granted in China (%)	Growth rate % inventions granted (%)	Annual avg. # utility models granted	% of total utility models granted in China (%)	Growth rate % utility models granted (%)	Annual avg. # designs granted	% of total designs granted in China	Growth rate % of designs granted (%)
Jiangxi	654	1	33	4369	1	37	2587	1	44
Jilin	1100	1	22	3158	1	17	691	0	14
Liaoning	3002	3	24	11,786	4	14	2075	1	23
Ningxia	138	0	31	540	0	29	253	0	51
Qinghai	74	0	30	219	0	38	155	0	78
Shaanxi	2908	3	34	8005	2	34	2484	1	68
Shandong	6223	6	39	40,111	10	26	8733	3	15
Shanghai	8429	9	25	21,866	6	22	11,829	5	13
Shanxi	1025	1	28	3495	1	27	912	0	38
Sichuan	3408	3	36	14,982	3	37	13,988	5	30
Tianjin	2450	3	20	11,268	2	35	2368	1	21
Tibet	28	0	45	38	0	24	58	0	20
Xinjiang	351	0	34	2346	1	25	744	0	47
Yunnan	953	1	24	2967	1	33	1088	0	20
Zhejiang	8829	8	40	61,291	14	37	59,861	20	22
Average	3336	3	34	13,668	3	30	9615	3	33

Source SIPO statistics, calculations

2016). However, on the other hand, Chinese SOEs may not be as efficient as private Chinese firms at turning resources into patentable inventions that actually generate value (World Bank 2013, pp. 170, 195; Zhou et al. 2016). In order to sustainably generate wealth through R&D or other means, firms need to develop smart and distinctive technological, organizational, and managerial processes inside the firm (Teece et al. 1997). Chinese SOEs often appear to lag in forming these dynamic capabilities.

3.1.3 Ownership

The majority of R&D expenditures in many innovative nations come from businesses, and almost 70% of such investments are spent on R&D personnel (Harhoff and Hoisl 2007). As such, service inventions—technical creations that result from an employee's duties under an employment contract, company know-how, and/or company R&D—make up the bulk of the invention stock in many innovative nations. (Non-service inventions are typically produced by individual inventors, who own the patents.) A high proportion of service inventions in an economy is a healthy indicator of innovation capacity because the business sector often drives patent commercialization whereas non-service inventions are often difficult to commercialize (e.g., Tuo 2009; Merges 1999). In fact, in many innovative nations, over 90% over the invention stock is derived from service inventions (Tuo 2009).

Put another way, firms should play a dominant role in an economy's NIS (e.g., Freeman 1987; Lundvall 1992; Nelson 1993). Firms provide critical resources for innovation that individuals going at it alone often do not have, including quality materials, equipment, collaborative inventing opportunities, marketing, and strategic direction. Further, within firms, most employee-inventions are made by teams—highlighting the importance of collaboration to innovation. For example, in Germany, over 70% of employee-inventions are made by teams of 2.5 inventors on average (Harhoff and Hoisl 2007).

Between 1985 and 2010, 45.9% of all patents filed in China (invention patents, utility models and designs) were non-service derived (54.1% were from service contracts).[2] Invention patents were far more likely to be service inventions than non-service inventions (78% were for service inventions).[3] In contrast, 60% of utility models were non-service inventions, and 56% of designs were non-service derived.[4] The section below on patent quality further discusses the implications of China's surge in utility model filings and grants derived from service-invention and non-service invention contracts. In short, the state, including provincial and local governments in China, should put further emphasis on invention patenting rather that utility

[2]See http://english.sipo.gov.cn/statistics/szslzljb/201101/t20110125_570591.html.

[3]Ibid.

[4]Ibid.

model patenting (design patenting seems to be declining), in particular non-service invention patenting.

Although the literature tells us that firms should play a strong role in patenting in a healthy NIS, beyond this there is no golden rule for what constitutes the optimal structure of patent ownership in an economy, including for foreign vs. domestic entities. In fact, innovative countries, including the US, Japan, South Korea, Germany, and the UK, adopt different approaches to technological development which are reflected in somewhat differing ownership shares of patents by foreign versus domestic entities.[5] As such, it is difficult to propose an optimal proportion of foreign versus domestic patent ownership that will enable China to transition to an innovation-driven economy. Different technological and economic development strategies have been followed in other successful economies and China can consider the merits of these approaches and how they fit with its own economic structure and state-set goals.[6]

All of this being said, it is worth noting that the share of invention patents filed by China-based entities (domestic Chinese firms and foreign affiliates in China) has risen dramatically from 47% in 2001 to 88% in 2015 (see Fig. 3.4). China-based entities currently make up the vast majority of invention patent filings in China today, which, in our opinion, represents a generally positive shift from reliance on imported and under-diffused knowledge to better transmission and exploitation of technological knowledge among firms and other entities in China (see Chap. 4 for a further discussion about transmission and exploitation of technological knowledge in China). It also may, albeit loosely, reflect rising indigenous innovation capacity.

At the same time, the majority of patents filed by China-based entities in key jurisdictions abroad are owned by foreign firms. For example, the majority of patents filed by China-based entities at the USPTO are granted to inventor teams working for foreign firms (Branstetter et al. 2014). This indicates that Chinese firms lag behind foreign MNCs in protecting their knowledge abroad through codified legal instruments. This is, to some extent, an intuitive trend and therefore not necessarily representative of any significant failure of the state to encourage indigenous innovation. Still, as part of its "going-out" (走出去战略) policy, the Chinese state may want to encourage indigenous Chinese firms to expand their appropriability via patenting more aggressively in nations such as the US.

Private enterprises in China (Chinese and foreign) patent and maintain patents far more than Chinese SOEs (see Table 3.3). This distribution of patent ownership in China between private firms and SOEs is expected (there are far more private enterprises in China than SOEs), and, generally-speaking, is a positive indication of the health of China's innovation trajectory.

---

[5]Analysis of statistics from national offices provided to WIPO here: http://www.wipo.int/ipstats/en/statistics/country_profile/.

[6]For example, Japan and Korea are well-known to have instituted laws and regulations that restricted foreign direct investment (FDI) in favor of cultivating domestic industry during their catch-up stages (e.g., Johnson 1982; Kim 1993; Morris-Suzuki 1994; Hobday 1995). In contrast, the US and UK are generally perceived to have been more open to foreign investment in modern times than Japan and South Korea. China has relied much more on FDI for its modern economic development than South Korea and Japan did for their own development (e.g., Lin 2012).

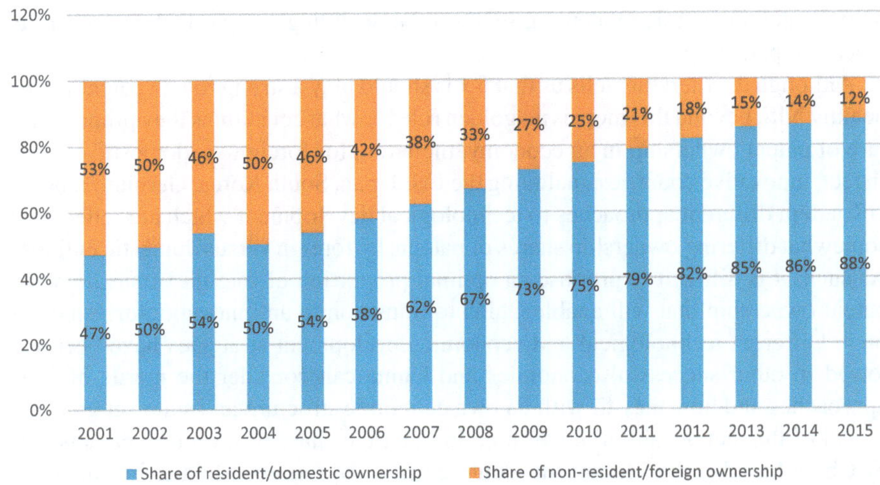

Fig. 3.4 Invention patent filings in China, by ownership type (2001–2015). *Source* SIPO statistics reported to WIPO (see http://www.wipo.int/ipstats/en/statistics/country_profile/profile.jsp?code=CN), calculations

Table 3.3 Innovation inputs and intermediate outputs, by firm ownership (2015)

Firm ownership	Full time equivalent R&D personnel (share of total) (%)	R&D expenditure (share of total) (%)	Number of invention patents in force (share of total) (%)
Domestic mainland Chinese private firms	77	77	77
Domestic mainland Chinese SOEs	3	3	3
HK, Macao, TW firms	11	9	9
Foreign firms	12	14	14

Source China Statistical Yearbook 2016, calculations. Data is for designated medium and large sized enterprises

World Bank (2013) uses the metric of a firm's share of patents in force per 100 R&D personnel in 2009 to conclude that Chinese SOEs are not as efficient as private Chinese firms at turning resources into patentable inventions that actually generate value (World Bank 2013, pp. 170, 195). However, in considering the same metric using statistics for 2015, this conclusion does not appear to be as forthcoming (see Table 3.3).[7] Nonetheless, recent empirical research using other approaches shows that Chinese SOEs are indeed less efficient at generating innovation than private Chinese firms (e.g., Zhou et al. 2016).

[7]The shortcomings of this metric (for example the lack of lag between R&D investment and patenting) should be considered.

The majority of patents owned by Chinese SOEs are utility models and designs (Prud'homme 2012). Utility models and designs in China require little and no inventiveness, respectively, and can only be protected for a fraction of the duration that invention patents can. As such, they are generally less valuable (although not necessarily without value) to firms than invention patents (Prud'homme 2012; Moga 2012). As such, it could be argued that China's SOEs, depending on the industry in which they operate (especially if they are technology-intensive), should be better incentivized/pressured to shift their patent portfolios to focusing more on invention patents.

3.1.4 Patent Quality

Although China is the foremost filer of domestic patent applications, it is not considered a leader in patent "quality". There has long been a debate about what the definition of "patent quality" should entail (e.g., Squicciarini et al. 2013; Guerrini 2014); however, generally speaking, the quality of a patent is associated with how well it is drafted (a definition often favored by patent attorneys), the extent to which it meets the legal standards for being granted (a definition often favored by legal scholars), and/or its technological and/or commercial worth (a definition often favored by economists).[8] A wide range of metrics are used to gauge patent quality.[9] The literature sometimes distinguishes patent quality from patent "value", with the latter often being measured through financial data related to patents (e.g., see OECD 2009; Munari and Oriani 2011). However, for simplicity, we use both terms interchangeably hereafter. There are a number of limitations of available patent quality metrics

[8]Perhaps one of the most fundamental economic conceptualizations of "quality" patents could be if they constitute inventions that are actually commercialized. Inventions that are not actually commercialized (which is the case for many low-quality patents), do not constitute *innovations* and therefore cannot contribute to economic growth (Schumpeter 1942).

[9]Patent quality metrics most commonly used include: (i) the lifespan of patents (whereby patents with longer lifespans are generally more valuable given that rational actors will only pay fees needed to maintain patents if they are valuable); (ii) forward citations (whereby more often cited patents are generally thought to be of higher value); (iii) size of patent families (with the logic being that patents filed in more offices internationally are generally of higher value given the costs required to do so, and the larger number of markets to which the patents are relevant); (iv) number of international patent classification (IPC) codes in which the patent is categorized (whereby the wider technological breadth is thought to make a patent more technologically impactful); (v) number of claims, including independent claims only or both independent and dependent claims (whereby a higher number of claims, especially independent claims, can indicate a more sophisticated invention which may indicate it has higher value); (vi) number of applicants (whereby a larger number of co-applicants may indicate higher value patents resulting from collaboration); and (vii) invalidation rates (whereby patents that are invalidated, as one aspect of a patent infringement lawsuit or as part of an invalidation case only, are proven to be of low quality). Yet other metrics (e.g., breadth of patent claims, backward citations in a patent to scientific and other non-patent literature (NPL), among various other measures) are sometimes used.

and therefore any individual metric should not be emphasized too heavily [for an overview of some of these limitations see Reitzig (2004), p. 941].

Proliferation of low-quality patents can restrain China's ability to transition towards an innovation-based economy. This process takes place through several interrelated mechanisms. First, an economy rife with low-quality patents is dangerously self-reinforcing because in such an environment rational firms seek more low-quality patents rather than higher-quality patents (Wagner 2009). In other words, poor patent quality creates path-dependency on inventions that do not significantly contribute to innovation. Second, poor patent quality generates uncertainty, which leads to lower incentives to innovate, which stifles technological development, entrepreneurship, employment, and ultimately growth and consumer welfare (Guellec and van Pottelsberghe de la Lotterie 2007; Hall et al. 2003). Third, poor patent quality can increase barriers to entry, i.e., more patents blocking freedom-to-operate (FTO), and raise IP-related transaction costs.[10] These barriers and costs are faced when merely identifying the rights in order to maintain FTO; otherwise navigating licensing of the rights; proactively invalidating the rights to maintain FTO; invalidating the rights as a defense in (frivolous or other) infringement disputes; otherwise defending against the rights, if they are difficult to invalidate, in infringement litigation; and defending against the rights if used as a basis for invalidity cases. These barriers and costs inhibit innovation.

An important, although not commonly used, indicator of the quality of a latecomer nation's patent stock is the ratio of utility models to invention patents. Lee and Kim (2010), Kim et al. (2012) suggest that a higher ratio of invention patents to utility models is one useful indicator of a country's transition to a more sophisticated stage of technological development. This is because the legal requirements for utility models around the world are generally lower than for invention patents. Specifically, many utility model regimes have lower substantive patentability requirements (often in terms of inventive step and/or novelty) than invention patents and, unlike many invention patent regimes, do not require a substantive examination to be conducted before the rights are granted to ensure that they actually fully meet the substantive statutory requirements for patentability (i.e., subject matter, novelty, inventiveness, and industrial applicability) (Prud'homme 2012, 2014b, 2015, 2017a, b). In China, utility models do not require a substantive examination prior to grant and have a lower inventive step requirement than the one used for invention patents. This regime per se does not create patent quality problems for countries with similar regimes; however, it has become problematic in China because it is coupled with state incentives for obtaining utility models that lack adequate patent quality requirements (Prud'homme 2014a, b, 2017b). These concepts are also more generally reflected in other literature, which finds that invention patent regimes with fewer safeguards to ensure granted patents meet a certain threshold of quality are more likely to enable lower quality patenting (de Saint-Georges and van Pottelsberghe de la Potterie 2013).

[10]FTO is the ability to utilize a product, process, or service without infringing on patents owned by other entities.

Table 3.4 Proportion of patent applications and grants in China, per right

Year	Applications (per right/all rights)			Grants (per right/all rights)		
	Invention patent (%)	Utility model (%)	Design (%)	Invention patent (%)	Utility models (%)	Design (%)
2006	37	28	35	41	11	47
2007	35	26	39	40	11	49
2008	35	27	38	37	13	50
2009	32	32	36	47	13	40
2010	32	34	34	43	11	46
2011	32	36	32	41	13	46
2012	32	36	32	39	12	49
2013	35	38	28	32	12	56
2014	39	37	24	29	13	58
2015	39	40	20	29	16	54
2016	39	43	19	23	52	25

Source SIPO statistics, calculations

Considering the aforementioned concepts, it is rather concerning to see the increasing proportion of utility model applications and grants in China in recent years. As illustrated in Fig. 3.1, there were more utility models filed in China as of 2010, and this trend has continued to date with a temporary change in 2014. Of course, these figures should be contextualized amidst declining design patent applications (see Table 3.4). But then again, as illustrated in Fig. 3.3, there has been a pronounced decline in the grants of invention patents relative to utility models since 2011. Further, in 2016, for the first time in the last decade, more utility models were granted than invention patents. From one perspective, a greater proportion of utility models than designs may reflect a recent shift in China away from design-based specialization towards more technological-based specialization. However, on the other hand, as discussed, there are significant risks from the proliferation of utility models and fewer returns from utility models in recent years.

Maintenance times of patents are one of the most commonly employed metrics of patent quality. Because patentees need to pay maintenance/renewal fees every year or every few years after they are granted a patent in order to maintain its validity, patents with longer lifespans are generally more valuable as rational actors will only pay fees needed to maintain patents if they are valuable (Pakes 1986). Available empirical literature using maintenance times as an indicator of patent quality shows that patents owned in China by domestic Chinese entities are of lower quality/value than those owned by foreign entities in China. Zhang and Chen (2012) find that, based upon analysis of patent renewal data from SIPO, the value of patents owned by domestic Chinese entities is much lower than those owned by foreign entities. Similarly, by analyzing patents filed in the late 1980s through the late 1990s in

China, Huang (2016) finds that domestically-owned patents are of lower value than foreign-owned patents. SIPO (2017a) identifies that, based on significantly shorter average maintenance times, the quality of patents owned by indigenous Chinese firms in many industries including but not limited to optics, audio-visual technology, semiconductors, transportation, and medical technology is far lower than the quality of foreign-owned patents.

Analyses of the maintenance times of patents granted internationally also shows that Chinese-owned patents are generally of lower quality than patents owned by firms from select developed countries. Thoma (2013) finds indigenous Chinese patents are maintained for shorter periods of time at the European Patent Office (EPO) than patents filed by foreign firms, including those with an office in China. Qiao (2017) finds the maintenance times of indigenous Chinese patents filed in China, the US, Germany, France, Japan, and South Korea is generally shorter than patents owned by foreign firms filed in those same jurisdictions.

Figure 3.5 indicates that the average lifespan of patents filed in China is currently shorter than all the countries used for comparative analysis in this book; however, the differences are not as significant as some may suspect. For example, according to data reported to WIPO, from 2014 to 2015 the average lifespan of an invention patent in China was 7.3 years, which is not exponentially shorter than the average patent lifespans in South Korea, the US, the UK, and Germany during that same time period (8.05, 10, 10.40, and 11.55 years, respectively).[11] Further, according to WIPO data, in 2010–2013, the average lifespan of patents in China was 7.25 years compared to an only marginally longer lifespan reported in the UK (7.35 years).[12] These figures indicate that although China somewhat lags behind our comparison countries on a core measure of patent quality, it does not lag as far behind as some might suspect and in fact seems to have fairly comparable quality (at least according to the metric) to some of the countries analyzed.

China also scores behind our reference countries on the patent quality metric of patent citations (Trajtenberg 1990). Forward patent citations, i.e. the citations in a patent to previously filed patents, are often considered to be one of the best indicators of patent quality (Jaffe and De Rassenfosse 2016). Similar to references/citations in academic literature, patent citations signal work that serves as a fundamental basis for subsequent work. (In patent law language, these citations signal relevant "prior art", i.e. evidence that an invention is known). Fisch et al. (2016) find that domestic Chinese entities experience a longer lag between when their patents are

[11]It is not fully clear how these figures mesh with other data sources on recent average patent lifespans in China (e.g., the 6 year average for 2015 cited in Table 3.1). Data for Fig. 3.5 inferably refers to both foreign and domestic applications in China while data in Table 3.1 inferably refers only to domestic applications, but clarifications from SIPO are warranted to confirm.

[12]See above footnote. Note that the average lifespan for patents in the UK reported to WIPO spiked in 2014 to 10.4 years. Also note, according to WIPO data, the average lifespan of patents in China from 2010–2013 (7.25 years) was actually longer than those in South Korea (6.65 years). However, WIPO data shows the average patent lifespan in South Korea in 2013 was 5.3 years, which is abnormally low compared to other years (and therefore may be a reporting error), thus weighing down its average lifespan.

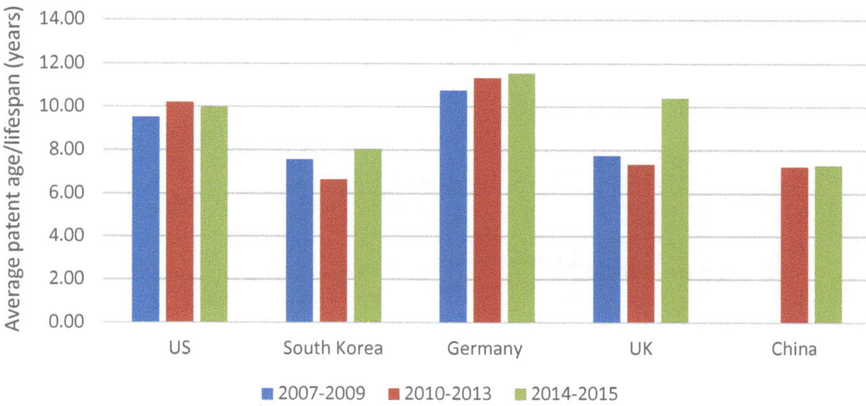

Fig. 3.5 Average patent lifespans (2007–2015) at IP offices. *Sources* data aggregated from WIPO (2013, 2014a, 2015, 2016). Data for prior years not available. Data for Japan not available, therefore excluded. Averages only reflect years for which data was available (data was missing for some years for some countries). Data shows average patent lifespan in South Korea in 2013 was abnormally low compared to other years and the average patent lifespan in the UK in 2014 was abnormally high

filed and cited than foreign firms (in five patent offices and at WIPO); although more recent filings experience a shorter lag, possibly indicating improvements in Chinese patent quality in recent years. Boeing and Mueller (2016), adjusting for a number of methodological limitations in using cross-country comparisons of patent citation data, find that patents originated from China score behind the US, South Korea, Germany, and Japan on numbers of forward citations in international search reports (ISRs) (see Fig. 3.6).[13]

Another indicator of patent quality is the rates of patenting abroad, with the logic behind the metric being that firms are only willing to pay the fees required to protect patents in other countries if they are actually valuable (Grupp and Schmoch 1999). The concept of foreign "patent families" is often used in such measures, which is a grouping of related patent applications filed in one or more jurisdictions to protect the same invention (In contrast, domestic patent families are patent families with only one filing in the first-named applicant's country of origin).[14] A number of patent quality metrics are based on patenting behavior abroad.

One of the most widely used foreign patenting measures of patent quality is "triadic" patent families, which are patents filed at the US Patent & Trademark Office (USPTO), EPO, and Japanese Patent Office (JPO) (Grupp and Schmoch 1999; Dernis and Khan 2004). Based on an analysis of triadic patents owned by Chinese entities, Boeing and Sandner (2011) suggest that the value of most Chinese patents is

[13]ISRs are the search reports used in the international phase of Patent Cooperation Treaty applications.

[14]Other related concepts may sometimes be used, namely 'foreign-oriented' or simply 'foreign' patent families, which are a subset of patent families with at least one filing office that is different from the one at the applicant's origin.

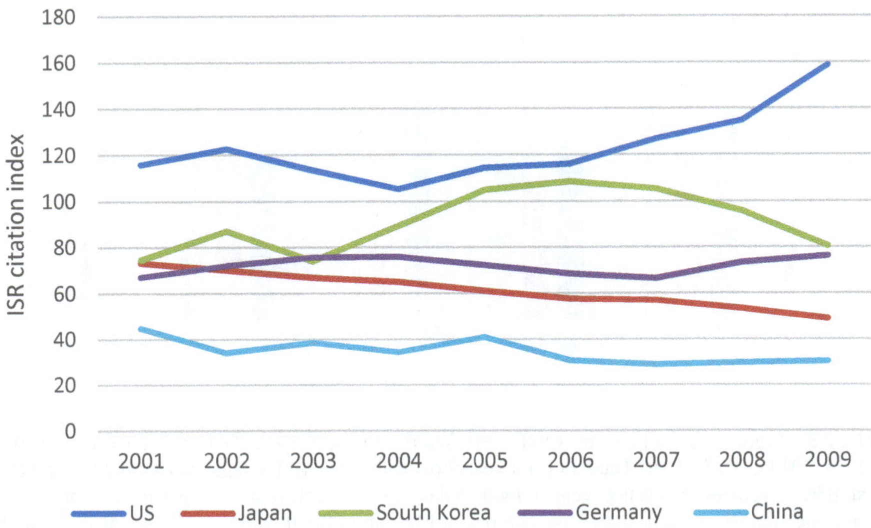

Fig. 3.6 International patent citations index (2001–2009) by patenting country of origin. *Source* Data from Boeing and Mueller (2016)

extremely low, especially when compared to patents owned by entities from the US and Germany. This being said, while providing useful contextual data, triadic patent filing data needs to be cautiously considered as it does not account for a range of understandable institutional, scale, and firm-related reasons why Chinese firms do not patent at all three triadic patent offices (Prud'homme 2014a).

Looking at a range of different foreign patent families, not just triadic patent families, WIPO (2014b) finds that Chinese patent filings abroad increased significantly after the year 2000. In the early 1990s, the number of Chinese foreign patent family filings was on a similar level to those from other fast-growing middle-income economies (WIPO 2014b). But by the end of the 1990s, China began to pull ahead of countries such as Brazil, India, Russia and South Africa (WIPO 2014b). Since the 1970s, far more invention patent applications than utility models have been filed by Chinese residents as part of foreign patent families (WIPO 2014b). Applications filed abroad by China-based entities have increased dramatically in recent years: from around 15,300 in 2010 to around 42,000 in 2015 (WIPO 2016, p. 24). China ranked as the 20th largest filer of invention patents abroad in 2001 but the 6th largest in 2015.[15]

Yet, despite this rise in foreign patenting by Chinese entities, these figures do not indicate that China is achieving levels of patent quality comparable to innovative developed nations. They also do not indicate what *proportion* of Chinese firms are patenting abroad. In fact, around 96% of total patent applications from China-based

[15]See China's statistical profile on the WIPO website, available at http://www.wipo.int/ipstats/en/statistics/country_profile/profile.jsp?code=CN.

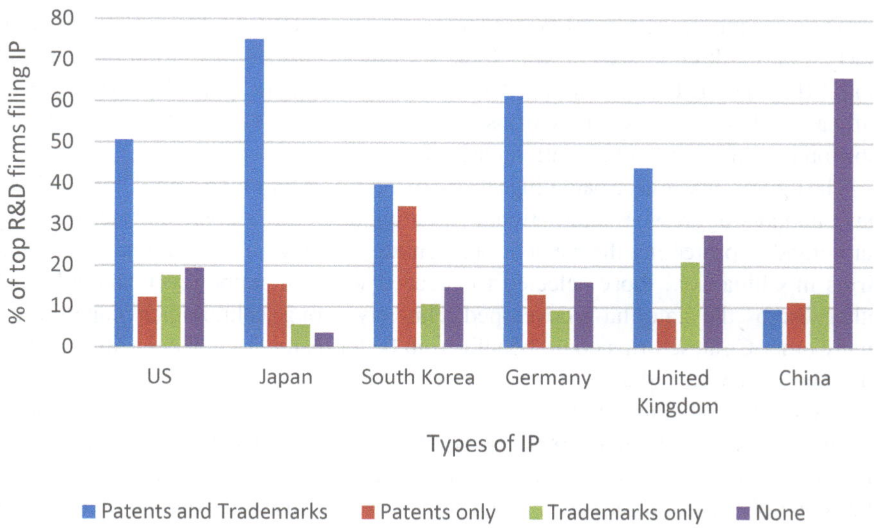

Fig. 3.7 Share of top R&D-investing firms filing IP rights in key offices, by origin. *Sources* OECD statistics, EU R&D Scoreboard data, EPO statistics, WIPO Statistics, OECD trademark database, calculations. Firms selected are those in the top 2000 corporate R&D sample from Dernis et al. (2015). IP rights counted are those filed at the USPTO, EPO, EUIPO (formerly "OHIM") (which registers designs), and JPO. Figures derived from average filings across the four IP offices

entities are filed exclusively in China, meaning only 4% of the total is filed abroad (WIPO 2016, p. 24). In contrast, Japanese and US entities file approximately 45% of their patents at home and abroad (WIPO 2016, p. 24).

Further, available data indicates that the vast majority of Chinese firms—even the most R&D-intensive ones—do not file IP rights abroad. Figure 3.7 shows that around 66% of even the most R&D-intensive Chinese firms do not file IP rights at key IP offices abroad—namely at USPTO, EPO, the European Union Intellectual Property Office (EUIPO) (formerly "OHIM") (which registers designs and trademarks), and JPO. This sharply contrasts with the IP filing behavior from R&D-intensive firms from the developed countries used as points of comparison throughout this book.

Another patent quality metric is numbers of patent filings via the Patent Cooperation Treaty (PCT). The PCT is a type of international patent filing mechanism administered by WIPO in cooperation with national IP offices via which entities can cost effectively file patents. The number of patents filed by Chinese entities through the PCT has rapidly increased in recent years; however, this has primarily been led by a relatively small number of firms. In 2016, China accounted for the third highest number of patents (behind the US and Japan, and surpassing Germany, South Korea, and the UK) via the PCT (WIPO 2017, p. 16). However, many of these PCT applications were from just a small number of Chinese firms. ZTE (who filed 4123 applications, more than any other firm in the world), Huawei (who filed 3692 applications, the second highest number of any firm in the world), and three other Chinese firms were among the top 50 PCT filers in the world (WIPO 2017, p. 19).[16] Similarly, Eberhardt et al. (2011), who look at Chinese entities' invention patenting at both SIPO and the USPTO (and SIPO alone) rather than via the PCT per se, find that only a small number of Chinese firms in one industry (ICT) account for a significant portion of China's recent invention patenting surge.

The figures on Chinese patenting abroad indicate that although some Chinese firms have adopted aggressive international patenting strategies, most Chinese firms lag far behind in protecting their inventions abroad. Although a few national champion firms in China (i.e., those selected to succeed who are supported financially and otherwise by the state) have developed relatively strong technological capabilities, many other Chinese firms could benefit from better technological capacity-building in order to survive and grow in the long-term.

The number of claims in a patent can also be taken as an indicator of its quality (Lanjouw and Schankerman 1999, 2004). Claims articulate the details of an invention in a patent application; they are divided into "independent" claims, which articulate the scope of the invention, and "dependent" claims, which narrow the focus of the invention described in the independent claim(s). Therefore, more claims, at least more independent claims, can indicate that a patent is more technologically complex and therefore of potentially higher value. Also, given that additional costs are often charged at the patent office for processing higher numbers of claims, patents with more claims may be of higher value. Data in Song and Li (2014) indicate that the average number of claims in patents filed in China (two per patent) as of 2012 is fewer than the average number of patents filed in the US, Japan, South Korea, Germany, and the UK. Similarly, data in Squicciarini et al. (2013, p. 31) indicate that among patents filed at the EPO, Chinese-owned patents on average have fewer claims than those owned from the aforementioned comparison countries.

The quality of the drafting per se of patent applications is also an important indicator of the quality of patent applications, particularly from the perspective of patent attorneys and litigators. Moreover, this metric is highly economically relevant because poorly drafted patents, if granted, can create serious complications in infringement and invalidation disputes via acting as barriers to entry and raising transaction costs to innovation. Song and Li (2014), analyzing the average number of pages and drawings (as well as claims) in patent applications around the world, find that Chinese patents are on average drafted significantly worse than patents owned by entities from the US, Japan, South Korea, Germany or the UK. This data confirms the finding in Gao et al. (2011) that the quality of the services offered by, and accreditation procedures for, patent agents in China should be improved, and that more Chinese firms should employee more and better-trained patent attorneys in-house.

---

[16]In 2016, the origins of the top 30 PCT firm filers were: Japan (18), the US (13), Germany (6), China (5), South Korea (3), two each from France and the Netherlands, and one from Sweden (WIPO 2017, p. 19). In 2016, the origins of the top 30 PCT filers from government and public research institutes were: South Korea (8), the US (6), China (4), three each from France and Japan, two from Germany, and one each from Australia, India, Malaysia, the Netherlands, Singapore and Spain (WIPO 2017, p. 20).

The findings in this section show that Chinese firms are inventing, and many are also innovating but not always as strongly as firms from forerunner countries. Much of the invention patenting surge from Chinese entities has historically been concentrated in the ICT sector, although recently there is a converging propensity to invention patent (and patent utility models) across different industries. At the same time, the surge in utility models and grants in China is dragging down the quality of China's overall patent stock. The question then becomes how has China's state policy impacted patent quality in China to date, and how might it be able to improve indigenous firms' patent quality in the future.

3.2 Factors Contributing to China's Patenting Surge, Including the Role of the Chinese State

The domestic patent explosion in China is owed to a number of factors, some of which involve innovation investments. For example, rising R&D intensity by Chinese firms is a significant contributor to the invention patenting surge in China (Hu and Jefferson 2009; Song et al. 2016). Some of this R&D expenditure has been supported by the Chinese state (Song et al. 2016). However, some sources indicate that if China had a healthier NIS we would see a greater number of valuable patents as a proportion of Chinese firms' R&D than we see at present (OECD 2017). Further, more research is needed to identify the precise extent to which R&D intensity has contributed to the incredible surge in utility model patenting in China to date. Given the lower technological sophistication threshold required to patent utility models compared to invention patents in China, it seems inevitable that their production, generally speaking, requires less intensive R&D.

Competition and learning has also contributed to the patenting surge in China. This includes classic competitive threat between foreign firms in China (Hu 2010) and between foreign and Chinese firms (Hu and Jefferson 2009; Thoma 2013). Foreign firms have also patented more in China in an attempt to ensure their FTO (Keupp et al. 2012) although, in the past at least, primarily patented "existing intellectual property that they created elsewhere" (Hu and Jefferson 2009, p. 66). An increasing awareness of why and how to patent, developed through firms' experience and encouraged by state efforts to limit information asymmetries, has also contributed to the patenting surge in China (Zhu 2013).

The domestic patenting explosion in China is also due to regulatory changes. For example, the strengthening of China's Patent Law in the 2000s and improvements in the processing of patent applications contributed significantly to the surge (Hu and Jefferson 2009; Hu 2010). This being said, some changes in the patent law contributed to heterogeneous patenting behavior by foreign firms compared with domestic firms (Huang et al. 2017). It is possible that improvements in the IP enforcement environment in China may also be facilitating more patenting, although further empirical research is needed to test this hypothesis.

Additionally, Chinese state policies directly meant to incentivize patenting have met their objectives. Political pressure in China via state-set patent targets tied to the performance evaluations of managers at SOEs, university and PRI staff, and government officials has contributed to the surge in patenting in China (Prud'homme, 2012; Song et al. 2016; Liefner et al. 2016; Cheng and Drahos 2017). "IP-conditioned government incentives"—measures imposed by the state that are intended to change economic behavior and are conditioned on meeting IP-related requirements—have also played a significant role in China's patent explosion (e.g., Li 2012b; Prud'homme and Song 2016). Some econometric studies suggest a significant amount of China's recent patent surge is attributed directly to these types of incentives (e.g., Xibao Li 2012; Dang and Motohashi 2015; Song et al. 2016; Long and Wang 2016).

From a strategy perspective, the Chinese state's efforts to increase patent quantity through heavy state intervention may have had its merits during the earlier stage of China's catch up trajectory (Zhu 2013; Prud'homme 2015, 2016).[17] After all, latecomer disadvantages created by incumbents' increasing usage of IP as barriers to entry and Chinese firms' lack of core IP are main factors restraining China's current catch-up process (Xiao et al. 2013; Song 2013).[18] Further, even though controversial, one might argue that there could be a role for the Chinese state to help Chinese firms develop strategically valuable patents, although doing so requires a careful balance between encouraging patenting that might undermine innovation with the reality that Chinese firms in some industries require strategic patents to effectively compete with incumbents (Prud'homme 2015, 2016, 2017c, 2018).

However, generally speaking, it is now essential for the Chinese state to foster patent quality over mere quantity to enable China to become an innovative economy that will avoid the middle-income trap. Prud'homme (2012), Song et al. (2016) discuss how overly simplistic patent targets set by the Chinese state since 2010

[17]The state approach of encouraging patent quantity is not always completely counterproductive for growth. The policy of encouraging patent filings was originally meant by the Chinese state to improve awareness about how to file IP and about the strategic benefits of filing IP (Zhu 2013). It was perceived that there was little to lose through this approach because many Chinese firms had low technological capabilities anyway, and therefore were not in a position to file high-quality patents even if the government set up incentives for doing so (Zhu 2013). Further, although not necessarily conducive to innovation, increasing the quantity of patents—even if they are not particularly high quality according to traditional metrics—in latecomer Chinese firms' portfolios provides them a valuable tool to compete with incumbents who leverage their own portfolios as barriers to entry (Prud'homme 2015, 2016, 2018). Such Chinese-owned patents can be used to block freedom-to-operate, raise licensing revenues, threaten or counter litigation, engage in cross-licensing, and in other strategic ways—especially in industries that are prone to incremental/sequential inventions and patent thickets and in which Chinese firms have at least basic technological capabilities (Prud'homme 2018). As such, at least during the early stages of the catch-up process, the strategy of boosting patent quantity has merit.

[18]Latecomer Chinese firms that are currently capable or could soon become perfectly capable of producing a product using a certain process at acceptable levels of quality and efficiency are legally excluded from doing so by patents held by incumbent firms (Xiao et al. 2013). And even if the incumbents do license their patents to Chinese latecomers, royalties charged can constrain latecomer profits while being reinvested by the incumbents to maintain their frontier lead (Xiao et al. 2013).

have incentivized recent patent filings without enough attention to their quality.[19] China has developed a massive system of IP-conditioned state incentives—including subsidies for patents, tax incentives tied to patenting, and other monetary and non-monetary awards—as one tool to meet these targets. Other countries (e.g., many in Europe) have instituted IP-conditioned incentives, however it appears that those in China are more plentiful and diverse (Prud'homme 2016).

The most prominent IP-conditioned tax incentive in China is the High and New Technology Enterprise (HNTE) program, which is administered at the provincial level in China and provides a 10% corporate income tax deduction (contingent on patenting inventions resulting from domestic R&D) and a 150% super deduction for R&D expenses per qualifying firm (Garcia et al. 2016). Yet other tax incentives tied to IP requirements exist in China (Long and Wang 2016; Garcia et al. 2016).

In terms of patent subsidies, Shanghai was the first province, in 1999, to institute such a scheme. Today, all 31 provinces/municipalities in mainland China have a patent subsidy scheme (Song et al. 2016). Provincial subsidies differ in their amounts and what they cover, although generally cover the costs of filing patents domestically at SIPO including patent application and examination fees. The subsidies sometimes also cover the costs of filing patents abroad. Further, some Chinese subsidies related to IP, patents included, are given as grants or rewards not specifically linked to, and/or covering costs far beyond, official patenting fees. The subsidies sometimes have covered annual maintenance/renewal fees and occasionally include patent attorney fees. A range of invention/patent awards also exist in China, for example but not limited to the Gold Award for China Patents; China Patent Excellence Award; and invention awards designated for youth, women, and others. (Additionally, although not often considered a "subsidy", it is worth noting that SIPO, like many patent offices around the world, also provides discounts on patent fees to entities with limited resources.)

Empirical research shows that Chinese patents receiving state support from some IP-conditioned incentives tend to be lower quality than those not receiving such support. For example, Lei et al. (2013) show that China's patent subsidy system has encouraged firms to break-up inventions in an attempt to capture a greater amount of patent subsidies. Boeing and Mueller (2015) find, based on an analysis of citations, that China's patent subsidies contribute to Chinese PCT applications achieving only a fraction of the quality level of PCT filings by entities from other countries. Dang and Motohashi (2015) show that patent subsidies have encouraged patents with a particularly narrow claim breadth, an indicator of low-quality patents. Long and Wang (2016) find that a range of China's patent promotion incentives, including

[19] During the 12th five-year policymaking period, this included the promulgation of over 10 national-level quantitative patent targets and over 150 provincial/municipal quantitative patent targets, mostly to be met by 2015 (Prud'homme 2012). The 12th Five Year Plan on National Social and Economic Development sets the target of 3.3 patents "owned" (note: the Chinese term here "拥有" is best translated as "owned" and is different from the term SIPO uses for "in force" [有效]) per 10,000 people; the National Patent Development Strategy (2011–2020) promulgated on November 11, 2010 prescribes that 2 million patents should be filed annually by 2015.

certain patent subsidies as well as tax policies, have created a decline in the quality of domestic utility models and designs as measured by low renewal rates.

There are a number of reasons why China's IP-conditioned state incentives contributed to low quality patenting. Most significantly, the criteria for qualifying for provincial subsidies and tax incentives in China have not been rigorous enough to safeguard against low-quality rights (Prud'homme 2012, 2016). This environment was especially easy for entities to exploit to claim government-provided incentives on utility models and registered designs, which technically did not even meet statutory patentability requirements. Further, in different provinces/municipalities, patentees have exploited the lack of coordination between local and provincial/municipal governments to make significant money from IP-conditioned incentives in ways not intended by policymakers.

Although not exclusively related to patent quality, it is worth noting that there are other shortcomings in the design of China's state incentives for patenting. Perhaps most importantly, the incentives are often not prioritized towards technology start-ups and other small and medium-sized enterprises (SMEs) to whom provision of state support is more economically justifiable compared to more established firms (Long et al. 2013; Song et al. 2016). This being said, some recent initiatives have been set up by China's State Council in 2017 to target more state financial support, including financing for IP, towards SME in particular (Chen 2017).

Official Chinese government policies in recent years clearly indicate the Chinese state is acutely aware of the shortcomings in Chinese patent quality, the role of the state in influencing this quality, and is firmly committed to improving patent quality (e.g., SIPO 2017a, b; Xinhua 2014a, b; State Council 2016; State Council Information Office 2017). Table 3.5 provides key examples of recent central-level initiatives to improve patent quality in China. The last initiative (from 2018) mentioned in Table 3.5 is further discussed in Chap. 5. Provincial-level governments have also recognized the need to improve patent quality and have included relevant initiatives into their IP development plans.[20] Our consultations with Chinese government policymakers affirmed their staunch commitment to improving patent quality in China. Generally speaking, these recent state initiatives appear to be well-designed and will likely help improve patent quality in China. Nonetheless, we provide a few recommendations in Chap. 9 of ways we believe the state might be able to further enhance patent quality.

[20]For a listing of such initiatives, see the annex in Prud'homme (2012), pp 172–185.

Table 3.5 Examples of key recent central-level initiatives to improve patent quality in China (non-exhaustive list)

Patent quality component	Initiative	Year instituted
Examination of utility models and designs	Revision to Implementing Regulations of Patent Law to expand the scope of Preliminary Examination for utility models to assess "obvious" non-compliance with industrial applicability and "obvious" lack of novelty	2010
Examination of utility models and designs	Patent Examination Guidelines revised to expand, albeit just slightly, the novelty assessment for utility models and designs	2013
IP-conditioned state financial incentives, patent targets, other	Several Opinions on Further Improving Quality of Patent Applications reforms China's system of subsidies and other incentives for all three types of patents, and proposes numerous other initiatives to improve patent quality	2013
Less promotion of utility models	Internally, SIPO sets a target to promote a higher number of invention patents than utility models	Circa 2014
Patent targets	More sophisticated, quality-oriented targets included in National IP Strategy 2014–2020 than in previous strategies	2014
Patent application drafting	Trainings for patent agents, revisions to guidelines governing patent agents	Multiple
Patent application drafting, other aspects	Regulation on Patenting Behavior seeks to discourage filing of "abnormal" patent applications by integrating applicants' data into the National Business Credit Information Sharing Platform; instituting liability for patent agents helping applications blatantly copy the prior art, "obviously fabricating" data, among other behavior; and restricting patent fee deductions and subsidies	2017
Coordination between central and local levels on IP policies	SIPO continually strengthens mechanism via which provincial IP authorities report on their IP strategies; award program for IP Demonstration Cities which, are geared to recognize provinces that perform well on patent-quality (and quantity) related criteria; other initiatives	Multiple
Multiple aspects	2017 Patent Quality Improvement Project Implementation Plan (2017 年专利质量提升工程实施方案推进计划) sets forth multiple initiatives for improving patent quality	2017
Multiple aspects	Memorandum of Understanding on Joint Disciplinary Action Against Serious Distrusted Entities in the Field of Intellectual Property (Patents) sets forth multiple initiatives which can help improve patent quality	2018

Sources Review of recent (2010–present) legal measures from SIPO [Of course, older reforms also improved patent quality in China (for example, but not limited to, the 2008 revision to the patent law to require absolute novelty for patents and limit conflicting applications)]. List is only an illustrative selection, it is not intended to be exhaustive

3.3 Summary

Chinese firms are inventing more than ever. Some Chinese firms are also innovating but, on aggregate, still not as strongly as firms from technological forerunner countries. The growth of patenting in China and by Chinese entities operating abroad has diverse implications for the direction of the Chinese economy. Some of the past increases in patent stocks have contributed to productivity growth and potentially stronger strategic competitiveness in Chinese firms. However, there are diminishing returns to some of the inventions in China, especially utility models which are being generated en masse.

Moreover, despite the surge in the quantity of patents in China in recent years, patent quality has not risen proportionately. Chinese state patenting targets tied to performance evaluations and IP-conditioned state financial incentives have contributed to this rising patent quantity at the expense of patent quality. On one hand, neither the quality of invention patents filed in China nor the quality of Chinese-owned invention patents filed abroad is alarmingly poor, although different patent quality indicators are more assuring than others and state-supported filings appear to be of lower quality on average. On the other hand, the surge in utility models in China—especially, but not only, those that are state-supported—appear to be dragging down the quality of the country's overall patent stock.

This patenting trajectory can create notable risks to businesses and China's national development. It can create path dependency on low quality inventions and unnecessary barriers to entry and transaction costs, which restrains China's ability to transition towards an innovation-based economy. The Chinese state has undertaken a number of important recent initiatives to improve patent quality, which appear generally well-designed and about which businesses should be aware. Still, further reforms could be made.

References

Boeing, P., and P. Sandner. 2011. The innovative performance of China's national innovation system. Frankfurt School Working Paper Series No. 158, available at https://papers.ssrn.com/sol3/papers.cfm?abstract_id=1769083.

Boeing, P., and E. Mueller. 2015. Measuring patent quality in international comparison—index development and application to China. Centre for European Economic Research Discussion Paper No. 15-051, available from ftp.zew.de/pub/zew-docs/dp/dp15051.pdf.

Boeing, P., and E. Mueller. 2016. Measuring patent quality in cross-country comparison. *Economic Letters* 149: 145–147.

Branstetter, L., G. Li, and F. Veloso. 2014. The globalization of R&D: China, India, and the rise of international co-invention. Mimeo, available at http://citeseerx.ist.psu.edu/viewdoc/download?doi=10.1.1.564.4629&rep=rep1&type=pdf.

Chen, C. 2017. Explosive growth in China's IPR pledge financing set to continue. Lexology, available at https://www.lexology.com/library/detail.aspx?g=3690c302-96d6-4708-99b6-e2240e7255ff.

Cheng, W., and P. Drahos. 2017. How China built the world's biggest patent office—The pressure driving mechanism. *IIC—International Review of Intellectual Property and Competition Law* 49:5–40.

Cohen, W., R. Nelson, and J. Walsh. 2000. Protecting their intellectual assets: Appropriability conditions and why US manufacturing firms patent (or Not). NBER Working Paper No. 7552, www.nber.org/papers/w7552.

Dang, J., and K. Motohashi. 2015. Patent statistics: A good indicator for innovation in China? Patent subsidy program impacts on patent quality. *China Economic Review* 35:137–155.

de Saint-Georges, M., and B. van Pottelsberghe de la Potterie. 2013. A quality index for patent systems. *Research Policy* 42:704–719.

Dernis, H., and M. Khan. 2004. Triadic patent families methodology. OECD Science, Technology and Industry Working Paper No. 2004/02, available at http://www.oecdilibrary.org/science-and-technology/triadic-patent-familiesmethodology_443844125004?crawler=true.

Dernis, H., M. Dosso, F. Hervás, V. Millot, M. Squicciarini, and A. Vezzani. 2015. World corporate top R&D investors: Innovation and IP bundles. A JRC and OECD common report. Luxembourg: Publications Office of the European Union.

Eberhardt, M., C. Helmers, and Z. Yu. 2011. Is the Dragon learning to fly? An analysis of Chinese patent explosion. Oxford Center for the Study of African Economies. Retrieved from http://www.csae.ox.ac.uk/workingpapers/pdfs/csae-wps-2011-15.pdf.

Eberhardt, M., and C. Helmers, and Z. Yu. 2017. What can explain the Chinese patent explosion? *Oxford Economic Papers* 69:239–262.

Fang, J., H. He, and N. Li. 2016. China's rising IQ (innovation quotient) and growth: Firm-level evidence. IMF Working Paper WP/16/249.

Fisch, C., J. Block, and P. Sandner. 2016. Chinese university patents: Quantity, quality, and the role of subsidy programs. *The Journal of Technology Transfer* 41:60–84.

Freeman, C. 1987. Technology policy and economic performance: Lessons from Japan. London: Pinter Publishers.

Gao, L., M. Li, and Y. Cheng. 2011. Report on the quality of patents for invention in China. Unpublished report commissioned under the "IPR2" Project.

Garcia, A., J. Jiang, C. Turley, and M. Wang. 2016. The evolving environment for intellectual property tax management in China. In: *Economic impacts of intellectual property-conditioned government incentives*, ed. D. Prud'homme and H. Song, 205–234. Springer.

Graham, S., and T. Sichelman. 2008. Why do start-ups patent? *Berkley Technology Law Journal* 23:1063–1097.

Griliches, Z. 1990. Patent statistics as economic indicators: A survey. NBER Working Paper No. 3301.

Grupp, H., and U. Schmoch. 1999. Patent statistics in the age of globalisation: New legal procedures, new analytical methods, new economic interpretation. *Research Policy* 28:377–396.

Guellec, D., and B. van Pottelsberghe de la Lotterie. 2007. *The economics of the European Patent regime: IP policy for innovation and competition*. New York: Oxford University Press.

Guerrini, C. 2014. Defining patent quality. *Fordham Law Review* 82:3091–3141.

Hall, B.H., and R. Ziedonis. 2001. The patent paradox revisited: An empirical study of patenting in the US semiconductor industry, 1975–1995. *RAND Journal of Economics* 32:101–128.

Hall, B.H., S. Graham, and D. Harhoff. 2003. Prospects for improving U.S. patent quality via post-grant opposition. NBER Working Papers No. 9731, available at www.nber.org/papers/w9731.

Harhoff, D., and K. Hoisl. 2007. Institutionalized incentives for ingenuity: Patent value and the German Employees' Inventions Act. *Research Policy* 36:1143–1162.

Hobday, M. 1995. *Innovation in East Asia*. Edward Elgar Publishing Ltd.

Hu, A.G., and G.H. Jefferson. 2009. A great wall of patents: What is behind China's recent patent explosion? *Journal of Development Economics* 90:57–68.

Hu, G.A. 2010. Propensity to patent, competition and China's foreign patenting surge. *Research Policy* 39:985–993.

Hu, A.G., P. Zhang, and L. Zhao. 2016. China as number one? Evidence from China's most recent patenting surge. *Journal of Development Economics* 124:107–119.

Huang, Z., and P. Yu. 2007. The effects of technical innovation to economic growth of our country in recent years: An empirical study based on panel data models (in Chinese). *Science and Technology Management Research* 8:74–77.

Huang, C. 2016. Estimates of the value of patent rights in China. In *Innovation and IPRs in China and India: Myths, realities and opportunities*, ed. K.C. Liu and U.S. Racherla, 181–209. Springer.

Huang, K., X. Geng, and H. Wang. 2017. Institutional regime shift in intellectual property rights and innovation strategies of firms in China. *Organization Science* 28:1–23.

Jaffe, A., and G. De Rassenfosse. 2016. Patent citation data in social science research: Overview and best practices. NBER Working Paper 21868.

Johnson, C. 1982. MITI and the Japanese Miracle: The growth of Industrial Policy, 1925–1975. Stanford, CA: Stanford University Press.

Keupp, M., S. Friesike, and M. von Zedtwitz. 2012. How do foreign firms patent in emerging economies with weak appropriability regimes? Archetypes and Motives. *Research Policy* 41:1422–1439.

Kim, L. 1993. National system of industrial innovation: Dynamics of capability building in Korea. In National innovation systems, ed. R. Nelson, 357–383. New York: Oxford University Press.

Kim, Y.K., K. Lee, W.G. Park, and K. Choo. 2012. Appropriate intellectual property protection and economic growth in countries at different levels of development. *Research Policy* 41:358–375.

Lanjouw, J.O., and M. Schankerman. 1999. The quality of ideas: Measuring innovation with multiple indicators. NBER Working Paper No. 7345, Cambridge, MA.

Lanjouw, J., and M. Schankerman. 2004. Patent quality and research productivity: Measuring innovation with multiple indicators. *The Economic Journal* 114:441–465.

Lee, K., and Y.K. Kim. 2010. IPR and technological catch-up in Korea. In *Introduction*, ed. H. Odagiri, A. Goto, A. Sunami, and R. Nelson. In *Intellectual property rights, development, and catch-up*, ed. H. Odagiri, A. Goto, A. Sunami, and R. Nelson, 133–167. Oxford, UK: Oxford University Press.

Lee, C.Y. 2011. China tops US, Japan to become top patent filer. Reuters, available at http://www.reuters.com/article/2011/12/21/us-china-patents-idUSTRE7BK0LQ20111221.

Lei, Z., Z. Sun, and B. Wright. 2013. Are Chinese patent applications politically driven? Evidence from China's domestic patent applications. OECD Published Working Paper. Available from http://www.oecd.org/site/stipatents/4-3-Lei-Sun-Wright.pdf.

Li, W. 2012a. Analysis of impact of different types of patents on technological advancement in China. *African Journal of Business Management* 6:3623–3629.

Li, X. 2012b. Behind the recent surge of Chinese patenting: An institutional view. *Research Policy* 41:236–249.

Liefner, I., H. Kroll, and A. Peighambari. 2016. Research-driven or party-promoted? Factors affecting patent applications of private small and medium-sized enterprises in China's Pearl River Delta. *Science and Public Policy* 43:849–858.

Lin, J.Y. 2012. *Demystifying the Chinese economy*. Cambridge: Cambridge University Press.

Liu, H. 2002. Patent regime and economic development: Theory & reality, analysis on the dynamic utility of China's patent regime. *China Software Science* 10:26–30.

Long, T., L. Yun, and Y. Fangjuan. 2013. Subsidy policy that supports coordinated development of patent quality and application quantity (in Chinese). *Science & Technology Progress and Policy* 30:99–104.

Long, C.X., and J. Wang. 2016. Evaluating patent promotion policies in China: Consequences on patent quantity and quality. In *Economic impacts of intellectual property-conditioned government incentives*, ed. D. Prud'homme and H. Song, 235–258. Springer.

Lundvall, B.A. 1992. National systems of innovation: Towards a theory of innovation and interactive learning. London: Pinter Press.

Merges, R. 1999. The law and economics of employee inventions. *Harvard Journal of Law & Technology* 13:1–53.

Moga, T. 2012. *China's utility model patent system: Innovation driver or deterrent*. US Chamber of Commerce Publications.

Morris-Suzuki, T. 1994. The technological transformation of Japan: From the seventeenth to the twenty-first century. UK: Cambridge University Press.

Munari, F., and R. Oriani. 2011. *The economic valuation of patents: Methods and applications*. Edward Elgar.

Nagaoka, S., K. Motohashi, and A. Goto. (2010). Patent statistics as an innovation indicator. In *Handbook of the economics of innovation*, vol. 2, ed. B.H. Hall, and N. Rosenberg, 1083–1127. Elsevier: Amsterdam, North Holland.

Nelson, R. (ed.). 1993. *National innovation systems: A comparative analysis*. UK: Oxford University Press.

OECD. 2009. OECD patent statistics manual. OECD publishing, available at http://www.oecd-ilibrary.org/science-and-technology/oecd-patent-statistics-manual_9789264056442-en.

OECD. 2017. OECD economic surveys: China 2017, available http://www.oecd-ilibrary.org/economics/oecd-economic-surveys-china-2017_eco_surveys-chn-2017-en.

Pakes, A. 1986. Patents as options. Some estimates of the value of holding european patent stocks. *Econometrica* 54:755–784.

Prud'homme, D. 2012. Dulling the cutting edge: How patent-related policies and practices hamper innovation in China. Beijing: European Chamber.

Prud'homme, D. 2014a. Rethinking what international patenting really says about Chinese innovation. *Journal of Intellectual Property Law & Practice* 9:986–992.

Prud'homme, D. 2014b. Creating a "model" utility model patent system: A comparative analysis of the utility model patent systems in Europe and China. IP Key Project Working Paper for China's State Intellectual Property Office, available at http://www.ipkey.org/en/resources/ip-information-centre/10-law-doc-category/3275-creating-a-model-utility-model-system-a-comparative-analysis-of-the-utility-model-systems-in-europe-and-china.

Prud'homme, D. 2015. "Soft spots" in China's utility model patent system: Perceptions, assessment and reform. *European Intellectual Property Review* 37:305–310.

Prud'homme, D. 2016. IP-conditioned government incentives in China and the EU: A comparative analysis of strategies and impacts on patent quality. In *Economic impacts of intellectual property-conditioned government incentives*, ed. D. Prud'homme and H. Song, 13–74. Springer.

Prud'homme, D. 2017a. Utility model patent "strength" and technological development: Experiences of China and other East Asian latecomers. *China Economic Review* 42:50–73.

Prud'homme, D. 2017b. Utility model regimes and innovation in China and beyond. In *Patents and innovation in Mainland China and Hong Kong*, ed. Y. Li, 29–78. Cambridge, UK: Cambridge University Press.

Prud'homme, D. 2017c. China's indigenous intellectual property incentives, global value chains, and latecomer catch-up. Macquarie Graduate School of Management, Sydney, Australia.

Prud'homme, D. 2018. Alternative responses to anti-commons: China's state patenting incentives and the strategic value of latecomers' patent portfolios. Paper presented at the Berkeley Intellectual Property Scholars Conference, University of Berkeley, CA, USA.

Prud'homme, D., and H. Song (ed.). 2016. Introduction. In *Economic impacts of intellectual property-conditioned government incentives*, ed. D. Prud'homme, H. Song, 1–12. Springer.

Qiao, Y. 2017. *Maintenance time and the industry development of patents*. Springer.

Reitzig, M. 2004. Improving patent valuations for management purposes—Validating new indicators by analyzing application rationales. *Research Policy* 33:939–957.

Sichelman, T., and Graham, S. 2010. Patenting by entrepreneurs: An empirical study. *Michigan Telecommunications Telecommunication Law Review* 17:111–142.

SIPO. 中国知识产权年鉴 (China IPR Yearbooks) (in Chinese). IPR Press.

SIPO. 2013a. 国家知识产权局关于进一步提升专利申请质量的若干意见 (Several Opinions on Further Improving Quality of Patent Applications) (in Chinese), available at http://www.sipo.gov.cn/zscqgz/2013/201312/t20131225_891833.html.

SIPO. 2017a. 实施专利质量提升工程 加快建设知识产权强国 (Implementing patent quality upgrading projects to accelerate the construction of an intellectual property power) (in Chinese). Interview with Zhang Mao, Deputy Director of SIPO, available at http://www.sipo.gov.cn/zscqgz/2017/201706/t20170609_1311996.html.

SIPO. 2017b. 年专利质量提升工程实施方案推进计划 (2017 Patent Quality Improvement Project Implementation Plan) (in Chinese).

Song, H. 2013. Indigenous innovation capability-building and the development of intellectual property rights (in Chinese). Beijing: Chinese Academy of Sciences Intellectual Property Rights Press.

Song, H., and Z. Li. 2014. Patent quality and the measuring indicator system: Comparison among Chinese provinces and key countries. Berkeley Center for Law & Technology IP Scholars Conference, August 6–8, 2014, Berkeley Law School, available at https://www.law.berkeley.edu/files/Song_Hefa_IPSC_paper_2014.pdf.

Song, H., Z. Li, and D. Xu. 2016. Study on policies to stimulate patenting in China: What led to the upsurge of China's domestic patent applications? In *Economic impacts of intellectual property-conditioned government incentives*, ed. D. Prud'homme and H. Song, 179–204. Singapore: Springer.

Squicciarini, M., H. Dernis, and C. Criscuolo. 2013. Measuring patent quality: Indicators of technological and economic value. OECD DSTI/DOC (2013)3.

State Council. 2016. 国务院关于印发"十三五"国家知识产权保护和运用规划的通知国发〔2016〕86号 (State Council's issuance of the 13th Five Year Notice on National Intellectual Property Protection and Planning, State Law (2016) #86) (in Chinese), available at http://www.gov.cn/zhengce/content/2017-01/13/content_5159483.htm.

State Council Information Office. 2017. Zhiding zhendui xing cuoshi tisheng zhuanli zhiliang (Formulating targeted measures to improve patent quality), available at http://www.scio.gov.cn/xwfbh/xwbfbh/wqfbh/35861/36536/zy36540/Document/1549510/1549510.htm.

Sui, G., G. Shen, and J. Song. 2005. The industrialization of China's high-tech industry based on the region regional differences of patent level (in Chinese). *Management World* 8:87–93.

Teece, D. 1986. Profiting from technological innovation: Implications for integration, collaboration, licensing and public policy. *Research Policy* 15:285–305.

Teece, D., G. Pisano, and A. Shuen. 1997. Dynamic capabilities and strategic management. *Strategic Management Journal* 18:509–533.

Thoma, G. 2013. Quality and value of Chinese patenting: An international perspective. *Seoul Journal of Economics* 26:33–72.

Trajtenberg, M. 1990. A penny for your quotes. Patent citations and the value of innovations. *RAND Journal of Economics* 21:172–187.

Tuo, Y. 2009. Turning more patents into profits. China Daily, available at http://www.chinadaily.com.cn/bw/2009-03/02/content_7524381.htm.

Wagner, R.P. 2009. Understanding patent-quality mechanisms. *University of Pennsylvania Law Review* 157:2135–2173.

WIPO. 2013. *World intellectual property indicators 2013*. WIPO publications, available at http://www.wipo.int/edocs/pubdocs/en/intproperty/941/wipo_pub_941_2013.pdf.

WIPO. 2014a. *World intellectual property indicators 2014*. WIPO publications, available at http://www.wipo.int/edocs/pubdocs/en/wipo_pub_941_2014.pdf.

WIPO. 2014b. International patent strategies of Chinese residents, in Committee on Development and Intellectual Property, 13th Session, pp 1–54, available at http://www.wipo.int/edocs/mdocs/mdocs/en/cdip_13/cdip_13_inf_9.docx.

WIPO. 2015. *World intellectual property indicators 2015*. WIPO publications, available at http://www.wipo.int/edocs/pubdocs/en/wipo_pub_941_2015.pdf.

WIPO. 2016. *World intellectual property indicators 2016*. WIPO publications, available at http://www.wipo.int/edocs/pubdocs/en/wipo_pub_941_2016.pdf.

WIPO. 2017. *Patent cooperation treaty yearly review 2017*. WIPO publications, available at http://www.wipo.int/edocs/pubdocs/en/wipo_pub_901_2017.pdf.

World Bank. 2013. China 2030: Building a modern, harmonious, and creative society. World Bank report #76299, available at http://documents.worldbank.org/curated/en/781101468239669951/China-2030-building-a-modern-harmonious-and-creative-society.

Xiao, Y., A. Tylecote, and J. Liu. 2013. Why not greater catch-up by Chinese firms? The impact of IPR, corporate governance and technology intensity on late-comer strategies'. *Research Policy* 42:749–764.

Xinhua. 2014a. China sees larger proportion of invention patent applications. Xinhua, available from http://news.xinhuanet.com/english/china/2014-04/22/c_133281638.htm.

Xinhua. 2014b. China eyes quality patent amid application surge. Xinhua, available from http://www.chinaipr.gov.cn/newsarticle/news/government/201404/1810614_1.html.

Zhang, G., and X. Chen. 2012. The value of invention patents in China: Country origin and technology field differences. *China Economic Review* 23:357–370.

Zhao, Y., and S. Liu. 2011. *Effect of China's domestic patents on total factor productivity: 1988–2009*. School of Statistics, Renmin University of China.

Zheng, L., and X. Lan. 2009. A tale of two cities: A comparison of patent-based innovative performance of domestic and multinational companies in China. Proceedings of the Joint Symposium of US-China Advanced Technology Trade and Industrial Development. *Journal of International Commerce & Economics*, available at http://www.usitc.gov/journals/entire_journal_2010_11_4.pdf.

Zhou, K.Z., G.Y. Gao, and H. Zhao. 2016. State ownership and firm innovation in China: An integrated view of institutional and efficiency logics. *Administrative Science Quarterly* 62:375–404.

Zhu, X. 2013. 辨证看待中国专利的数量与质量 (Dialectical perspective of patent quantity and quality in China) (in Chinese). *Bulletin of Chinese Academy of Sciences* 4:003.

Chapter 4
IP Measures for Transmission and Exploitation of Technological Knowledge

The ability of technological knowledge to be efficiently created and shared among different economic agents in a NIS is a fundamental determinant of the ability of an economy to sustainably generate innovation (Freeman 1987; Lundvall 1992; Nelson 1993). Mechanisms for transmission and exploitation of technological knowledge are central to this process. International transmission of technological knowledge is achieved through direct learning from technology transfer (of tacit or codified/explicit knowledge) and technological spillovers (i.e., spread of knowledge at a lower cost than the costs of its production) (Keller 2002, 2004). (Some sources interchangeably use the terms technology "transmission" or "transfer" with technology "diffusion", although some argue the latter term should refer to a different process).[1] Exploitation of technology via commercialization and sale of technology-intensive products and services is also fundamental to the spread of technology. Many factors, ranging from firm strategies and dynamics of technological change to state institutions and societal norms determine the rates of technology transfer, exploitation, and diffusion across firms and economies (Cohen 2004). This chapter only focuses on key IP-related aspects of what we call "transmission and exploitation of technological knowledge"—including direct technology transfer, spillovers, and commercialization—in China.

4.1 Firms' Patent Commercialization and Technology Transfer: Major Trends and Policies

Latecomer disadvantages created by incumbents' increasing usage of IP as barriers to entry and Chinese firms' lack of core IP significantly restricts legally-compliant

[1]Rogers (1995) defines technological diffusion as the *adoption* of a technology within a society, organization (such as a firm), or group of individuals. Stewart (1987) is careful to distinguish technological diffusion (the process of adoption of technology in the market) from technology transfer (exchange of knowledge and legal rights to produce a new product).

D. Prud'homme and T. Zhang, *China's Intellectual Property Regime for Innovation*, https://doi.org/10.1007/978-3-030-10404-7_4

Table 4.1 Progress meeting IP value targets in China's National IP Strategy (2014–2020)

Targets	2015–target	2015–actual
Total transaction amount of the technology contracts registered on the national technology market (in trillions of yuan)	1.0	0.98
Annual amount of IP pledge financing (in 100 millions of yuan)	750	931.7
Export income from royalties and franchise fees from proprietary rights (in 100 millions of USD)	20	11[a]

Sources Annual Report on National Technology Market Statistics 2016, Speech by Shen Changyu of SIPO at National Internet Information Office news conference in 2016 (https://www.yuanchuangyun.com/newsList/info/2016/2348.html), [a]from readily available data on China's balance of payments (http://www.safe.gov.cn)

transmission and exploitation of knowledge in China (Xiao et al. 2013; Song 2013). It is well recognized by the Chinese government that Chinese firms face difficulties obtaining and commercializing valuable IP and technology. As such, a number of targets were included in China's 2014–2020 National IP Strategy specifically focused on improving IP commercialization levels. These include (i) total transaction amount of the technology contracts registered on the national technology market, (ii) annual amount of IP pledge financing, and (iii) export income from royalties and franchise fees from proprietary rights. The 2015 targets for IP pledge financing and technology contract value have been exceeded or nearly met, respectively, but the IP export income target was not met (see Table 4.1). These figures indicate that while some improvements may have been made to the ability of Chinese firms to commercialize technology, additional improvements are needed to meet the state's own targets.

It is well-documented that China's historically ineffective IP regime has discouraged transfer of foreign technology, especially frontier technology, to domestic firms (Bruun and Bennett 2002; Asakawa and Som 2008; Chan and Daim 2011; Maskus et al. 2005; Zhou 2006; Fu 2015). At the same time, foreign firms dominate technology-intensive segments of the Chinese economy: 90% of high-tech exports from China are from foreign firms, not domestic ones (OECD 2008, p. 16).

Further, although foreign firms do transfer some forms of technology to China, the benefits of this to indigenous Chinese enterprises' ability to indigenously innovate is limited. Although FDI in China is increasing, this is mostly confined to building plants incorporating capital, technology, and managerial expertise controlled by foreigners (Moran 2011). While foreign FDI payments for Chinese materials and labor used in the operations of foreign plants have increased as domestic value-added has increased, these domestic value-added increases have been concentrated in the lower-skilled segment of the export frontier (Moran 2011). The sub-optimality of China's IP regime contributes to "isolated innovation poles" created by foreign firms, whereby even though foreign firms may increase overall innovation inputs and outputs, their benefits to the technological capability-building of indigenous entities remains to be seen (Fu 2015). In other words, the ineffectiveness of China's IP regime has effectively limited knowledge spillovers in China from foreign firms.

Further, some state policies appear to inhibit Chinese firms from in-licensing valuable foreign patents. Chinese firms are increasingly in-licensing patents, which when absorbed have been shown to help improve their indigenous technological capabilities (Wang et al. 2014a; Li-Ying et al. 2012). Yet, most of the patenting licensing in recent years has been between indigenous Chinese firms, potentially reflecting the Chinese state's attempt to encourage transfer of indigenous technology (Wang et al. 2014b). This state strategy may be somewhat shortsighted given that indigenous firms that in-license and properly absorb foreign technology often perform better than those that only in-license indigenous technologies (Wang et al. 2013; Li-Ying and Wang 2015).

There are a number of specific areas of IP law and policy we have identified that appear to most significantly restrain investment, especially by foreign firms, in technological innovation and technology transfer in China. These include concerns about certain aspects of statutory IP laws (see Chap. 2) and IP enforcement in China (see Chap. 7). Several other important legal measures were also identified as problematic.

China's Technology Import Export Regulation (TIER), effective as of 2002, has long contained both ambiguous and overly burdensome provisions that may have restrained the willingness of firms to transfer technology and invest in innovation in China and/or increased the costs of doing so. These provisions include: (i) Article 27, which set the burdensome requirement that subsequent improvements on technology development in contractual relationships are owned by the party making the improvements; (ii) Article 24.3, which set overly burdensome requirements mandating foreign technology licensors bear liability for any accusation of infringement that may be brought against a technology importer in relation to the use of licensed technology; (iii) lack of clarity in the TIER's technology catalogue about what technologies are covered within the category of "restricted" and "prohibited" import/export technology; and (iv) Article 2, which provides an overly ambiguous definition of "technology import and export" (Prud'homme 2012). Article 29 of the TIER, especially Article 29.3, has also been identified as restricting foreign firms' appropriability on their innovations, whereby it specified that a technology import contract must not contain provisions that prevent a receiving party in a technology contract from improving upon the technology supplied by the supplying party or otherwise restrict the receiving party from using improved technology (USTR 2018, p. 52); this being said, it is debatable about how detrimental this provision is to innovation in China. Although some firms have used the apparent flexibility in China's Contract Law to circumvent some of these requirements (especially Article 27), thinking of creative solutions in this regard has required time and resources, constituting arguably unnecessary transactions costs, and the legality of such approaches has long been uncertain. Further, at China's current stage of development, where many Chinese firms now have strong technological capabilities and are looking to engage in high-value contract research without having their knowledge appropriated by those they contract, the aforementioned provisions in the TIER can disadvantage Chinese firms. Minding these concerns, China's Ministry of Commerce (MOFCOM) contemplated revisions to the TIER meant to better facilitate innovation in China (IP Key 2016).

While this book was in the proofing phase, China's State Council made several highly important revisions to the TIER. These changes appear to be motivated by long-standing discussions on the TIER between Chinese and foreign authorities, and expedited by the recent WTO complaint brought by the US (DS 542) and EU (DS 549) involving the TIER and the US-China trade war partially meant to repeal FTT policies in China (Cohen 2019). Specifically, provision 38 in State Council Order No. 709 (Decision of the State Council to Revise Several Regulations),[2] issued and effective on March 2nd 2019 abolishes (deletes) Article 24.3, Article 27, and Article 29 of the TIER. These changes should, at a minimum, reduce some arguably unnecessary transaction costs previously faced by foreign firms to investing in innovation activities involving Chinese entities. They may even make foreign firms somewhat more likely to conduct more advanced forms of innovation in China and/or to transfer more advanced technology to China.

For over a decade, the Regulations for the Implementation of the Law on Sino-Foreign Equity Joint Ventures (hereafter the "equity JVs regulation"), issued by the State Council, set-forth several provisions which may have made foreign firms less likely to participate in certain innovation activities in China. Article 43.3 of the regulation stipulated that technology contracts are "generally" restricted to a duration of ten years. Moreover, Article 43.4 of the regulation stipulated that the technology importing party in the JV should be granted the right to use such technology "continuously" after the term of the contract expires.[3] These terms weakened the appropriability of foreign innovations and therefore may, depending on how they interacted with a range of other factors, have incentivized foreign firms participating in equity JVs to only transfer and develop technology well behind the frontier.

While this book was in the proofing phase, major revisions were made to the equity JVs regulation. Specifically, provision 33 of State Council Order No. 709 (the same measure previously mentioned in the context of the TIER) abolishes the third and fourth paragraphs of Article 43 (i.e., Article 43.3 and Article 43.4) of the equity JVs regulation. These changes may have a positive impact on innovation activities by foreign firms in China in ways similar to those previously described in the context of the versions to the TIER.

Up until several years ago, the interface between IP and anti-trust was governed by very broad provisions in China's Anti-Monopoly Law. This loose legal framework was perceived by firms as insufficient to protect against of abusive behavior of IP rights in a way that could inhibit innovation. In the last few years, several measures have been introduced providing more specific guidance to the authorities on how to govern the abuse of IP rights: SAIC promulgated the Provisions on the Prohibition of the Abuse of IPR to Eliminate or Restrain Competition in 2015 (hereafter "SAIC Provisions"), the NDRC released the draft Anti-Monopoly Guidelines on the Abuse of IPR (hereafter "NDRC Draft Guidelines") in 2015, SAIC released the Draft Anti-

---

[2]Full text of the measure (in Chinese) available from http://www.gov.cn/zhengce/content/2019-03/18/content_5374723.htm.

[3]For more information on other IP and technology issues related to China's laws on JV's and foreign investment see USTR (2018).

Monopoly Enforcement Guidelines on the Abuse of IPR (hereafter "SAIC Draft Guidelines") in 2016, and the Anti-Monopoly Commission of the State Council (AMC) promulgated the Guidelines on General Conditions and Procedures for the Exemption of Monopoly Agreements (hereafter "AMC Guidelines") in 2016.

Despite the aforementioned revisions to China's new legal framework regulating the interface between IP and anti-trust, some provisions therein are overly ambiguous and therefore create legal uncertainty which can inhibit innovation investments. Perhaps the most ambiguous and impactful provision in this regard is (i) the so-called "essential facilities" doctrine in Article 7 of the SAIC Provisions that states an economic agent (an "operator") with dominant market position may not, without justification, refuse to license its IP rights to other economic agents on reasonable terms so as to exclude or restrict competition if such IP is considered to constitute an "essential facility" for relevant production and other business operations. Although there is some specificity in the regulation about how the essential facilities doctrine might be applied,[4] there is concern from both Chinese and foreign firms that unreasonable application of the concept will violate IP rights holders' reasonable use of their IP as a means of appropriability. In effect, the provisions institutionalize the threat of a compulsory license in rather unclear circumstances, which raises transaction costs to innovation in China and thereby may dis-incentivize valuable innovation investments in favor of ones that firms are less weary of losing to state appropriation.

There is also legal ambiguity in other areas of the SAIC Provisions that are not particularly conducive to innovation: (ii) ambiguous scope of the "safe harbor" clause (Article 5) in the SAIC Provisions; (iii) the fact that the SAIC Provisions can only be enforced against non-price monopolistic conduct related to IP, giving them a limited scope of application; and (iv) the fact that the provisions may be replaced in the near future. Further, there is some inconsistency among certain provisions in the SAIC Provisions, NDRC Draft Guidelines and SAIC Draft Guidelines (for example related to market power thresholds for safe harbor) that should be addressed in order to create more legal certainty for innovators in China (Zhang et al. 2017).

Elements of China's legal framework regulating the interface between IP and technical standards are rather ambiguous or burdensome to firms and therefore may restrain innovation investments by both foreign and Chinese firms in China. The Regulations on National Standards Involving Patents, promulgated by SIPO and the Standardization Administration of China (SAC) (hereafter "SIPO & SAC Regulation") which came into force in 2014, contains a number of ambiguities that may restrain innovation investments. The most significant of these include (i) uncertainty about the exact definition of "standard essential patents" (SEPs), (ii) ambiguity about related disclosure obligations for patents that may be essential to technical standards, and (iii) burdensome requirements for companies participating in standards to license their IP under fair, reasonable and non-discriminatory (FRAND) condi-

[4]According to Article 7 of the SAIC Provisions, several factors need to be taken into account when determining what constitutes an essential facility: the reasonable substitutability of the IPR, the adverse impact of refusal to license on competition or innovation in the relevant market or on consumers' or the public's interests, whether the IP licensing will cause unreasonable damage to the IP holder, among potentially other factors.

tions. Moreover, perhaps the most significant ambiguity in the regulation is (iv) a provision stating that SAC, SIPO and "relevant departments" will negotiate licensing terms with patentees or applicants for a patent slated for inclusion in a compulsory national standard if they otherwise refuse to license that patent under FRAND terms for a fee or free. This latter provision indicates that there will be a compulsory license issued for patents to be included in compulsory national standards, though it is not explicitly required that this is done under FRAND terms, is unclear what form such negotiations with the authorities will take, and is uncertain how often this compulsory licensing situation will arise (Prud'homme 2014). These legal provisions compound the often-reported discriminatory nature through which certain firms are excluded from substantial roles in patent pools and technical standards-setting in China.

An area of Chinese IP and technology policy including some of the aforementioned measures are so-called "forced-technology transfer" (FTT) policies. What are often characterized by businesses, government officials, and scholars as "forced" technology transfer policies in fact do not always appear to technically "force" technology transfer—if the common definition of "force" is used, i.e. being compelled by threats (physical or otherwise), violence, or an utter lack of alternatives. With the important exception of one group of policies called "no choice" policies, which are further described in the next paragraph, foreign firms are allowed some flexibility to decide whether or not they want to comply with China's so-called "FTT" policies. In this sense, "forced" may not be the most accurate word to describe many controversial technology transfer policies in China. However, and importantly, the choice not to comply with the policies that most often appear to be considered to "force" technology in China is always met with consequences, some significant. In this sense, FTT policies attempt to compel technology transfer through negative (rather than positive) incentives/repercussions; in other words, the Chinese state institutes FTT policies in an attempt to shift the bargaining power in commercial transactions from foreign to Chinese firms (Prud'homme et al. 2018). While fully appreciating the complexity of these dynamics, which are further discussed in Table 4.2, for simplicity and to be consistent with well-established lingo, this section retains the term "forced" technology transfer policies but only for policies that meet the corresponding definition provided in Prud'homme et al. (2018): government policies meant to increase foreign-domestic technology transfer that simultaneously weaken appropriability of foreign innovation.

Existing scholarly studies into what might be labelled FTT policies in China largely focus on technology for market access requirements, often related to local content requirements, or other foreign investment catalogue restrictions (e.g., Pearson 1991; Bruun and Bennett 2002; Thun 2006; Hout and Ghemawat 2010; Grimes and Sun 2014; Holmes et al. 2015).[5] However, China also employs other types of FTT policies. Prud'homme et al. (2018) categorizes FTT policies based upon commonalities in how they shift foreign-Sino technology transfer bargaining

[5]US government reports look at some of these, and some other, controversial Chinese FTT policies and indigenous innovation policies. See, for example, BEA (1999), CECC (2010), Linton et al. (2010), Hammer et al. (2011).

Table 4.2 How forced technology-transfer policies encourage and discourage tech transfer

With the exception of the "No choice" policies, foreign firms are allowed some flexibility to decide whether or not they want to comply with China's FTT policies. Yet all are accompanied by consequences for non-compliance
The concept of policy "*leverage*" is integral to understanding the ability of FTTs to contribute to technology transfer. FTT policy "leverage" is herein defined as the ability of the policy to shift bargaining power in foreign-domestic technology transfer arrangements to favor domestic firms. In other words, leverage is tantamount to the ability of the state to pressure (what some would call "force") technology transfer
Not only does the design of FTT policies per se help determine if they exert leverage over frontier technology transfer, but the environment/circumstances in which they are deployed is equally important. Prud'homme et al. (2018) find that FTT policies exert the most leverage over frontier technology transfer when accompanied by seven conditions: (1) strong state support for industrial growth, (2) oligopoly competition, (3) other policies closely complementing FTT policies, (4) high technological uncertainty, (5) policy mode of operation offering basic appropriability and tailored to industrial structure, (6) reform avoidance by the state,[a] and (7) stringent policy compliance mechanisms. Prud'homme et al. (2018) then create an FTT Risk and Strategy Forecasting Matrix to identify specific strategies that the state might adopt to maximize the leverage of FTT policies and, on that basis, forecast the overall leverage of individual FTT policies
In sum, some Chinese FTT policies might force domestic acquisition of frontier foreign technology if accompanied by all seven conditions determining policy leverage, and if all these conditions are fully exploited by the state. However, if not, the policies have weaker leverage and may even discourage technology transfer. As a rule of thumb, FTT policies will generally only contribute to sustained technology transfer if they do not deprive foreign firms of a minimum level of appropriability and allow them to at least somewhat benefit from technology transfer arrangements

Source Prud'homme et al. (2018)

[a]Some aspects of reform avoidance regard the extent to which FTT policies may conflict with China's WTO obligations on technology transfer requirements, if violations are actually disputed at the WTO, and the details of the WTO ruling on such issues (e.g., Shea 2012; USTR 2018; WTO 2018a, b)

dynamics to favor domestic firms. The typology the authors develop is as follows: (1) "Lose the market" policies—where foreign firms should transfer technology in line with the policy or lose market access; (2) "No choice" policies—where foreign firms do not have a reasonable choice about whether or not to transfer technology because the state interprets the letter of the law governing such transfer in a highly dubious way/one that is clearly unreasonable vis-à-vis what is written; and (3) "Violate the law" policies—where foreign firms should choose to transfer technology in line with the written policy/law (which itself may be ambiguous or burdensome but nonetheless can at least generally be planned around) in order to be cautious and avoid potentially being subject to administrative or judicial actions enforcing that policy/law. Examples of "lose the market" policies include market access preconditioned on meeting technology transfer requirements, more specific examples of which are discussed in subsequent paragraphs. Examples of "no choice" policies include unfair IP civil litigation rulings, which are further discussed in

Chap. 7 hereto, and some cases of requiring excessive divulgation of trade secrets to receive regulatory approvals and then sharing that information with competitors. Examples of "violate the law" policies include the aforementioned legal provisions governing the interface between anti-trust and IP, IP and technical standards, and the TIER.[6]

Perhaps the most well-known "lose the market" FTT policies involve requirements imposed on foreign firms to transfer their technology to a foreign-Sino JV as a precondition for market access in China. The literature on these policies often focuses on those in the traditional auto industry and high-speed trains industry (e.g., Moran 2011; Zhou et al. 2016). Yet, broadly similar policies have also been reported in the big-power-generation turbines industry, telecom industry, and elsewhere. Further, there is also a controversial recent lose the market policy in the new energy vehicles (NEVs) industry that started in 2009 and was tightened in 2017. The 2009 policy required "mastering" of one of three core NEV technologies within a foreign-Sino JV in order to receive an NEV production license and access to government procurement and subsidies. The 2017 policy required mastering of all (not just one of three) core NEV technologies; further, as of January 2019, the 2017 measure still appeared to be in effect. However, meanwhile, the JV requirements in the auto industry have changed following statements by President Xi JinPing and the NDRC, and issuance of the Special Administrative Measures for Admittance of Foreign Investment, effective as of July 28th 2018 (Schaub and Zhao 2018). The aforementioned statements and measure indicate that foreign ownership restrictions were removed on NEVs in China as of 2018, and will be removed on commercial vehicles in 2020 and on passenger cars by 2022 (Schaub and Zhao 2018).

There are other types of lose the market policies in China. One type, which depending on the details thereof could also be considered a "violate the law" and/or perhaps a "no choice" policy, involve over-disclosure of trade secrets in order to receive regulatory approvals. These include, for example, requirements to disclose trade secrets as a precondition for receiving regulatory approvals for pharmaceuticals, authorization to invest in chemical plants, among activities in other industries. Such disclosure should not be necessary to grant regulatory approvals; worse, the confidential business information disclosed is sometimes shared with competitor firms. Another type of lose the market policy, which sometimes overlaps with those mentioned in the prior paragraph, are local content requirements as a precondition to win government procurement contracts or qualify for other government support. These policies have, at times in the past, been found in the wind turbines industry (e.g., Lewis 2011) among various other industries.

There is an ongoing debate about how FTT policies in China actually work to spur foreign-Sino technology transfer. The possibility that FTT policies may not exert leverage over frontier technology transfer, or might even discourage technol-

[6]Yet other, arguably less significant policies include: restrictions on IP resulting from government-funded research, overly strict sufficiency of disclosure and inventiveness requirements for biopharmaceutical patents, insufficient patent linkage, subsidies for indigenous patents, and the burdensome requirements in the High and New Technology Enterprise (HNTE) tax scheme. See Prud'homme et al. (2018) for a discussion.

ogy transfer if not smartly designed, represents potentially high stakes risk-taking by Chinese policymakers. If not formulated smartly, FTT policies (in China or any other country) may create a zero-sum game where foreign firms are actually discouraged from transferring technology and domestic firms therefore do not acquire new technology (Blomstrom et al. 2000; Kokko and Blomstrom 1995; Prud'homme et al. 2018). Table 4.2 provides insights on the workings of FTT policies in China.

While this book was in the proofing phase, on March 15th 2019 the National People's Congress adopted a new Foreign Investment Law (FIL), which includes provisions meant to address rising concerns from businesses and foreign governments about China's FTT policies.[7] The new FIL is set to take effect on January 1st 2020. While it typically takes several years for a change to the law to be approved in China, the changes to the FIL were expedited in just a few months given heavy backlash against China's investment policies—manifested in the WTO complaints against China and US-China trade war previously mentioned—at the time of finalizing this book. Article 21 of the FIL explicitly allows foreign firms more flexibility in transferring royalties from IP outside of China. Of even greater interest, Article 22 of the FIL proposes that "…administrative agencies and their staff must not use administrative methods to force transfer of technology".[8] This article builds on a similar provision in Part IV, Article 14 of the Notice of the State Council on Certain Measures for Actively and Effectively Utilizing Foreign Investment to Promote Quality Economic Development (State Council Document No. 19 [2018]), effective in June 2018. In addition, Article 23 of the new FIL requires confidentiality of trade secret information learned by Chinese government officials during regulatory approvals. Further, Article 39 of the new FIL sets-forth the grounds for penalties, including criminal ones, for the involvement of government officials in misappropriating trade secrets.

Taken together, Articles 22, 23, and 39 of the new FIL can help provide foreign firms a more certain business environment in which to innovate, although several factors limit the effect they will have. Articles 23 and 39 should be generally welcomed by foreign firms. And perhaps Article 22 could be used to push back against administrative agencies that de facto require excessive divulgation of trade secrets as a precondition for receiving state regulatory approvals. Further, Article 22 potentially can be strategically politicized and/or referenced in appeals by well-resourced MNCs in Chinese courts or other venues to somewhat help limit FTT and/or its effects in practice. This being said, it is not clear what activities Article 22 is meant to govern, i.e., exactly what the Mandarin Chinese term "force" ("强制") entails. Further, the Mandarin Chinese term for "transfer" used in Article 22 ("转让") specifically refers to ownership transfer/assignment and therefore does not appear to govern instances of "forced" licensing (exclusive or non-exclusive). While the intentionality of this language is unclear, considering the aforementioned concerns about the effect of

---

[7]Full text of the measure (in Chinese) available from: http://www.npc.gov.cn/npc/xinwen/2019-03/15/content_2083532.htm.

[8]The corresponding Chinese text reads as follows: "…行政 机关及其工作人员不得利用行政手段强制转让技术." (emphasis added).

perceived-to-be-unreasonable de facto and de jure government policies in China on licensing terms, the wording in Article 22 could more explicitly offer more confidence to foreign investors that the returns for their licensed innovations will be appropriated on perceived-to-be more reasonable terms.

In the final proofing phase for this book, yet other revisions were made to Chinese law that somewhat help address concerns surrounding FTT policies. On April 23rd 2019, the Administrative Licensing Law, which governs business licenses/certain regulatory approvals in China, was reformed. Article 5 of the revisions prohibits the individuals (including not only government officials, but also external experts, among others) involved in licensing procedures to disclose applicants' trade secrets and other confidential business information without the applicants' consent, except in situations required by law or justified under national security or public interest grounds. Presumably in an attempt to limit the uncertainty created by the aforementioned exceptions, Article 5 further specifies that applicants can object to the sharing of their information under such exceptions—although it remains unclear how this will happen. Article 5 also states that an applicant has equal rights to obtain administrative licenses and the state should not discriminate against applicants. Article 31 of the revised law stipulates that government bodies and their personnel must not make technology transfer a prerequisite for administrative licensing, and in the process of governing the licensing should not indirectly or directly require applicants to assign (transfer ownership of) their technology. These provisions complement similar ones in the new FIL, collectively helping, at least somewhat, deter and provide recourse against some FTT policies previously experienced by firms in China.

Several other relatively recent reforms to China's IP legal framework directly related to technology transfer and patent commercialization have been made which will likely have mixed effectiveness in stimulating transmission and exploitation of technological knowledge. First, as of 2018, several provisions intended to improve the commercialization of IP rights have been introduced into the draft fourth revision of China's Patent Law. These include provisions aimed at creating a platform administered by SIPO and supported by sub-central IP offices via which entities can out-license their patents. Generally, these revisions seem to limit information asymmetry and therefore may be useful to facilitate patent commercialization in China. However, their workings deserved to be clarified. As mentioned in Chap. 2, the provision on compulsory licensing of SEPs introduced in the 2015 draft patent law, which would create significant legal uncertainty for innovators, is absent from the 2018 draft of the law.

Second, the new draft of the Service Invention Regulations (SIR) sets forth monetary amounts for remunerating and rewarding individual service inventors. The first draft SIR was published in 2012, and subsequent drafts were published in 2014 and 2015. The draft SIR attempts to add further flesh to Article 16 of the current Patent Law which allows firms to be exempt from statutory approaches to remuneration and rewards (e.g., which specify specific percentages of operating profit to be paid to an employee inventor upon commercialization of his/her invention) if they institute "reasonable" remuneration and reward policies. However, it is not fully clear in the draft SIR (or Patent Law) what constitutes "reasonable" remuneration and rewards.

This major ambiguity, amongst others in the draft SIR, may add burdensome compliance and other financial costs to large foreign and Chinese firms in China that may hinder patent commercialization (Lutze 2016). As of 2017, our consultations with Chinese government officials indicate the draft SIR may not be finalized in the near future given significant concerns from Chinese and foreign industry over the burden it may impose on firms that already have effective remuneration schemes in place.

Still, in the absence of a legally effective SIR, Chinese courts are issuing decisions about service invention remuneration and rewards that may discourage R&D in China. For example, in a second instance civil judgment in Zhang Weifeng versus 3M in 2015, the Shanghai High People's Court decided that the statutory remuneration claim for service inventors in China should be calculated from the employer's global turnover figures and shall extend to the whole group of affiliated companies of the employer. Such clarifications may make the state-mandated terms in China the highest state-mandated standard globally (Lutze 2016). These high remuneration amounts may discourage R&D investments in China.

Judging from our consultations with legal scholars in China, there seems to be a misperception that state-mandated service inventor remuneration and reward laws (which only a few countries in the world actually have) have clearly been useful for incentivizing innovation in foreign countries. In fact, the literature generally finds that these state schemes create more negative economic impacts than positive impacts. For example, Merges (1999) finds the schemes create significant compliance costs and dis-incentivize R&D collaboration because individual inventors try to maximize their own remuneration and rewards. Owan and Nagaoka (2011) find that the schemes incentivize safer/less disruptive research that is more certain to be financially rewarded. Kappos and Nagasawa (2014) find that the schemes effectively require that significant money is spent within the firm on administering compliance programs and on litigation costs, and this money could be better spent on innovation. Onishi (2013) finds the schemes may have a positive impact on increasing revenue from patents in small firms; however, Kanama and Nishikawa (2017) find the schemes have negative impacts on the development of new products and services in large firms. Harhoff and Hoisl (2007) find mixed impacts of the schemes on employee and firm-wide performance. Further, in general, effective firm-determined pay, management structures, training, and stock options might be better tools to incentivize innovation than state-mandated inventor remuneration schemes (Lynch and Black 1995; Lerner and Wulf 2007; Cosh et al. 2007; Yanadori and Cui 2013; Chang et al. 2015). Considering this evidence, it appears that Chinese policymakers would benefit from rethinking the centrality of statutory and judicial approaches to service inventor remuneration and rewards as part of their innovation strategy.

4.2 University Technology Commercialization and Transfer: Major Trends and Policies

Universities play an integral role in the "triple-helix" model, which emphasizes the efficient connections between universities/PRIs/academia, government, and industry/firms in order to generate innovation (Leydesdorff and Etzkowitz 1996). Similarly, universities have played a strong role in the patent explosion in China (Hu and Mathews 2008). In 2015, Chinse universities and PRIs were granted 21% of China's invention patents, 9% of its utility models, and 2% of its designs, and 10% of its patents overall.[9]

Figure 4.1 illustrates that universities and PRIs in China have contributed to at least 10% of all patents out-licensed in China in recent years, which is a sizeable amount relative to the proportion of the patent stock held by universities and PRIs in China. There is evidence that Chinese universities and PRIs are slower at out-licensing their patents than comparable institutions in developed countries (Chen et al. 2014). However, there remains disagreement in the literature about whether universities and PRIs in China should put greater emphasis on technology commercialization or basic research (Chen et al. 2016). Most patents out-licensed by Chinese universities fall within three international patent classification (IPC) categories, namely chemistry & metallurgy, performing operations & transporting, and physics (Liu et al. 2016). Most patent out-licenses from universities in China are exclusive licenses for invention patents and most out-licensing universities are based in Eastern China (Liu et al. 2016).

Of course, patent licensing data is an imperfect measure of technology commercialization and transfer and therefore should be cautiously considered. Technology can of course be transferred via hiring new human resources, learning new management practices, sharing trade secrets, and numerous other means that do not require patents. In fact, in appropriability environments that are perceived to be weak, such as China's (at least in the recent past), FDI and exchange of tacit rather than codified knowledge (e.g., that in patents) is the preferred method of technology transfer (e.g., see Mansfield 1994). Still, despite these limitations, the patent licensing data have broad descriptive value.

There are a variety of challenges that have made linkages between Chinese universities and industry less than optimal for diffusing academic inventions (OECD 2008, pp. 41–42). It is well beyond the scope of this book to discuss all of these challenges; however, this chapter briefly highlights several challenges related to Chinese IP law and policy.

China's Law of Scientific and Technology Progress (LSTP) (mentioned in Chap. 2), first adopted in 1992, intends to promote the commercialization of scientific and technological achievements. The law, which is similar in several ways to the US' Bayh-Dole Act, provides several important provisions governing the ownership of IP generated by public funding. For example, it allows "the authorized

[9]Calculations using data from National Statistical Yearbook 2016 (http://www.stats.gov.cn/tjsj/ndsj/2016/html/2013EN.jpg).

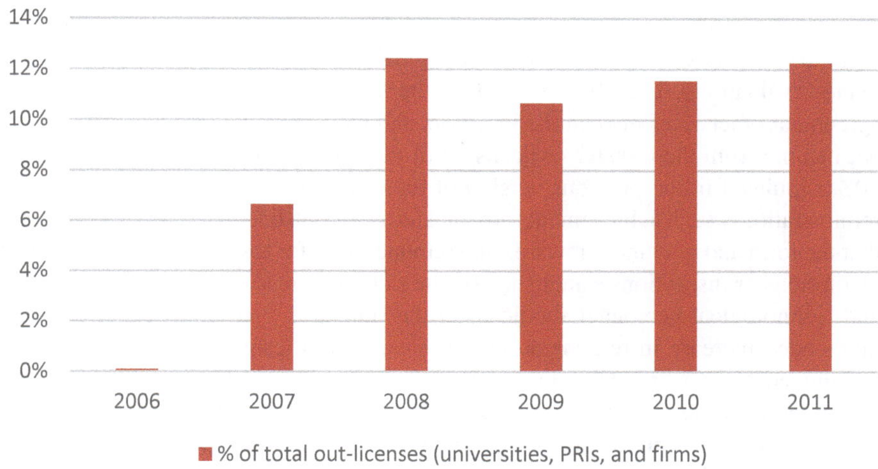

Fig. 4.1 Patent out-licenses from Chinese universities and PRIs. *Source* Data manually collected and classified by licensor type from SIPO's patent database. Data for invention patents, utility models, and designs. Limitations of the data should be noted (First, although Chinese law requires certain information to be reported to SIPO for all patent licenses, it appears quite possible that not all entities have reported their patent licenses. Second, the method used to classify the licensor and licensees is based upon our manual working classification, as no official sorting tool by entity type was available in the database we used)

undertaker of the project" i.e. the public institutes such as universities to have the ownership of invention supported by public fund and therefore stimulate universities to prosecute and commercialize patents via their specialized Technology Transfer Offices or Patent Licensing Offices. There is evidence that the law has contributed to increasing patenting by Chinese universities (Tang 2006), although not necessarily high-quality patents (Chen et al. 2016). The LSTP was revised in 2007 because its prior version was considered too vague to effectively stimulate innovation and patent commercialization. Despite these revisions, China's LSTP could benefit from more clarity about the legal interests of different parties involved in the patent commercialization process (Wu 2016). Also, as mentioned in Chap. 2, the LSTP could benefit from clarification about the circumstances in which firms can expect the state to exercise march-in rights.

China's Law on the Promotion of Transformation of Scientific and Technological Achievements (LPTSTA) was introduced in 1995 to encourage R&D research institutions, colleges and universities, and other institutions to join efforts with manufacturers in order to transform and commercialize their scientific and technological achievements. The LPTSTA is a subordinate law to the LSTP, meant to provide more specific advice to implement the LSTP. The law was revised in 2015 to strengthen coordination of the government's various policies to create a stronger environment for the transformation of S&T achievements.

It is unclear if all the provisions in the LPTSTA will improve technological commercialization in China, and in fact some appear too vague to do so at present.

Amongst various other provisions, the LPTSTA requires Chinese universities and PRIs to put greater emphasis on technological commercialization in their performance evaluations. The 2015 revision to the law also requires that, if there is no agreement otherwise between the inventors and their units, no less than 50% of the net income from the transfer or licensing of the S&T achievements (instead of the 20% stipulated in the previous version of the law) should be taken as awards and remuneration if such achievements are transferred or out-licensed.[10] It also stipulates that the form and amount of rewards and remuneration for research and development institutions or institutions established by the state or agreed upon with the scientific and technological personnel should meet the standards.[11] It is unclear if this recommended increase in remuneration will have a significant impact on innovation, and university-industry technology transfer in particular, in China. As mentioned in the previous discussion about the draft SIR, state-mandated remuneration schemes for technological commercialization may not be an optimal approach to encouraging innovation. Further, in other countries, for example those in Europe, there is evidence that similar legislative remuneration approaches do not have significant positive impacts on innovation and university-industry technology transfer (Sobrero 2016).[12] At the same time, the 2015 revision to the LPTSTA regarding remuneration allows freedom to contract that did not exist in the same way under the 1995 version of the law; as such, rigid compliance with the remuneration figures proposed in the new law are not necessarily required. This new flexibility may have a positive impact in terms of reducing compliance costs once associated with commercialization technology in China. At the same time, the vagueness of many provisions in the LSTP and LPTSTA in effect require that authorities at different levels in China create more specific implementing rules in order for the laws to have a significant impact on patent commercialization (Zhang et al. 2017).

Although the LSTP and LPTSTA encourage Chinese universities and PRIs to develop technology transfer offices (TTOs), many TTOs in China are not particularly efficient or effective. For example, many TTOs in China are rather poorly equipped to write solid patent applications, patent licensing contracts, or devise a smart overarching patent management strategy (Liu et al. 2016).

As mentioned, several provisions intended to improve the commercialization of IP rights, including by universities and PRIs, have been introduced into the draft fourth revision of China's Patent Law. The provisions may limit information asymmetry by setting up public licensing platforms, thereby supporting the patent commercialization efforts of Chinese universities and PRIs.

The Chinese government has introduced several important national research funding programs to support knowledge generation. These include, for example, Project

---

[10]See Art. 45, Section 1, LPTSTA.

[11]See Art. 45, Section 2, LPTSTA. This parallel system in the LPTSTA stipulates a higher and more ambitious standard of remuneration in favor of inventors and scientists than that required in China's Patent Law.

[12]This being said, the situation in Europe may not be as comparable to China given differences in levels of knowledge accumulation, technological development, and efficiency of the triple helix.

'211' (1991), the Engineering Program '985' (1998), and Program '2011' (2012), to enhance the research capacity of universities. Additionally, National Science and Technology programs such as Program '863' (1986) and Program '973' (1997), are mostly implemented by universities. From the available literature on the subject, these programs appear to have had mixed effectiveness in terms of supporting patent commercialization (Chen et al. 2016). Further research appears warranted to provide an up-to-date assessment about how each of these programs are working to facilitate patent commercialization and technology transfer in China.

4.3 Other Policies

Various other initiatives have been developed by the Chinese state to try and increase patent commercialization and licensing. For example, central-level and provincial-level initiatives aim to start Patent Banks for funding cultivation of IP; encourage banks to control loan risk for better funding IP development; accept IP-based collateral as security for loans; establish venture capital funds for investment in IP-intensive areas; expand pledge financing for IP; among other initiatives (Prud'homme 2012). Similarly, provincial/municipal technology markets sometimes focus explicitly on IP development—for example CTEX, a Beijing-based government-supported technology exchange created an IP Ventures Fund to purchase IP in foreign markets and the Shanghai Silicon IP Exchange is developing a similar mechanism.[13] By way of another example, Ruichuan IPR Funds, a Chinese state-owned non-practicing entity (NPE), aims to acquire IP from domestic and foreign firms, support Chinese firms in obtaining and financing commercialization of their patents, and helps provide a portfolio of patents that Chinese firms can use to shield against infringement suits from foreign entities (Larson 2015).

Additionally, the state has developed a variety of initiatives to aid Chinese firms in developing and acquiring "indigenous intellectual property rights" (自主知识产权), i.e. IP owned by wholly-Chinese-owned firms. These policies are intent on eroding incumbents' IP-derived barriers to entry facing indigenous Chinese firms. Prior to 2011, the policies once spanned government procurement preferences, although now focus more on subsidies, grants, and tax incentives (Prud'homme 2012, 2013). While potentially strategically useful in some value chains that are less reliant on intermediate products owned by foreign incumbents, restricting state support to "indigenous" IP rights limits potentially useful IP that indigenous Chinese firms could use to compete in internationalized/truly global value chains (GVCs) (Prud'homme 2017). In fact, as mentioned previously, recent research shows that Chinese firms that in-licensed foreign patents subsequently outperformed firms that primarily in-licensed fully indigenous Chinese patents (Wang et al. 2013; Li-Ying and Wang

[13]Transaction value in technology markets in China rose dramatically from RMB 476.4 billion in 2011 to RMB 983.6 billion in 2015. Calculations using data from National Statistical Yearbook 2016 (http://www.stats.gov.cn/tjsj/ndsj/2016/html/2001EN.jpg).

2015). And, more generally, absorption of external resources from foreign firms (including patented technology) alongside development of internal capabilities is necessary for sustainable indigenous innovation (Fu et al. 2011; Fu and Gong 2011).

China's state incentives for IP consultants and attorneys to design and oversee suitable IP and technology licensing agreements can also influence patent commercialization and technology transfer. For example, some Chinese provinces have established rules for reducing the business tax, education surcharge, amongst other state fees associated with developing patented technology. To the extent that these policies include sufficient requirements to ensure they are only incentivizing quality patents and quality technology transfer agreements, they may enable innovation in China.

4.4 Summary

The Chinese state has formulated a plethora of IP-related regulations and policies to try and increase transmission and exploitation of technological knowledge – including direct technology transfer, spillovers, and patent commercialization. Many of these measures are very recent. The measures include the technology import and export regulations (TIER), regulations governing Sino-foreign equity JVs, regulations governing the interface between anti-trust and IP/abuse of IP, regulations and practices governing the interface between technical standards and IP, other policies considered by foreign firms to "force" technology transfer, a draft regulation for service/employee inventor remuneration and rewards (draft SIR), laws governing scientific and technological progress and achievements, state-supported technology markets and funds for IP development, financial incentives for development of "indigenous" IP, amongst other policies.

The Chinese state currently faces the challenge of proactively encouraging transmission and exploitation of technological knowledge in an economy where firms are often reluctant or unable to do so. Further, the Chinese state faces the challenge of balancing the strategic goal of eroding incumbents' IP-derived barriers to entry with the reality that absorption of external resources from foreign firms alongside dynamic use of internal capabilities is needed for sustainable indigenous innovation. These ongoing challenges are reflected by the fact that parts of the aforementioned IP measures are arguably not optimal for encouraging innovation investments, technology transfer (especially of frontier technology), patent commercialization, or spillovers in China because they are overly ambiguous or burdensome. This raises transaction costs of compliance and otherwise creates an uncertain legal environment for innovation in China.

In 2018 and 2019 the Chinese state made several very commendable revisions to some of these measures, although additional reforms could still be made. Several ambiguous, overly-burdensome, or otherwise suboptimal provisions in some of the measures should be revised or removed entirely.

References

Asakawa, K., and A. Som. 2008. Internationalization of R&D in China and India: Conventional wisdom versus reality. *Asia Pacific Journal of Management* 25: 375–394.

BEA. 1999. U.S. Commercial technology transfers to the People's Republic of China. U.S. Department of Commerce's Bureau of Export Administration Office's Strategic Industries and Economic Security Defense Market Research Report, available at https://fas.org/nuke/guide/china/doctrine/dmrr_chinatech.htm.

Blomstrom, M., A. Kokko, and M. Zejan. 2000. *Foreign direct investment: Firm and host country strategies*. New York: Palgrave.

Bruun, P., and D. Bennett. 2002. Transfer of technology to China: A Scandinavian and European perspective. *European Management Journal* 20: 98–106.

CECC. 2010. Will China protection intellectual property? New developments in counterfeiting, piracy, and forced technology transfer. Hearing before the US Congressional-Executive Commission on China, available at https://www.cecc.gov/sites/chinacommission.house.gov/files/documents/hearings/2010/CECC%20Hearing%20-%20Will%20China%20Protect%20Intellectual%20Property%20-%209.22.10.pdf.

Chan, L., and T. Daim. 2011. Technology transfer in China: Literature review and policy implications. *Journal of Science and Technology Policy in China* 2: 122–145.

Chang, X., K. Fu, A. Low, and W. Zhang. 2015. Non-executive employee stock options and corporate innovation. *Journal of Financial Economics* 115: 168–188.

Chen, K., X. Li, and G. Yang. 2014. A comparison of technology transfer efficiency of domestic and foreign universities: Based on the DEA-Malmquist method (in Chinese). *Science of Science and Management of Science & Technology* 35: 98–106.

Chen, A., D. Patton, and M. Kenney. 2016. University technology transfer in China: A literature review and taxonomy. *Journal of Technology Transfer* 41: 891–929.

Cohen, G. 2004. *Technology transfer: Strategic management in development countries*. London: Sage Publications.

Cohen, M. 2019. The TIER is revised. China IPR, available at https://chinaipr.com/2019/03/18/thetier-is-revised/.

Cosh, A., X. Fu, and A. Hughes. 2007. Management characteristics, managerial ownership and innovative efficiency in high-technology industry. Oxford University, SLPTMD Working Paper Series No. 007 available at https://ora.ox.ac.uk/objects/uuid:426cbee0-22c4-4e2c-a83a-26a897904c02.

Freeman, C. 1987. *Technology policy and economic performance: Lessons from Japan*. London: Pinter Publishers.

Fu, X. 2015. *China's path to innovation*. UK: Cambridge University Press.

Fu, X., and Y. Gong. 2011. Indigenous and foreign innovation efforts and drivers of technological upgrading: Evidence from China. *World Development* 39: 1213–1225.

Fu, X., C. Pietrobelli, and L. Soete. 2011. The role of foreign technology and indigenous innovation in the emerging economies: Technological change and catching-up. *World Development* 39: 1204–1212.

Grimes, S., and Y. Sun. 2014. Implications of China's on-going dependence on foreign technology. *Geoforum* 54: 59–69.

Hammer, A., et al. 2011. China: Effects of intellectual property infringement and indigenous innovation policies on the US economy. USITC Publication 4226, available at https://www.usitc.gov/publications/332/pub4226.pdf.

Harhoff, D., and K. Hoisl. 2007. Institutionalized incentives for ingenuity: Patent value and the German Employees' Inventions Act. *Research Policy* 36: 1143–1162.

Holmes, T.J., E.R. McGrattan, and E.C. Prescott. 2015. Quid pro quo: Technology capital transfers for market access in China. *The Review of Economic Studies* 82: 1154–1193.

Hout, T., and P. Ghemawat. 2010. China's vs. the world—Whose technology is it? *Harvard Business Review* 88: 94–103.

Hu, M.C., and J. Mathews. 2008. China's national innovative capacity. *Research Policy* 37: 1465–1479.

IP Key. 2016. Proceedings of EU-China Innovation Policies Workshop (unpublished), organized by the European Commission, China's Ministry of Commerce, and Xiamen University at Xiamen University.

Kanama, D., and K. Nishikawa. 2017. Does an extrinsic reward for R&D employees enhance innovation outcomes? Evidence from a Japanese innovation survey. *R&D Management* 47: 198–211.

Kappos, D., and K. Nagasawa. 2014. Japan's article 35: Are employee-inventor monetary award laws impeding Japanese innovation? *Japarn AIPPA Journal* 39–46.

Keller, W. 2002. Trade and the transmission of technology. *Journal of Economic Growth* 7: 5–24.

Keller, W. 2004. International technology diffusion. *Journal of Economic Literature* 42: 752–782.

Kokko, A., and M. Blomstrom. 1995. Policies to encourage inflows of technology through foreign multinationals. *World Development* 23: 459–468.

Larson, K. 2015. The emergence of non-practising entities in China. In *Governance of intellectual property rights in China and Europe*, ed. N. Lee, N. Bruun, and M. Li, 287–302. Cheltenham, UK: Edward Elgar.

Lerner, J., and J. Wulf. 2007. Innovation and incentives: Evidence from corporate R&D. *Review of Economics and Statistics* 89: 634–644.

Lewis, J. 2011. Building a national wind turbine industry: Experiences from China, India and South Korea. *International Journal of Technology and Globalisation* 5 (3): 281–305.

Leydesdorff, L., and H. Etzkowitz. 1996. Emergence of a triple helix of university-industry-government relations. *Science & Public Policy* 23: 279–286.

Linton, K., A. Hammer, et al. 2010. China: Intellectual property infringement, indigenous innovation policies, and frameworks for measuring the effects on the US economy. USITC Publication 4199.

Liu, Y., L. Tan, and Y. J. Cheng. 2016. University patent licensing and its contribution to China's National Innovation System. In *Economic impacts of intellectual property-conditioned government incentives*, ed. D. Prud'homme and H. Song, 259–277. Springer.

Li-Ying, J., and Y. Wang. 2015. Find them home or abroad? The relative contribution of international technology in-licensing to 'indigenous innovation in China. *Long Range Planning* 48: 123–134.

Li-Ying, J., Y. Wang, S. Salomo, and Vanhaverbeke. 2012. Have Chinese firms learned from their prior technology in-licensing? An analysis based on patent citations. *Scientometrics* 95: 183–195.

Lundvall, B.A. 1992. *National systems of innovation: Towards a theory of innovation and interactive learning*. London: Pinter Press.

Lutze, O. 2016. Incentives for Chinese inventors: A proposal for a new inventor remuneration scheme with German elements. In *Economic impacts of intellectual property-conditioned government incentives*, ed. D. Prud'homme and H. Song, 157–175. Springer.

Lynch, L., and S. Black. 1995. Beyond the incident of training: Evidence from a National Employers Survey. NBER Working Paper No. 5231.

Mansfield, E. 1994. Intellectual property protection, foreign direct investment and technology transfer. International Finance Corporation Discussion Paper 19.

Maskus, K.E., S.M. Dougherty, and A. Mertha. 2005. Intellectual property rights and economic development in China. In *Intellectual property and development: Lessons from recent economic research*, ed. C. Fink and K.E. Maskus, 295–332. Washington, D.C.: World Bank and Oxford University Press.

Merges, R. 1999. The law and economics of employee inventions. *Harvard Journal of Law & Technology* 13: 1–53.

Moran, T. 2011. Foreign manufacturing multinationals and the transformation of the Chinese economy: New measurements, new perspectives. IIE Working Paper 11-11, available at http://www.iie.com/publications/wp/wp11-11.pdf.

Nelson, R. (ed.). 1993. *National innovation systems: A comparative analysis*. UK: Oxford University Press.

OECD. 2008. OECD review of innovation policy: China. Available at www.oecd.org.

Onishi, K. 2013. The effects of compensation plans for employee inventions on R&D productivity: New evidence from Japanese panel data. *Research Policy* 42: 367–378.
Owan H., and S. Nagaoka. 2011. Intrinsic and extrinsic motivations of inventors. RIETI Discussion Paper Series 11-E-022.
Pearson, M. 1991. *Joint ventures in the People's Republic of China*. Princeton: Princeton University Press.
Prud'homme, D. 2012. *Dulling the cutting edge: How patent-related policies and practices hamper innovation in China*. Beijing: European Chamber.
Prud'homme, D. 2013. China's indigenous IP policies—Here to stay? *Managing Intellectual Property* 233: 24–27.
Prud'homme, D. 2014. FRAND and other requirements in China's Announcement on Releasing (Provisional) Administration Regulations of National Standards Involving Patents. *Journal of Intellectual Property Law & Practice* 9: 346–349.
Prud'homme, D. 2017. China's "indigenous" intellectual property incentives, global value chains, and latecomer catch-up. Sydney, Australia: Macquarie Graduate School of Management.
Prud'homme, D., M. von Zedtwitz, J. Thraen, and M. Bader. 2018. "Forced technology transfer" policies: Workings in China and strategic implications. *Technological Forecasting and Social Change* 134: 150–168.
Rogers, E.M. 1995. *Diffusion of innovation*. New York, NY: The Free Press.
Schuab, M., and A. Zhao. 2018. Impact of China removal of foreign ownership restrictions in auto sector. Lexology, available at https://www.lexology.com/library/detail.aspx?g=184f92db-2a7f-4233-bc05-4e042566ea15.
Shea, D., 2012. The impact of international technology transfer on American research and development. Testimony of Hon. Dennis C. Shea before US House of Representatives, available at https://science.house.gov/sites/republicans.
Sobrero, M., 2016. Experiences with technology transfer policies in EU Member States. Presentation at the EU-China Innovation Policies Roundtable organized by China's Ministry of Commerce, the European Commission, IP Key, and Xiamen University. Presentation available at http://www.ipkey.org/en/activities/upcoming-activities/item/4091-eu-china-innovation-policies-roundtable.
Song, H. 2013. *Indigenous innovation capability-building and the development of intellectual property rights (in Chinese)*. Beijing: Chinese Academy of Sciences Intellectual Property Rights Press.
Stewart, C. 1987. Technology transfer vs. diffusion: A conceptual clarification. *The Journal of Technology Transfer* 12: 71–79.
Tang, M.F. 2006. The effect of China's "Bayh-Dole Act" on university research and technology transfer (in Chinese). *Journal of Central South University of Technology* 13: 26–33.
Thun, E. 2006. *Changing lanes in China: Foreign direct investment, local governments, and auto sector development*. New York: Cambridge University Press.
UNCTAD, United Nations, New York, available at http://unctad.org/en/Docs/iteiia20056p2_en.pdf.
USTR. 2018. Findings of the investigation into China's acts, policies, and practices related to technology transfer, intellectual property, and innovation under Section 301 of the Trade Act of 1974. Office of the United States Trade Representative, available at https://ustr.gov/sites/default/files/Section%20301%20FINAL.PDF.
Wang, Y., N. Roijakkers, and W. Vanhaverbeke. 2013. Learning-by-licensing: How Chinese firms benefit from licensing-in technologies. *IEEE Transactions on Engineering Management* 60: 46–58.
Wang, Y., N. Roijakkers, and W. Vanhaberbeke. 2014a. How fast do Chinese firms learn and catch up? Evidence from patent citations. *Scientometrics* 98: 743–761.
Wang, Y., J. Li-Ying, J. Chen, and Z. Lu. 2014b. Technology licensing in China. *Science and Public Policy* 42: 293–299.
WTO. 2018a. US' WTO request for consultations regarding certain measures on the transfer of technology in China, available at https://www.wto.org/english/tratop_e/dispu_e/cases_e/ds542_e.htm.

WTO. 2018b. EU's WTO request for consultations regarding certain measures on the transfer of technology in China, available at https://www.wto.org/english/tratop_e/dispu_e/cases_e/ds549_e.htm.

Wu, H. 2016. The evolution and normalization of Chinese Bayh-Dole Rules (in Chinese). *Journal of Nanjing University of Science and Technology* 29.

Xiao, Y., A. Tylecote, and J. Liu. 2013. Why not greater catch-up by Chinese firms? The impact of IPR, corporate governance and technology intensity on late-comer strategies. *Research Policy* 42: 749–764.

Yanadori, Y., and V. Cui. 2013. Creating incentives for innovation? The relationship between pay dispersion in R&D groups and firm innovation performance. *Strategic Management Journal* 34: 1502–1511.

Zhang, T., D. Prud'homme, and O. Lutze. 2017. China's new patent commercialization strategy. *Journal of Intellectual Property Law & Practice* 12: 474–488.

Zhou, Y. 2006. Features and impacts of the internationalization of R&D by transnational corporations: China's case, in Globalization of R&D and Development Countries, 297.

Zhou, Y., W. Lazonick, and Y. Sun. 2016. *China as an innovation nation*. New York, NY: Oxford University Press.

Chapter 5
New/Experimental IP-Related Measures

The growth of Internet-intensive and other emerging industries in China has posed new challenges to governance of IP, to which the Chinese state has proactively responded. The Chinese state has recently attempted to regulate corresponding business models and other commercial activities in a way that ensures healthy competition and safeguards the public interests while also not restricting innovation.[1] However, there is a dearth of literature that provides an integrated review of all of these different recent initiatives, which we call "IP experiments".

We divide these new IP initiatives into two groups and offer a preliminary evaluation of their effectiveness. The first group of experiments we discuss is "technology-reactionary experiments", named after the initiatives which appear to have developed in response to emerging new technologies and business models. This group of experiments could be regarded as the China's direct implementation of its National Intellectual Property Strategy 2008 and revision of its IP system in line with the development of strategic technologies and industries (Lipu 2013; Xiaoqing 2011).[2]

[1] About the Chinese government's attitude to offer better IP protection to emerging business models and new technologies, see for example CPC Central Committee and State Council, 'Several Opinions on Deepening the Reform of Institutional Mechanisms and Accelerating the Implementation of Innovation-driven Development Strategies' (2015) No. 8 [中共中央国务院, '关于深化体制机制改革加快实施创新驱动发展战略的若干意见' (中发 〔2015〕 8 号)]; State Council, 'Several Opinions on Accelerating the Construction of Powerful Intellectual Property Rights under the New Situation' (2015) No. 71 (国务院, '关于新形势 下加快智慧财产权强国建设的若干意见' [国发 〔2015〕 71 号)]; SIPO, 'Explanation of the Draft Revision of Patent Examination Guideline' (2016) (国家知识产权局, '国家知识产权局关于《专利审查指南修改草案 (征求意见稿)》的说明' (2016)).

[2] As to China's State IP strategy and its relationship with the emerging technologies and industries, see Lipu (2013) and Xiaoqing (2011); as to the need to revise the IP system in line with changes in technology, see for example Samuelson (1990).

D. Prud'homme and T. Zhang, *China's Intellectual Property Regime for Innovation*, https://doi.org/10.1007/978-3-030-10404-7_5

The second group of IP experiments we discuss is "other experiments" which capture all other types of recent experimental IP initiatives and programs not discussed [with the exception of the draft service Invention Regulation (SIR)] in other chapters of this book. This group of experiments is designed to improve the internal and external innovation environment of market players.

5.1 Technology-Reactionary Experiments

5.1.1 Graphical User Interface (GUI)

In 2014, the State Intellectual Property Office of China (SIPO) revised its rules to remove electronic screen designs from excluded subject matter for design patent protection. Specifically, on May 1, 2014, SIPO issued Order No. 68 which opened the gate for design applications for graphical user interfaces (GUIs) in China (SIPO 2014). This reform was part of an attempt to bring China's laws on designs further in line with those of foreign countries and in recognition of the competitive advantage that development of GUIs may provide Chinese industry. This policy change seems to have already contributed to appropriability in the GUI industry in China: at the end of 2016, more than 14,741 GUI design patents were granted by SIPO (Chen 2017). With the development of industry, relevant legal disputes also arise. The first GUI design patent infringement case was filed at the Beijing IP Court in 2016[3] and the first GUI invalidation case was decided in 2017.[4]

There are, however, important limitations of GUI design protection in China. First, a GUI must be combined with an industrial product, such as a smart phone, in order to meet SIPO's requirements for patentability. In other words, a mere GUI without any corresponding physical product will not be granted a design patent. Second, no partial design protection is available under the current Chinese Patent Law (although this may change in future amendments). Therefore, a Chinese design patent is only protected by the law if the entire design of the same product is infringed upon. If a GUI design can be used on different products such as laptops, smart phones and tablets, an applicant needs to apply for a separate GUI design patent for each of these products.

In practice, SIPO has paid increasing attention to the nature of the GUI design itself. Some design applications have been submitted with the name "GUI applied to smart devices" or with only the main view of the product instead of six-sided views required, and these applications have successfully passed SIPO's (non-substantive) examination for designs (Chen 2017). This phenomenon may indicate some filers

[3]Qihu 360 claimed that defendant's software infringes on its three GUI design patents. See [2016] Qihu 360 v. Jiang Ming Technology, 2016 (北京奇虎科技有限公司, 奇智软体(北京)有限公司诉北京江民新科技有限公司侵犯外观设计专利案, (2016) 京73民初276号).

[4]Decision of Patent Reexamination Board, Decision No. 31958 (2017) (国家知识产权局专利复审委员会, 217年第31958号专利无效审查决定).

of low quality patents are exploiting the new GUI patentability allowance and lack of substantive examination for designs in China. Chinese policymakers may weaken the product element of design protection and extend protection for partial designs in future legal amendments.

5.1.2 *Software and Business Method Patents (BMP)*

On October 27, 2016, SIPO published a Draft of Revisions to the Patent Examination Guidelines (interchangeable with "the Guidelines" hereafter) that appears to reduce the barrier to patenting software and business methods in China. This revision became effective on April 1, 2017 according to SIPO's Order No. 74 (SIPO 2017a, b, c). According to the revised Patent Examination Guidelines, patent applicants will be able to claim a software medium plus computer program process in their patents. According to the new rules, previously ineligible patent claims directed at "a computer program product" or "a machine-readable medium" will now be eligible for patent protection in China.

With regards to business method patents (BMPs), according to SIPO's previous rules, BMPs involve a type of mental activity that should be excluded from the scope of patent-eligible subject matter in China. The revised Guidelines ease the former BMP ban by noting that "*If a claim related to a business model involves not only content of business rules and methods but also technical characteristics, it shall not be excluded from the possibility of being granted a patent right according to Article 25 of the patent law*". Moreover, in the official explanation of the revision, it is explicitly stated that SIPO welcomes and encourages inventions in the fields of finance, insurance, bond/securities, leasing, auctions, investment, marketing, advertising, and management that clearly are considered "business" activities (SIPO 2017a, b, c). This pioneering patentability rule has no precedent in the US or Europe and suggests that China is adopting a more liberal approach to patentability in some areas compared with leading developed countries (Lu and Hausman 2016).[5] Consequently, it will become more common to see SIPO's rejections for BMP applications based on lack of novelty or inventive step rather than dismissing the subject matter per se as outright ineligible for patent protection (Xu 2018).[6]

SIPO attributes the aforementioned changes regarding software patents and BMPs largely to the boom of Internet-intensive innovations in China in recent years. Chinese legislators surveyed industry in China and discovered that innovative firms hoped that the patent system could provide protection to innovative technical solutions relating to software and business methods (SIPO 2016). However, to strike a good balance

---

[5]There are yet other ways in which China's patent regime offers more appropriability for innovations than the regimes in some developed countries. For example, in practice, important biotechnology and software inventions are patentable in China but not in the US (Madigan and Mossoff 2017).

[6]Before the end of 2017, the granting rate of BMP was 12% and most of the BMP applications were denied due to the lack of inventiveness.

between stimulating innovation in the industry and discouraging patent trolls from taking advantage of BMPs with claims that are normally full of unclear functional languages (Merges 1999a, b; Cohen and Lemley 2001), it would be wise for the SIPO to develop intricate official guideline in detail to tell how to examine the BMP applications and reject those of poor quality. Such guidelines are still not available.

5.1.3 Expedited Patent Examination for Select Industries

In 2012, SIPO established a prioritized examination track for invention patents in SEIs and other key areas (SIPO 2012).[7] This mechanism provides firms (especially Chinese SOEs, who often use the mechanism) a faster effective term for an issued patent and the ability to more quickly raise funds and accelerate business decisions (Liu 2017). This mechanism can accelerate product launches and investment returns and therefore should generally be conducive to innovation in Chinese firms who use the mechanism (Department of Treaty and Law of SIPO 2012).

A 2017 revision to the mechanism now allows utility models and designs, not just invention patents, to qualify for expedited examination.[8] If examination of only quality utility models and designs is expedited via this mechanism, this could have a positive impact on innovation in China; however, in absence of a more substantive examination for utility models and designs (see Chap. 3) the quality of such rights cannot necessarily be assured. Meanwhile, observers also point out that expedited patent examination could sometimes be inefficient due to a lack of clear definition of specific technology and could even lead to discrimination among industries and reduce the quality of patent examination given the shortage of qualified examiners and the backlog of patent applications (Li and Zheng 2014).

5.1.4 E-Commerce Regulation

China's e-commerce market became the largest in the world as of 2015 and is still growing at breakneck speed. A joint report by Bain Consultancy and Alibaba shows that by 2020, the total value of China's e-commerce market will reach 10 trillion RMB (Bain and Alibaba 2016). Business to consumer (B2C) sales, mobile electronics and cross-border electronic businesses will be the main driver of this future growth (Bain and Alibaba 2016).

---

[7] SIPO prescribed a non-exhaustive list of technical fields which are considered to be China's key technical fields, including environmental protection, energy conservation, new-generation IT, biotechnology, high-end equipment manufacturing, new energy, new materials, new energy vehicles, and so on.

[8] See http://www.haseltinelake.com/media-centre/news/2017/july/china-broadens-scope-for-accelerated-examination.

To keep up with the new challenges posed by these new developments, various laws and regulations on e-commerce have been enacted by different Chinese authorities. For example, in 2010, the Administrative Measures for the Payment Services of Non-financial Institutions was released to promote the development of the payment service market; in January 2014, SAIC released the Internet Transaction Management Measures to improve customer rights protection and discourage the sale of fake or damaged goods; in 2015, the State Council issued the Opinions on Strengthening the Governance of Infringement and Counterfeiting on the Internet; in 2015, the State Administration of Quality Supervision, Inspection and Quarantine released draft Regulations for the Safety Supervision and Administration of Cross-border E-commerce of Imported Food via the Bonded Warehouse Model, which raised the regulatory bar for distributing food via cross-border e-commerce; in April 2016, the government published the List of Products Eligible for Cross-border E-commerce (known as the "Positive List" by industry); among other measures.

Despite these developments in the legal framework for e-commerce in China, many challenges still remain to the healthy development of China's e-commerce market. These include uncertainties regarding related taxation, obligations and liabilities of e-commerce platforms, and protection of IPRs and the security of personal information collected by the platforms. In an attempt to address these issues, Chinese lawmakers published a draft of the nation's first comprehensive e-commerce law (the "Draft E-Commerce Law") in December 2016. The Draft E-Commerce law was finalized and officially promulgated on August 3, 2018, and went into effect on January 1, 2019.

Under the E-Commerce Law, all e-commerce operators must register with the proper government authority. Individual e-commerce operators have an obligation to acquire business licenses and pay taxes (Art. 12–15). A key element here is the recognition of non-traditional shopping channels as places of e-commerce, bringing popular Apps such as WeChat and Duoyin under the new legislation.

Section II, Chapter II of the E-Commerce Law clarifies the obligations and liabilities of e-commerce third party platforms. These include the need for these entities to: (1) review and supervise operators on their own platforms; (2) make and enforce open and transparent platform rules; (3) record and keep important information; and (4) allow exit from platforms. The new law also requests e-commerce operators to establish internal control systems and technology management measures to avoid information leakage, loss or damages, and to ensure the safety of e-commerce data (Art. 30). However, these rules need to be clarified and tested in court in China to clarify the exact scope of associated obligations and liabilities.

The new law also tries to improve the protection of IP involved in e-commerce. It requires e-commerce operators to protect IPR by establishing notice and take-down provisions for infringing products being offered for sale. To address the issue of take-down complaints filed in bad faith which is quite common in China in recent years, Chinese policy makers introduced "multiple damages" for take-down notices that are filed in bad faith and cause damage to platform sellers (Article 42). Article 43 of the new Law further provides that IP right holders must file civil or administrative complaints with the relevant authorities or courts within 15 days of receiving a seller's "counter notice' from the platform. However, there are still ambiguities to be addressed in these notice and take-down provisions.

For example, on the one hand, observers correctly point out that the application of Article 43 would be worrisome to IP right holder not only because of its failure to offer clear standards for determining the validity of counter notice but also the impossibility for foreign companies to acquire such complaints within the 15-day filing deadline due to the lengthy procedure to notarize and legalize relevant documents (Palmer and Ye 2018). On the other hand, the 15-day waiting period following complaints of bad faith could also lead to great losses for platform sellers even if they could come up with clear evidence and declaration of non-infringement (Liu 2018).

Joint liability is imposed on a platform operator if it knows or should know that an operator doing business through its platform is infringing IPR but fails to take the necessary measures, such as deleting, blocking, disconnecting, and terminating transactions or services (Art. 45). It is obvious that the new rule codifies current court practice under Article 36 of the Tort Liability Law and other IP law such as the Copyright Law and Patent Law. It does, however, continue to leave open for interpretation the meaning of "knows or should know" and "promptly notify" (Palmer and Ye 2018).

The law also explicitly prohibits misuse of dominant market position (Art. 22), unfair competition behaviors (Art. 85), and behavior that may otherwise damage the e-commerce credit system such as fake transactions, malicious ratings or evaluations contrary to the facts to damage others' business credibility, deleting unfavorable ratings/evaluations, amongst others (Art. 81).

Among all of these measures, the rules regarding data security proposed in the draft law are of the most concern to some foreign firms. The draft law includes the requirement, for example, that personally identifiable information be stored domestically. This is said to increase costs for foreign firms that must develop their own server or contract out to domestic suppliers (Melnicoe 2017). Requirements that companies share data with the government also raise privacy concerns (Melnicoe 2017). In the newly promulgated law, the requirement of local storage no longer exists. Operators of e-commerce, however, should still offer the data of e-commerce to relevant authorities when the latter require them to do so "according to the laws and regulations". The authorities shall take necessary measures to protect the security of these data and protect the personal information, privacy, and trade secret from disclosure to others (Art. 25). According to the drafters of this new law, it is necessary for government agents to access to the personal and trade information of the operators when they commit illegal activities on the e-commerce platform (Drafting Team of the E-commerce Law 2018).

Generally speaking, with some reservations mentioned, the law should improve the ecosystem for e-commerce in China and can help discourage the sale of fakes and counterfeits.

5.1.5 *Data Storage and Protection*

China's regime for data protection has received increasing scrutiny in recent years. Although China has not enacted a general data protection act that specifically addresses the collection, storage, transmission and operation of personal information, rules of data protection are still to be found in a multitude of sector-specific legal instruments.

The General Principle of the Civil Code offers protection to reputation rights (Art. 101), individuals' rights regarding personal names, portraits, and honors (Articles 99, 100 and 102). For example, unauthorized disclosure of personal information can be treated as a potential infringement of reputation rights if such individual's reputation has been harmed. And via the "civil rights and interests" provision in Art. 2 of the Tort Liability Law, network service providers or netizens can be liable for violations of privacy.

In 2012, the Standing Committee of the National People's Congress released its Decision to Strengthen Protection on Internet Information (2012 SC-NPC Decision). To date, this Decision is the highest level of law in China to deal specifically with data protection issues. The law imposes the obligation on Internet Service Providers and other enterprises and institutions to legally collect and use personal electronic information in the course of their business. However, this instrument focuses only on Internet-based activities and lacks an enforcement mechanism.

Aside from the provisions in the Draft E-Commerce Law, mentioned earlier in this chapter, there are other Chinese laws and regulations that govern the protection of personal information of specific industrial sectors (for example, the telecommunications sector) or that govern information of a specific nature (for example, individual financial credit information, consumer information, population health information, and medical records) (Marissa 2016). The following are some of examples of these legal measures:

- Guideline on Personal Information Protection in Public and Commercial Service Information System under Information Security Technology (Ministry of Industry and Information Technology 2013);
- The Decision of the Standing Committee of the National People's Congress on Revising the Consumer Rights Protection Law of the PRC (Revision of Consumer Rights Law 2013);
- Personal Information Security Measures for Mailing and Courier Services (State Post Office 2014);
- Medical Records Administration Measures of Medical Institutions (National Health and Population Commission and National Chinese Medicine Administration 2013);
- Measures for Administration of Population Health Information (NHPC 2014); and
- Regulation on Personal Information Protection of Telecom and Internet Users (MIIT 2015).

Considering the depth of the aforementioned legal instruments, it could be said that China's data protection is "aimed exclusively at the individual as a consumer" (instead of aiming to institutionalize fundamental human rights). In other words, data protection recipients in China are not individuals or a "data subject", but are consumers (de Hert and Papakonstantinou 2015).

The new General Principles of Civil Law promulgated in March 2017 define the right of personal information as a basic civil right. Article 111 of this law provides that the personal information of natural persons is protected by law. Any organization and individual that needs to obtain personal information of others should obtain information in accordance with the law and ensure the information's security; should not illegally collect, use, process, or transmit personal information; and should not illegally trade, offer, or disclose personal information.

Another new law, the Network Security Law, which came into effect in June 2017, also changes the landscape for data protection in China. It clearly states core principles on collection and use of personal information (namely, secrecy maintenance, legality, reasonableness, and necessity) (Art. 40–41). The law requires that data on Chinese consumers be stored within the country and bans the export of "personal and important data" that could threaten national security or the public interest (Art. 37). This means that multinational corporations operating "key information infrastructure" need to set up data centers within Chinese borders and that the state needs to review and authorize the export of any sensitive data "due to business need(s)". Should any violation occur, the Chinese government may impose fines on the firm and individual employees who are deemed to be responsible for the violation, and may, at its discretion, revoke or cancel commercial licenses, suspend operations, and/or shut down a firm's website (Art. 66).

These new data storage and protection laws, especially the Network Security Law, appear to have had a rapid impact on the data market in China. On May 20, 2017, the Supreme People's Court and the Supreme People's Procuratorate jointly issued the Measures to Crackdown on Illegal Trading Citizen Privacy Data, which created some legal barriers to commerce by some firms in the Big Data market. Many data companies have been investigated and shut down because of their involvement in illegal data transaction activities.

The Chinese government assumedly believes the data storage regulation and data export requirements are a necessary step towards safeguarding against threats such as hacking and terrorism. However, some stakeholders from foreign industry in particular have indicated that the measures unfairly target foreign businesses (Cappella 2017).[9] This being said, the extent of the commercial effect of these legal barriers, including their impact on innovation, is not yet fully clear. Nonetheless, at a minimum it seems that Art. 37 of the new Network Security Law should be limited to specific enterprises and data. In fact, at present the Chinese government is attempting to formulate advice highlighting that it does not intend to overly restrict cross-border data flows (Gao and Liu 2017).

[9] Also see https://www.amchamchina.org/about/press-center/amcham-statement/amcham-china-statement-on-cybersecurity-law.

5.1.6 Regulation of the Sharing Economy

The Chinese state has strongly supported development of the sharing economy, also called the "collaborative economy", and related innovations in recent years. This support is clearly stated in the CPC's 13th Five Year Plan for National Economic and Social Development (promulgated in 2015) and repeated by the official Government Work Report from 2015 and 2016. In March 2017, the National Development and Reform Commission (NDRC) issued the Sharing Economic Development Guideline (draft) to guide the development of the sharing economy in China.

A variety of sharing economy start-ups have proliferated in China in recent years. To date, perhaps the most hyped example of the sharing economy in China is the free-floating bike-sharing model made famous by Mobike and Ofo. These two Chinese start-ups have now gone global: for example, Mobike planned to introduce 1000 bikes in Manchester and Salford in the UK at the end of June 2017 (China Daily 2017). Ride-sharing firms such as Didi Chuxing and apartment-sharing firms such as Airbnb and Tujia are also popular sharing economy businesses in China. Many other new kinds of sharing and renting start-ups are sprouting up around China, such as Molisan's umbrella rent-out, Xiaodian's portable battery stations in shopping malls, and Zhulegeqiu's basketball rent-out (Daxueconsulting 2017).

The growth in sharing and renting out assets or services appears to have a pronounced impact on China's economic output. According to the National Information Center, the collaborative economy in China rose to about 508 billion USD in 2016 and is expected to grow 40% annually until 2020, reaching a value of 1921 trillion USD (National Information Center 2017).

As the sharing economy expands, competition and litigation, including IP litigation, in related industries will also increase. For example, in August 2017 Mobike was sued for patent infringement for a patented lock system and Mobike has successfully defended itself in Shanghai's IP Court and Shanghai Higher People's Court (Shanghai IP Court 2017).

According to the NDRC and the other seven government departments, the Chinese government will continue to encourage innovation in the sharing economy while regulating the sector in a tolerant and prudent manner. More sophisticated regulations will be passed in the coming years to govern different industries in the sharing economy in order to reduce barriers to market entry and guard against commercial risks. The government also intends to maintain orderly competition and will regulate monopolies. Specific employment and taxation policies will be developed in China to assure the sharing economy's growth (Xinhua 2017).

5.2 Other Experiments

5.2.1 Protection of Pharmaceutical and Chemical Test Data

The State Food and Drug Administration (SFDA) and several departments of the State Council released a draft regulation titled "Relevant Policies for Encouraging Innovations of Drugs and Medical Devices and Protecting Innovators' Rights and Interests" (No. 55 of 2017) for public comments in May 2017 in an attempt to promote innovation in the pharmaceutical medical equipment industry and allow the industry to otherwise better meet the needs of the public (The State Food and Drug Administration 2017). One of the major concerns with this Draft regards the improvement of the drug test data protection system. According to the draft, a generic applicant bears the obligation to notify the relevant drug patentee within 20 days after the drug application is submitted. The patentee is then given 20 days to notify the SFDA and respond by filing a lawsuit within one of the Chinese courts having jurisdiction over patent matters. During the litigation proceedings, the SFDA may set a 24-month stay of approval and continue evaluating the abbreviated new drug application (ANDA) application (The State Food and Drug Administration 2017; Addison 2018). However, observers point to a number of challenges that may arise from these proposed rules, especially the contradiction with the existing patent law (Lai 2017). According to Article 69 (5) of the Patent Law of PRC, a generic drug applicant can file the ANDA application without being deemed to be conducting any patent infringing activity, rendering some litigation groundless.[10]

Another major concern with this Draft regards the improvement of the drug test data protection system. According to the Draft, applicants may submit a test data protection application when submitting a drug marketing application. During the data protection period, a designated review body will not approve other applications for the same variety of products, except when the data is independently obtained by the applicant.

It is worth noting that different time periods for data protection have been suggested in the Draft. An innovative drug can enjoy six years of data protection; 'innovative' drugs as well as medicines meant to treat rare diseases and diseases particularly affecting children can enjoy 10 years of data protection; 'improved' drugs as well as medicines for treating rare diseases and diseases particularly affecting children can enjoy 3 years of data protection; and innovative biological products for medical treatments can enjoy 10 years of data protection. Also, 1.5 years of data protection will be granted to new drugs that successfully challenge an existing patent or those drugs already sold abroad but which were first marketed as a generic drug in the domestic market. The proposal to introduce different time periods for drug test data

[10] Article 69 (5) of Patent Law of PRC states: "The following shall not be deemed to be a patent infringement: (5) any person who produces, uses, or imports patented drugs or patented medical apparatus and instruments, for the purpose of providing information required for administrative examination and approval, or any other person who imports patented drugs or patented medical apparatus and instruments especially for that person".

protection is affected by current regulations in the U.S. and EU or relevant provisions in the TPP Agreement. Since it's difficult to make special exceptions in the present patent system, the extension of the protection period of the above-mentioned types of new drug test data and improved new drugs will be reasonable incentive policies (Cheng et al. 2017).

Another major development for firms in the field of China's IP regime for pharmaceutical, chemical, and biotech industries involves state treatment of post-filing experimental data and its fulfillment of the sufficient disclosure requirement according to the Patent Law. Before late 2013, SIPO strictly interpreted Article 26.3 of the Chinese Patent Law to require specifications in every patent application to disclose the invention clearly and completely enough by a person skilled in the art. Additionally, post-filing experimental data could not be used to address a sufficiency of disclosure rejection under the law. However, representatives from the pharmaceutical, biotech, and chemicals industries, concerned with the unavoidable delay in obtaining experimental data on medical and/or biological effects, argued that these data requirements were inherently difficult to fulfill. Recognizing the negative impact of their prior practices on several industries, SIPO clarified in late 2013 that post-filing experimental data could be submitted in the patent examination process in some instances, e.g. to support the sufficient disclosure requirement under the law and in order to confirm that the technical solution has the use or effect specified by the applicant (Greenfield 2014; AIPLA 2013). Consultations with industry indicate differing perceptions among firms regarding how thoroughly this regulatory change was implemented. SIPO's newly revised Patent Examination Guideline also confirms this clarification to allow post-filing experimental data "when the technical effect to be proved could be acquired in the disclosed patent application by a person skilled in the art" (SIPO, Patent Examination Guideline, Section II, Chapter 10, 3.5, 2017).

In 2018, several changes were made to China's system of governing generic drugs and their interface with the patent system. On March 21st 2018, the Opinion on Reforming and Improving Policies Supply Guarantee and Use of Generic Drugs (No. 20 [2018]) was issued by the General Office of the State Council. In an effort to stimulate R&D involving generic drugs, the Opinion proposes to (1) develop catalogs of encouraged generic drugs by (a) establishing an interdepartmental drug manufacturing and use information sharing mechanism, (b) encouraging the production of generic drugs necessary for clinical practices, those for preventing and treating major infectious diseases and rare diseases, those for public health emergencies, those for children, and drugs without a registration application submitted one year before corresponding patent(s) expires; (2) strengthening the research on generic drug technology by inter alia establishing a generic drug technology research alliance and collaboration in R&D involving raw materials and auxiliary materials, packaging materials; and (3) to improve the protection of IPR for drugs by sufficiently balancing the interests between patentees of drugs and the public, nurturing more 'essential' and 'original' IPRs in drugs, and intensifying anti-monopoly law enforcement involving IPR and preventing the misuse of IP rights.

To improve the quality and therapeutic effect of generic drugs, the Opinion proposes to (1) accelerate the advancement of generic drug quality and therapeutic-effect consistency assessments; (2) improve the quality of raw materials, auxiliary materials, and packaging materials for drugs in order to reduce heavy dependence on imports of raw materials, auxiliary materials, and packaging materials for drugs while also satisfying a demand for quality; (3) to upgrade development and manufacturing in the industry; and to (4) strictly review and approve generic drugs according to the principle of consistency with original drugs in terms of quality and therapeutic effect.

The Opinion sets out additional provisions for developing the generic drugs industry. It proposes to (1) advance the substitution of generic drugs by including those consistent with original drugs in terms of quality and therapeutic effect in the catalogs of drugs available for mutual substitution with original drugs and disclosing related information in a timely manner to the public to facilitate the choice and use of such drugs by medical staff and patients. The Opinion also (2) specifies methods to exploit compulsory licensing of patents on drugs to improve the accessibility of drugs. Specifically, the Opinion reiterates the stipulations in China's Patent Law that entities or individuals meeting the conditions for exploiting compulsory licensing can apply to SIPO (now CNIPA) for a compulsory license in accordance with the law. It also mentions that when there is a serious threat to public health or safety, or in other special circumstances, the National Health Commission shall, to protect public health, conduct an assessment and provide a justification for compulsory licensing in conjunction with the Ministry of Industry and Information Technology, the State Drug Administration, and other authorities. Then a proposal for compulsory licensing should be submitted to CNIPA and CNIPA shall decide to grant permission or reject the proposal in accordance with the law. Additionally, the Opinion recommends (3) to institute certain tax incentives and other pricing policies to develop new technology, new products, or new crafts.

Although there are scant specifics available about how the Opinion will be implemented, several provisions in the measure may raise concerns amongst firms in the pharmaceutical industry (Mak 2019). Some provinces or cities such as Guangdong Province have issued measures to implement the Opinion (General Office of the People's Government of Guangdong Province 2018); however, how exactly the Opinion will be implemented throughout China is indeed still uncertain. Such uncertainty may somewhat restrain the willingness of actors in China's NIS to invest in the country's pharmaceutical industry to the extent they would amidst more certainty and assurance of reasonable appropriability over their innovations.

5.2.2 Employee Invention Remuneration and Reward Regulations[11]

As mentioned in Chap. 4, the new draft of the Service Invention Regulations (SIR) sets forth monetary amounts for remunerating and rewarding individual service inventors. The first draft SIR was published in 2012, and subsequent drafts were published in

[11] This section is repeated verbatim in Chap. 4.

2014 and 2015. The draft SIR attempts to add further flesh to Article 16 of the current Patent Law which allow firms to be exempt from statutory approaches to remuneration and rewards (e.g., which specify specific percentages of operating profit to be paid to an employee inventor upon commercialization of his/her invention) if they institute "reasonable" remuneration and reward policies. However, it is not fully clear in the draft SIR (or Patent Law) what constitutes "reasonable" remuneration and rewards. This major ambiguity, amongst others in the draft SIR, may add burdensome compliance and other financial costs to large foreign and Chinese firms in China that may hinder patent commercialization (Lutze 2016). As of 2017, our consultations with Chinese government officials indicate the draft SIR may not be finalized in the near future given significant concerns from Chinese and foreign industry over the burden it may impose on firms that already have effective remuneration schemes in place.

Still, in the absence of a legally effective SIR, Chinese courts are issuing decisions about service invention remuneration and rewards that may discourage R&D in China. For example, in a second instance civil judgment in Zhang Weifeng versus 3 M in 2015, the Shanghai High People's Court decided that the statutory remuneration claim for service inventors in China should be calculated from the employer's global turnover figures and shall extend to the whole group of affiliated companies of the employer. Such clarifications may make the state-mandated terms in China the highest state-mandated standard globally (Lutze 2016). These high remuneration amounts may discourage R&D investments in China.

Judging from our consultations with legal scholars in China, there seems to be a misperception that state-mandated service inventor remuneration and reward laws (which only a few countries in the world actually have) have clearly been useful for incentivizing innovation in foreign countries. In fact, the literature generally finds that these state schemes create more negative economic impacts than positive impacts. For example, Merges (1999a, b) finds the schemes create significant compliance costs and dis-incentivize R&D collaboration because individual inventors try to maximize their own remuneration and rewards. Owan and Nagaoka (2011) find that the schemes incentivize safer/less disruptive research that is more certain to be financially rewarded. Kappos and Nagasawa (2014) find that the schemes effectively require that significant money is spent within the firm on administering compliance programs and on litigation costs, and this money could be better spent on innovation. Onishi (2013) finds the schemes may have a positive impact on increasing revenue from patents in small firms; however, Kanama and Nishikawa (2017) find the schemes have negative impacts on the development of new products and services in large firms. Harhoff and Hoisl (2007) find mixed impacts of the schemes on employee and firm-wide performance. Further, in general, effective firm-determined pay, management structures, training, and stock options might be better tools to incentivize innovation than state-mandated inventor remuneration schemes (Lynch and Black 1995; Lerner and Wulf 2007; Cosh et al. 2007; Yanadori and Cui 2013; Chang et al. 2015).

Considering this evidence, it appears that Chinese policymakers would benefit from rethinking the centrality of statutory and judicial approaches to service inventor remuneration and rewards as part of their innovation strategy. The problems that have arisen from the state's attempt to draft the SIR should serve as a cautionary tale about the downsides of "over-experimentation" with IP initiatives in China.

5.2.3 IP Demonstration Cities

SIPO began to develop IP and technology "demonstration" bases in the late 1990s. These have evolved into what are known as "IP Demonstration Cities" (IPDC) today. The objective of this program is to create an incentive mechanism for rewarding geographical regions in China that score well on certain indicators related to IP and technology creation, utilization, management, and protection/enforcement. In addition to serving as a positive signal, recognition as an IPDC is accompanied by state funding for developing IP.

In January 2004, SIPO issued the Guidance on the Work of IP Pilot and Demonstration, in which cities, S&T parks, companies and institutions were incorporated in an IP Pilot and Demonstration scheme. That 2004 measure formulated selection criteria and application procedures for the IPDC program. Subsequently, several revisions were made to the program requirements. Table 5.1 provides an overview of the composition of current indicators used in the IPDC program. SIPO oversees a complex system through which geographical regions in China are judged on the criteria, monitors the regions to see if they maintain good performance on the criteria, and governs graduation between different levels of the program (Zhang et al. 2016). At the end of 2015, there were 64 official IPDCs and another 80 cities were deemed fit to apply for the title.

Surprisingly, there is sparse scholarly research (although SIPO does publish an IP Demonstration Cities Report, which provides a useful descriptive review in its own right) evaluating how China's IPDCs program is working to achieve its immediate objectives, let alone its ability to spur technological innovation. Zhang et al. (2016) provide some useful analysis on the program. The authors find that the IPDC program has likely led to an increase in IP creation, the growth of IP-related industries, the improvement of both firms' IP awareness and the governments' IP administrative system, and potentially an increase in the inflow of foreign direct investment. However, at the same time, the authors find that the effect of the program within many provinces appears to be relatively limited, although it may be stronger in less-developed provinces. Furthermore, the marginal economic return of the current IPDC Program appears to decrease as more IPDCs are introduced, although in the long term a greater number of IPDCs may eventually generate more general nationwide economic returns.

Table 5.1 Overview of requirements in China's IP Demonstration Cities program

Main indicators	Sub-indicators (score)[a]	Number of sub-indicators	Scoring
Overarching indicators	Creation (15), utilization (20), protection (20), management (30), service (15)	22	100
Institution establishment	Establishment of an IP administrative system (35), establishment of IP culture and talent (12), establishment of IP awareness and ability in companies (20), law enforcement work and assertion of IP rights (17), work on special themes (11), other work (5)	45	100
Special work	Special measures (5), excellent achievements (5)	2	10

Sources Evaluation and Management Method of SIPO's Pilot and Demonstration Cities (districts), and Zhang et al. (2016). [a]The number in parenthesis indicates the score of the corresponding indicator

5.2.4 *Blacklists for IP Infringers*

A "blacklist" regulatory system is not a completely new addition to China's IP regime. Since 2007, Chinese Customs have established a blacklist system relating to infringing goods for export. For goods declared by those blacklisted enterprises, the Customs must increase the inspection rate of shipments within a limited period.

However, new initiatives have been proposed expanding the scope of the blacklist system in China. China's State Council released the Notice Concerning Issuance of the Planning Outline for the Establishment of a Social Credit System (2014–2020) on June 14, 2014 in order to establish a "social credit system". The plan includes rules for judging the integrity of people in China, and includes specific indicators in the fields of government affairs, commercial affairs, the judiciary, and other social aspects (Office of State Council 2014).

In 2015, the Office of State Council issued the Notice of Work Plan to Crackdown IPR Infringement and Manufacture and Sale of Fakes (Office of State Council 2015). Part of the work to be undertaken by the state, according to this Notice, is to establish an IP protection-related social credit system administered by SAIC, State Administration of Press, Publication, Radio, Film, and Television (SAPPRFT), and SIPO. And the Ministry of Industry and Information Technology (MIIT) was designated to construct the Internet Credit System in a way that covers IP infringement activities. The work plan also proposes the establishment of a nationwide social credit code system and information sharing platform, blacklist of dishonest and illegal businesses, and joint disciplinary mechanism for non-compliance.

In November 2016, SIPO issued the Notice on the Rapid Collaborative Protection of Intellectual Property Rights (SIPO 2016). According to this Notice, SIPO intends to establish a Rapid Collaborative Mechanism to protect IPRs. The following measures are included in this system: (i) establish IPR centers and simplify the enforcement procedures to aid rapid handling patent infringement and other IP disputes; (ii) establish a rapid and comprehensive response mechanism to receive complaints and process infringement feedback quickly; (iii) connect with large-scale e-commerce platforms to promote consultations for online patent infringement disputes; (iv) increase the punishment against bad faith activities. The Notice suggests establishing a credit blacklist for IP infringers, especially those that repeatedly commit infringement, patent passing-off, refuse to implement administrative decisions, continuously submit "abnormal" applications, and/or illegally register patent agents.

In 2017, the Office of State Council issued a new version of the Notice of Work Plan to Crackdown IPR Infringement and Manufacture and Sale of Fakes. The National Development and Reform Commission (NDRC) and the People's Bank of China are assigned, in cooperation with other authorities, to establish a blacklist system to crack down on IPR infringement and manufacturing and selling of counterfeit and shoddy goods.

In the past two years, the blacklists of enterprises and individual businesses that committed IPR infringements have been released by the local Bureau of Civilization, Administration of Industry and Commerce, and China's different IP offices. The blacklist system may, to some degree, discourage repeated IP infringement by the same enterprises and improve the efficiency of IP administrative enforcement in China. However, none of the present rules governing the blacklist are codified in high-level legislation, i.e., laws or regulations, in China. Instead, most of these measures are merely normative documents issued by different authorities and lack a uniform standard. This approach creates cross-governmental department conflicts and confusion when administering the system (Liu 2016). Moreover, the scope of dishonest behavior is rather ambiguous in current measures governing the IP blacklist, making the scope of state power to administer the list rather uncertain.

On December 4th 2018, 38 ministries and commissions in China including the National Development and Reform Commission, the People's Bank of China, and CNIPA issued the Memorandum of Understanding on Joint Disciplinary Action Against Serious Distrusted Entities in the Field of Intellectual Property (Patents) (国家发展改革委, 人民银行, 国家知识产权局等印发《关于对知识产权(专利)领域严重失信主体开展联合惩戒的合作备忘录》的通知, 发改财金〔2018〕1702号), No. 1702 [2018]) (hereinafter referred to as the "Memorandum"). According to the Memorandum's preamble, it is intended to "accelerate the development of a credit system in the field of intellectual property (patents) and establish and improve a system of joint punishment for dishonesty".

According to the Memorandum, the principal implementer of 'serious dishonesty' in the field of IP including patents shall be subject to joint disciplinary action. The principal implementer can either be a legal person and legal representative, principal in charge, person directly responsible and actual controller, an unincorporated organization and its person in charge, or a natural person. Operating through the National Credit Information Sharing Platform, CNIPA shall provide, at regular intervals, a list of 'seriously dishonest' parties in the field of IP (patents) to other departments and entities. Then one or more disciplinary actions shall be taken by one or more of the departments.

Six major types of serious dishonesty in the field of IP (patents) are listed in the Memorandum: (1) repeated patent infringement; (2) refusal to implement effective decisions regarding administrative treatment or administrative punishment, or hindering local IP offices from carrying out investigations and obtaining evidence in accordance with the law; (3) serious illegal acts by patent agents; (4) altering, reselling, leasing or lending the qualification certificate of a patent agent; (5) involvement with abnormal patent applications; and (6) providing false documents during patent prosecution.

The disciplinary provisions adopted by CNIPA include intensifying supervision, severely punishing illegal acts; canceling authorization for patents to enter into the expedited channel and rapid enforcement channel, canceling patent fee reductions and priority examination, among other provisions. Inter-departmental joint disciplinary provisions include restricting government financial support, restricting subsidy funds and social security fund support, restricting participation as a supplier in government procurement activities, recording dishonesty status in the Basic Financial Credit Information Database and the Internet credit system, refusal to accept the application for issuance of corporate bonds, among other provisions.

In general, the Memorandum is an interesting and potentially useful measure for improving patent quality in China and disincentizing behavior that can be counterproductive to the functioning of a healthy NIS. This being said, it remains to be seen how exactly the measure will be implemented and transparent protocols are needed to ensure it is applied consistently and fairly.

5.3 Summary

The growth of Internet-intensive and other emerging industries in China has posed new challenges to governance of IP, to which the Chinese state has proactively responded. Such technological change has led to a sharp increase of IP applications and more IP disputes in China in these new areas of economic activity. The Chinese state has recently attempted to regulate corresponding business models and other commercial activities in a way that ensures healthy competition and safeguards the public interests while also not restricting innovation. The state has expanded patentable subject matter in China (e.g., for graphical user interfaces, software, and business methods); better protected pharmaceutical and chemical test data; formulated a new policy towards generic drugs; protected data usage and storage; regulated e-commerce activities; regulated the sharing economy; expedited patent examination; drafted a SIR; administered and reformed the IP Demonstration Cities Program; and set-forth a blacklist for IP infringers and other initiatives to penalize "serious dishonesty" involving IP.

These state initiatives appear to be generally well-designed, although improvements could still be made. With the exception of the draft SIR and perhaps some aspects of the recent policy on generic drugs, the aforementioned experiments/new initiatives generally seem to be creating an environment that is more conducive for innovation in growth industries in China. Then again, there are still some shortcomings in the drafting and administration of several of the initiatives and close oversight is needed to ensure they are working as hoped. The Chinese government should continuously reform its legislative, administrative and judicial approaches to the initiatives as the industries which they attempt to regulate evolve. Specific recommendations for reform are provided in Chap. 9.

References

Addison, Bradford G. 2018. Taiwan and China introduce the patent linkage system (1 December 2018), available at http://www.btlaw.com/Taiwan-and-China-Introduce-the-Patent-Linkage-System-01-12-2018/. Accessed 3 Mar 2018.

AIPLA. 2013. SIPO clarifies the examination standard on sufficient disclosure of chemical/medical inventions. CCPIT, available at http://www.aipla.org/committees/committee_pages/IP_Practice_in_China/Chinese%20IP%20Law%20%20Regulations/SIPO%20Clarifies%20the%20Examination%20Standard%20on%20Sufficient%20Disclosure%20of%20Chemical%20Medical%20Inventions.pdf.

Bain, Alibaba. 2016. Annual research report of China's e-commerce market 2015. Internet Branding and Brand Internet, available at http://b2b.toocle.com/detail–6297170.html.

Cappella, N. 2017. New Chinese regulation requires security assessment for data export, available at https://thestack.com/data-centre/2017/04/12/new-chinese-regulation-requires-security-assessment-for-data-export/.

Chang, X., K. Fu, A. Low, and W. Zhang. 2015. Non-executive employee stock options and corporate innovation. *Journal of Financial Economics* 115: 168–188.

Cheng, Fang et al. 2017. 从《关于鼓励药品医疗器械创新保护创新者权益的相关政策_(征求意见稿)》看中国专利连接和药品试验数据保护制度 [Comments on China's patent linkage and drug test data protection system from the perspective from the relevant policies for encouraging innovations of drugs and medical devices and protecting innovators' rights and interests (Draft)], available at https://hk.lexiscn.com/topic/legal.php?tps=ip&act=detail&id=217238&newstype=3&isEnglish=N.

Chen, Yang. 2017. GUI外观设计专利发展趋势及侵权裁判规则 (The development tendency and the referee rules of the infringement of GUI design patent) (in Chinese) *Electronic Intellectual Property* 1–2: 21.

China Daily. 2017. China's sharing economic is now exporting innovations, available at http://www.chinadaily.com.cn/opinion/2017-06/27/content_29897191.htm.

Cohen, J., and M. Lemley. 2001. Patent scope and innovation in the software industry *California Law Review* 89: 1–57.

Cosh, A., X. Fu, and A. Hughes. 2007. Management characteristics, managerial ownership and innovative efficiency in high-technology industry. Oxford University, SLPTMD Working Paper Series No. 007, available at https://ora.ox.ac.uk/objects/uuid:426cbee0-22c4-4e2c-a83a-26a897904c02.

Daxueconsulting. 2017. "Sharing Economy" only as one part of exploding collaborative economy in China, available at http://daxueconsulting.com/exploding-collaborative-economy-in-china/.

de Hert, P., and V. Papakonstantinou. 2015. The data protection regime in China. Report for the European Commission, available at http://www.europarl.europa.eu/studies.

Department of Treaty and Law of SIPO. 2012.《发明专利申请优先审查管理办法》政策解读 (Administrative Measures for Priority Examination of Patent Applications) (in Chinese) 9 CHINA INVENTION & PATENT 68–69.

Drafting Team of the E-commerce Law. 2018. Interpretation of the e-commerce law, 137–138. China Legal Publishing House.

Gao, Shanxing, and Weiqi Liu. 2017. 资料跨境流动规制及其应对——对《网路安全法》第三十七条的讨论(Regulation and reaction of cross—Border data flows—A study of Article 37), Cybersecurity Law) (in Chinese) 37 *Journal of Xian Jiaotong University* (Social Sciences), 2, 85–91.

Greenfield, M. 2014. Update from China: Supplemental evidence in pharmaceutical patent applications. Patent Docs, available at http://www.patentdocs.org/2014/02/update-from-china-supplemental-evidence-in-pharmaceutical-patent-applications.html.

Harhoff, D., and K. Hoisl. 2007. Institutionalized incentives for ingenuity: Patent value and the German Employees' Inventions Act. *Research Policy* 36: 1143–1162.

Hans, S. 2018. China mulls "leapfrog appeal" for patent and other technical cases, available at https://www.linkedin.com/wukong-web/articleShare/6460141770821943296?trk=wukong-web_wecaht-share_message&from=singlemessage.

Huang, C. 2017. Recent development of the intellectual property rights system in China and challenges ahead. *Management and Organization Review* 13: 39–48.

Kanama, D., and K. Nishikawa. 2017. Does an extrinsic reward for R&D employees enhance innovation outcomes? Evidence from a Japanese innovation survey. *R&D Management* 47: 198–211.

Kappos, D., and K. Nagasawa. 2014. Japan's article 35: Are employee-inventor monetary award laws impeding Japanese innovation? *Japarn AIPPA Journal* 39–46.

Lai, Karry. 2017. China's new linkage scheme will transform pharmaceutical patenting' Asialaw (27 July 2017) available at https://www.asialaw.com/articles/chinas-new-linkage-scheme-will-transform-pharmaceutical-patenting/arosyfjy.

Lerner, J., and J. Wulf. 2007. Innovation and incentives: Evidence from corporate R&D. *Review of Economics and Statistics* 89: 634–644.

Li, Weiwei, and Youde Zheng. 2014. 绿色专利申请快速审查制度的实施效果评价与完善 (Evaluation and Improvement of Expedited Censorship for Green Patent Application) (in Chinese) 3 Huazhong University of Science & Technology (Social Science) 49–56.

Liu, W. 2016. 对黑名单制度实体法律问题的几点思考:以地方黑名单立法规定为依据分析 (Some thoughts on substantial legal issues of blacklist system—Analysis based on the stipulations of blacklist system in local legislations) (in Chinese). *Citizen and Law* 10: 33–35.

Liu, Xiaochun. 2018. 电商法知产条款 15天等待期隐忧 (The 15-day waiting period introduced by the IP clause in E-commerce law is worrisome) (in Chinese). *Finance*, available at: https://mp.weixin.qq.com/s/wRon0m6ao6nFHoXyv5HdLQ.

Liu, Xiuxiang. 2017. 从专利法及专利优先审查管理办法看专利保护—以民营航太企业的角度 (Patent protection from patent law and patent priority approach: From the perspective of private aerospace companies) (in Chinese) *11 Legal System and Economic* 26.

Lipu, T. 2013. 深入实施知识产权战略, 有效支撑创新驱动发展—写在《国家知识产权战略纲要》颁布5周 (Deepen the implementation of intellectual property strategy and effectively support development of innovation) (in Chinese) *Science Technology and Law* 3: 72–74.

Lu, R., and E. Hausman. 2016. China may become more liberal towards business method and software related patents, available at http://www.rcip.co.il/en/article/china-may-become-more-liberal-towards-business-method-and-software-related-patents/.

Lutze, O. 2016. Incentives for Chinese inventors: A proposal for a new inventor remuneration scheme with German elements. In *Economic impacts of intellectual property-conditioned government incentives*, ed. D. Prud'homme and H. Song, 157–175. Springer.

Lynch, L., and S. Black. 1995. Beyond the incident of training: Evidence from a National Employers Survey. NBER Working Paper No. 5231.

Marissa, X. 2016. Data protection in China: Overview, Thomas Reuters Practical Law, available at https://uk.practicallaw.thomsonreuters.com/4-519-9017?transitionType=Default&contextData=(sc.Default)&firstPage=true&bhcp=1.

Melnicoe, M. 2017. China E-commerce proposed law includes data security, available at https://www.bna.com/china-ecommerce-proposed-n57982083151/.

Merges, R. 1999a. The law and economics of employee inventions. *Harvard Journal of Law & Technology* 13: 1–53.

Merges, R. 1999b. As many as six impossible patents before breakfast: Property rights for business concepts and patent system reform. *Berkeley Technology Law Journal* 14, 577.

Madigan, K., and A. Mossoff. 2017. Turning gold into lead: How patent eligibility doctrine is undermining U.S. leadership in innovation. *George Mason Law Review* 24: 939–960.

Mak, T. 2019. *China: Generic drugs*. Mondaq, available at http://www.mondaq.com/china/x/787212/food+drugs+law/Generic+Drugs.

Ministry of Industry and Information Technology. 2013. Guideline on personal information protection in public and commercial service information system under information security technology.

MIIT. 2015. Regulation on personal information protection of telecom and internet users.

National Health and Population Commission and National Chinese Medicine Administration. 2013. Medical records administration measures of medical institutions.

National Information Center. 2017. 2017 年度中国共享经济发展报告 (Report on the development of China's sharing economy in 2017) (Beijing, 2 March 2017) (in Chinese), available at http://www.100ec.cn/zt/2017gxjj/.

NHPC. 2014. Measures for administration of population health information.

Office of State Council. 2014. 社会信用体系建设规划纲要2014-2020年 [The notice concerning issuance of the planning outline for the establishment of a social credit system (2014–2020)] (in Chinese), available at http://www.gov.cn/zhengce/content/2014-06/27/content_8913.htm.

Office of State Council. 2015. 2015 年全国打击侵犯知识产权和制售假冒伪劣商品工作要点 (The notice of work plan to crackdown IPR infringement and manufacture and sale of fakes) (in Chinese), available at http://www.gov.cn/gongbao/content/2015/content_2853605.htm.

Onishi, K. 2013. The effects of compensation plans for employee inventions on R&D productivity: new evidence from Japanese panel data. *Research Policy* 42: 367–378.

Owan H., and S. Nagaoka. 2011. Intrinsic and extrinsic motivations of inventors. RIETI Discussion Paper Series 11-E-022.

Palmer, S., and W. Ye. 2018, *China promulgates electronic commerce law*, available at: https://www.chinaiplegalreport.com/2018/09/china-promulgates-electronic-commerce-law/.

Samuelson, P. 1990. Digital media and the changing face of intellectual property law. *Rutgers Computer & Technology Law Journal* 16: 323.

Shanghai IP Court. 2017, 上海知产法院受理摩拜单车被控侵害发明专利权纠纷案 (Shanghai IP Court accepted patent infringement case against Mobike) (in Chinese), available at: http://www.kankanews.com/a/2017-04-26/0037967749.shtml.

SIPO. 2012. 发明专利申请优先审查管理办法 (2012) (局令第65号令) (Administrative measures for priority examination of invention patent applications) (Order No. 65) (in Chinese).

SIPO. 2014. 国家知识产权局关于修改<专利审查指南>的决定 (局令第68号) (2014) [Amendments to the Guidebook of Patent Examination (No. 68)] (in Chinese) http://www.sipo.gov.cn/zwgg/jl/201403/t20140314_916952.html.

SIPO. 2016. 国家知识产权局关于《专利审查指南修改草案 (征求意见稿)》的说明 (Explanation of the draft revision of patent examination guideline) (in Chinese).

SIPO. 2017a. 国家知识产权局关于修改《专利审查指南》的决定 (局令第74号) (2017) (Decision to revise the Patent Examination Guidelines (2017) Order No. 74) (in Chinese).

SIPO. 2017b.《专利审查指南》(Patent Examination Guideline) (in Chinese).

SIPO. 2017c. 2016 年中国专利调查数据报告 (SIPO's Survey Report on Chinese Patents in 2016) (in Chinese), available at http://www.gov.cn/xinwen/2017-07/01/content_5207170.htm.

SPC. 2018. 建立国家层面知识产权案件上诉审理机制 (Establish a review mechanism for appeals at the national level) (in Chinese), available at https://www.thepaper.cn/newsDetail_forward_2574376.

Standing Committee of the National People's Congress, 2013. The Decision of the Standing Committee of the National People's Congress on Revising the Consumer Rights Protection Law of the PRC.

State Food and Drug Administration. 2017. 关于征求《关于鼓励药品医疗器械创新保护创新者权益的相关政策 (征求意见稿)》意见的公告 [Relevant policies for encouraging innovations of drugs and medical devices and protecting innovators' rights and interests (Draft)] (2017 Order No. 55) (in Chinese).

State Post Office. 2014. 寄递服务用户个人信息安全管理规定 (Personal information security measures for mailing and courier services) (in Chinese).

Xiaoqing, F. 2011. 国家产业技术政策, 技术创新体系与产业技术创新战略联盟—兼论知识产权战略的作用机制 (National industrial and technology policy, technology innovation system and the construction of strategic alliances for technological innovation—On the mechanism of intellectual property strategy) (in Chinese) 8 CONTEMPORARY ECONOMY & MANAGEMENT, 19.

Xinhua. 2017. *China issued guidelines Monday on the sharing economy*. Available at: http://news.xinhuanet.com/english/2017-07/03/c_136414158.htm.

Xu, Jiahui. 2018. 商业方法类专利创造性要求的分析 (Analysis of the patent's creative requirements for business methods) (in Chinese), available at: https://mp.weixin.qq.com/s?__biz=MjM5OTI0OTU3Ng==&mid=2447676667&idx=1&sn=f66228a8ba031d778bff6db039e0cc98&chksm=b32e673c8459ee2aa7f4f191a0d03f53ee94b310e176577c99dc2699344a7d7c536ae8b264e1&mpshare=1&scene=1&srcid=0313NUxnVDIIwjiEQbG9rgXq#rd>.

Yanadori, Y., and V. Cui. 2013. Creating incentives for innovation? The relationship between pay dispersion in R&D groups and firm innovation performance. *Strategic Management Journal* 34: 1502–1511.

Yu, P. 2007. Intellectual property, economic development, and the China puzzle. In *Intellectual property, trade and development: Strategies to optimize economic development in a TRIPs plus area*, ed. D. Gervais, 173–220. Oxford: Oxford University Press.

Zhang, Y., L. Haibo, and Z. Jin. 2016. A study on the effects of intellectual property policies in China: Evidence from China's 'IP Demonstration City' Program. In *Economic impacts of intellectual property-conditioned government incentives*, ed. D. Prud'homme and H. Song, 279–308. Singapore: Springer.

Chapter 6
Administration of IP Rights

A relatively complex state system for administering IP rights has been developed in China since the 1980s. This chapter provides a brief overview of this system and offers a general assessment as to how it has functioned to enable innovation and entrepreneurship in China.

6.1 Snapshot of IP Administration in China

See Table 6.1.

Aside from the central-level bureaus, there are normally four levels of local government administration in China: (i) the government of provinces, autonomous regions, or direct-controlled municipalities (e.g., Beijing and Shanghai); (ii) the government of prefectures; (iii) the government of counties or districts; and (iv) the government of townships and villages. When IP rights holders identify cases of infringement, depending on the scope of relevant legal provisions for different IP, he or she may petition the relevant department at the provincial or a lower level of government to stop the infringement, seize the infringing goods, and fine the infringer. (See more on this point in Chap. 7). However, normally only local government officials at the city or township level are responsible for governing IPR in their administrative areas.

D. Prud'homme and T. Zhang, *China's Intellectual Property Regime for Innovation*, https://doi.org/10.1007/978-3-030-10404-7_6

Table 6.1 Key[a] IP-related institutions at the central-level and their main responsibilities

Name		IP-related responsibilities	Historic development
State Administration of Market Regulation (SAMR)	China National Intellectual Property Administration (CNIPA), part of SAMR	Governs multiple types of IP	Founded in 2018
		Patents: 1. Patent Office is responsible for patent examination and granting, and for registration of integrated circuit layout-designs 2. Patent Reexamination Board (PRB) is responsible for the review of patent invalidation disputes	"China's Patent Office" founded in 1980 and changed to the State Intellectual Property Office (SIPO) in 1998; then changed in 2018 to CNIPA and to be an affiliate of SAMR
		Trademarks and anti-unfair competition: 1. Trademark Office is responsible for the registration and administration of trademarks throughout China 2. Trademark Review and Adjudication Board (TRAB) is responsible for the review of trademark invalidation cases 3. Antimonopoly and Anti-Unfair Competition Enforcement Bureau is responsible for the administrative enforcement of unfair competition	Trademark Office was established in 1978 under the State Administration for Industry and Commerce (SAIC) and it, as well as the unfair competition functions of SAIC, dismantled to be part of CNIPA (under SAMR) in 2018 Local AICs/AMRs have five levels, corresponding to the five levels of government in China
		GIs: 1. Registration and administration of collective or identification GI marks 2. GI functions formerly administered by AQSIQ	Part of Trademark Office devoted to GIs now under CNIPA (under SAMR) as of 2018; Part of AQSIQ devoted to administering GIs now under CNIPA (under SAMR) as of 2018

(continued)

Table 6.1 (continued)

Name		IP-related responsibilities	Historic development
	Administration for Quality Supervision, Inspection and Quarantine (AQSIQ)	1. Develops product quality standards 2. Investigates and handles counterfeits and inferior commodities	Leading National Standards Committee and State Certification and Accreditation Administration; now an affiliate of SAMR
	Standards Administration of China (SAC)	1. Undertake streamlined management, supervision and overall coordination of technical standardization in China 2. Approves and organizes the implementation of international cooperation and exchange projects on technical standardization	Established in April 2001; now part of SAMR
	Anti-monopoly bureau	1. Draft relevant regulations and policies involving concentration of operators 2. Conducts anti-monopoly reviews of the concentration behavior of operators, processes corresponding complaints, and investigates and punishes anti-monopoly behavior (including that involving IP rights)	Established under the Ministry of Commerce in 2008; became part of SAMR since 2018

(continued)

Table 6.1 (continued)

Name	IP-related responsibilities	Historic development
National Copyright Administration (NCA) [shares the same staff with State Administration for Press and Publication]	1. Implements the copyright law and regulations 2. Examines and approves the collective administration of copyrights 3. Guides the work of local copyright administration agents and investigates copyright infringement cases that have significant impact	NCA was founded in 1985 under the Ministry of Culture and combined with the State Administration of Press, Publication, Radio, Film and Television in 2013. The functions of administration of copyright, publication and press have been under the Propaganda Department of Central Committee since 2018
Ministry of Agriculture and Rural Affairs (MoARA) [formerly the Ministry of Agriculture (MoA)]	1. Examines and grants rights for agricultural plant varieties 2. Examines and grants GI certificates for agricultural products	Founded in 1949; combined with other authorities (1970–1988); rebuilt in 1988 as the Ministry of Agriculture (MoA) and changed to the Ministry of Agriculture and Rural Affairs (MoARA) in 2018
State Administration of Forestry and Grasslands (SAFG) [formerly the State Administration of Forestry (SFA)]	1. Examines and grants forestry plant varieties 2. To examine and grant GIs for forestry products (see the draft Regulation of the GIs for Forestry Products)	Founded in 1949; combined with other authorities (1970–1998); rebuilt in 1998 as the State Forestry Administration of (SFA) and changed to the State Administration of Forestry and Grasslands (SAFG) in 2018
General Administration of Customs	1. Receives registrations and manages records of cross border IPR 2. Investigates and detains suspected infringing goods	Founded in 1949

(continued)

Table 6.1 (continued)

Name	IP-related responsibilities	Historic development
Ministry of Commerce	Governs IPR matters in domestic and foreign trade and international economic cooperation Established the Office of the Leading National Group on the Fight Against IPR Infringement and Counterfeiting	Founded in 1949; Ministry of Foreign Trade and Economic Cooperation (1993–2003)

Source The authors. [a]*Note* There are many other Chinese bodies not listed in the above table that govern IP enforcement specifically (for more discussion see Chap. 7)

Table 6.2 Average processing time for patents in China in the 1990s (in months)

Year	1985	1986	1988	1990	1992	1994	1996
Process time	50.3	51.6	13.6	20.0	46.6	60.6	63.8

Source Xia (2003)

Table 6.3 Average caseload of single examiner in the US, Japan and China (2000)

	U.S.	Japan	China
Number of patent applications	7503	8300	51,747
Number of examiners	4000	3000	350
Average caseload of single examiner	1.88	2.77	147.85

Sources Xia (2003), data collected from China Statistical Yearbook

6.2 Main Administration Challenges at Different IP Offices

6.2.1 Processing Times

SIPO

According to Xia (2003), the average pendency (i.e., the time to grant) for patents in China in the 1990s was four years or even longer. See Table 6.2.

By 2000, the workload of patent examiners in China increased. The main reasons for this were the rapid growth of applications and the shortage of examiners. This impacted patents in China. Table 6.3 compares numbers of patent applications, examiners and caseloads in China, the US, and Japan in 2000, showing the significant caseload of Chinese examiners in 2000.

The rise in patent applications and lengthening of patent pendency time pushed SIPO to take several measures to speed up patent pendency in China. First, SIPO greatly enlarged the team of its patent examiners after 2001. At present, SIPO is the biggest IP office in the world with nearly 13,000 patent examiners. Second, SIPO continues to improve information management for its patent examinations. Third, SIPO strictly controls its reexamination cycle by introducing new models of review. These measures seem to have contributed to a decrease in patent pendency times in China (see Fig. 6.1).

According to SIPO, during the Eleventh Five-Year period (2006–2010), the average examination period for invention patents was 24.8 months, and during the "second five" period (2010–2015), the average examination period dropped to 22.3 months. In 2015, the average examination period for invention patent applications was 21.9 months, which is shorter than that of USPTO (25.3 months) and the EPO (26.5 months). In 2016, the average examination period for invention patents applications was 22 months. In 2016, the average examination period for utility models and designs application was within 2.9 months and 3.0 months, respectively, as counted from the date of filing. Meanwhile, SIPO has opened up an expedited patent exami-

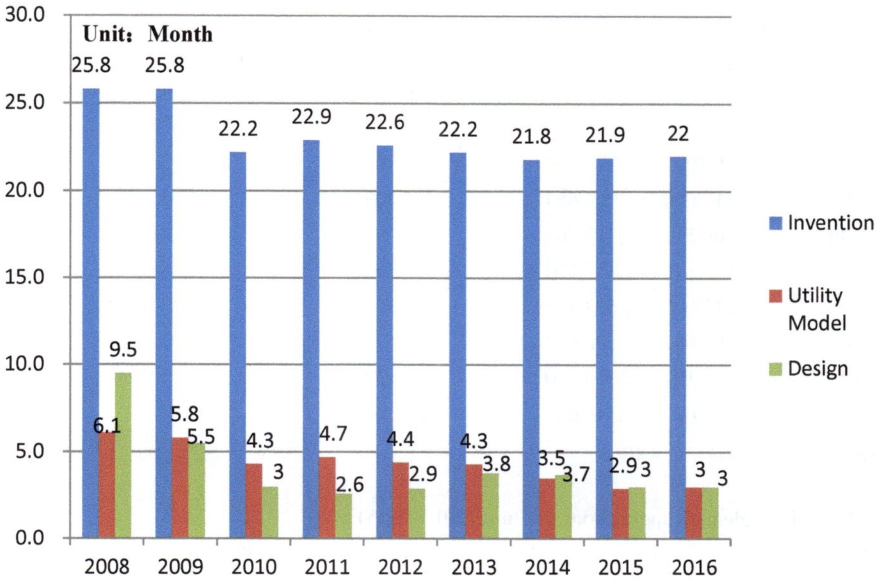

Fig. 6.1 Average patent pendency times in China (2008–2016). *Source* Annual Report of SIPO

nation channel (see Chap. 5) to give priority to patent applications in technological fields of major national interests and industrial core technologies. Invention patents subject to this channel can be granted in as few as eight months (Shen 2017).

Comparing the present caseload per SIPO examiner (see Table 6.4) with that in 2000 (see Table 6.3), it is clear that the present average caseload of a single examiner is higher. Some suggest that rising case-load experienced by SIPO examiners has had detrimental impacts on patent quality in China (Liang 2012). However, other data and analysis suggests that, in fact, the examinations provided by SIPO are of relatively high quality, for example when compared to other large patent offices (Song and Li 2014).

Trademark Office (TMO)

Entities apply for more trademarks annually in China than any country in the world. And these filings are still growing exceptionally fast (see Table 6.5).

Backlog for trademark examinations has been a serious problem for the China Trademark Office since 2000. A large part of this backlog is owed to the rapid growth of trademark applications in China. By the end of 2007, the examination period for a trademark application was more than 36 months on average. This led to the reform of trademark examination procedure. In 2008, SAIC formulated a series of measures to speed up the review of trademarks. According to a report from SAIC, by the end of 2010, China's trademark examination period had been shortened to about 12 months. In 2013 and 2016, it was further reduced to 10 months and then

Table 6.4 Average caseload of single examiner in China (2008–2016)

Year	Patent granted	Examination cases concluded	Number of examiners	Average caseload of single examiner
2008	411,982	567,520	2932	193.6
2009	581,992	846,403	3074	275.3
2010	815,000	1,064,654	3094	344.1
2011	960,513	1,217,706	2954	412.2
2012	1,255,138	1,355,000	7207	188.0
2013	1,313,000	1,622,406	8601	188.6
2014	1,302,687	1,890,000	8701	217.2
2015	1,718,192	2,080,000	10,302	201.9
2016	1,772,000	2,310,000	11,600	199.1

Source Annual Report of SIPO

Table 6.5 Trademark applications in China (2012–2015)

Year	2012	2013	2014	2015	2016
Number of filings	1,648,000	1,881,500	2,285,400	2,876,000	3,691,400
Growth rate	16.3%	4.1%	21.5%	25.9%	28.4%

Sources China's Intellectual Property Protection (2012–2016) issued by SIPO; Annual Report on China's Trademark Development Strategy

9 months, respectively, on average. Still, some firms we consulted experienced slower trademark examination periods in recent years.

Geographical indication (GIs) by TMO, AQSIQ, and MoA before 2019

The China Trademark Office issues special marks, i.e. a certificate mark and collective mark, for GI products. In 2014, there were 507 GI filings and preliminary grants, reflecting a growth of 16.3% compared with the previous year (436). As of the end of 2014, the cumulative registration number of these marks was 2697, nearly nine times the figure in 2007 (301). Among these marks, 81 are filed by foreigners (SAIC 2015). It normally takes 7–9 months to get a GI certificate from SAIC.

Aside from the Trademark Office, the General Administration of Quality Supervision, Inspection and Quarantine of the PRC (AQSIQ) and Ministry of Agriculture (MoA) also issue GI certificates. So far, there are no public figures on examination times for these certificates. There does not appear to be a backlog problem reported so far, perhaps primarily because of the limited amount of applications. According to the information offered by practitioners we consulted, it normally takes 6–10 months to get a GI certificate from AQSIQ or MoA.

It is worth noting that, AQSIQ promulgated the Measures on the Protection of Foreign Geographical Indications Products (the Measures) on March 28, 2016. According to the Measures, a formality examination for GI certificates should be made within a maximum of 30 days, which should be followed by a period of 60 days for opposition after publication, and then a technical examination stage without a clear time limitation (Art. 11–15 of the Measures).

With the establishment of CNIPA and SAMR in 2018, the situation that TMO, AQSIQ, and MoA separately receive and issue certificates for various GIs is scheduled to change. However, at the time of writing this book the fragmented management approach had not yet changed. Further, it appears that only GI administration by TMO and AQSIQ is slated to be streamlined under CNIPA (which is under SAMR), while it appears MoA (now (MoARA) will continue to separately administer GIs specifically for agricultural products and, if its request is authorized, SFA (now SAFG) may separately administer GIs specifically for forestry products.[1] In reaction to this continually fragmented system, it is possible that some rights holders will continue a practice we have observed where they apply for GI protection to TMO and AQSIQ (now under CNIPA) even if their products directly involve agriculture or forestry.

New plant varieties

Plant variety protection (PVP) rights in China have increased rapidly over the years. At the end of 2016, China's total applications for new varieties of agricultural plants was more than 18,000 (see Table 6.6). The total granted amount was more than 8000, and the annual application number ranked first for any individual country among International Union for the Protection of New Varieties of Plants (UPOV). As of the end of 2016, there were 2188 new varieties of forestry plants granted. In 2016, the State Forestry Administration received a total of 400 new varieties of forestry plants, and granted 195 new varieties of forestry plants rights.

No data concerning the examination time of new plant variety rights has been issued by any official authority in China. Due to the relatively small amount of applications in the PVP field, there may be limited problems with examination backlog. Judging from data made available to us by practitioners we consulted, PVP examinations will be concluded within the statutory maximum time, i.e. 14 months.

6.2.2 *Quality of Examination*

The quality of IPR examinations can be determined, to some extent, from quality satisfaction surveys conducted by third parties. The challenge of intermediate examination decisions and the final examination outcome can be another indicator of the quality of IP examination. This book offers only some perspectives on the quality of IP examination in China based on the limited available information on the subject.

Patents

According to several surveys, the patent examination process in China has improved over the last several years. The 2012 IP5 Statistics Report issued by IP5, a coalition

[1]In 2013, SFA produced a draft regulation governing GI applications related to forestry products, although the regulation still remains in draft form.

Table 6.6 Applications for new varieties of agricultural plants in China (2012–2015)

Type of institution		Total applications	Total granted	2012	2013	2014	2015
Domestic	Research institutes	6470	3159	485	494	598	704
	Enterprises	6181	2023	584	618	932	990
	Teaching institutes	1085	516	116	65	108	93
	Individuals	827	272	73	52	82	95
Foreign	Research institutes	27	9	8	3	3	1
	Enterprises	895	268	89	98	48	161
	Teaching institutes	10	1	2	1	1	6
	Individuals	57	10	4	2	0	19
Total		15,552	6258	1361	1333	1772	2069

Source China IP Statistical Yearbook

Table 6.7 Annual survey of the quality of patent examination in China (2010–2016)

Year	2010	2011	2012	2013	2014	2015	2016
PSI	81.1	81.5	81.6	81.8	81.9	82.8	82.7

Source Annual Report of SIPO. PSI = Public Satisfaction Index

of the world's five largest patent offices, shows that SIPO's examination process in 2011 improved the most relative to the improvements experienced at the other five IP offices around the world that receive the most patent applications (IP5 2013). Similarly, a survey conducted by Thomson-Reuters and the IP practitioner magazine Intellectual Asset Management from 2009 to 2010 shows that SIPO's examination process improved the most relative to the improvements experienced at the other five IP offices around the world that receive the most patent applications. Around the same time, SIPO commissioned the annual quality satisfaction survey of patent examination (He 2011). Investigators participating in this audit include patent applicants, patent owners, patent agencies, and entities that request patent invalidation. Through face to face, telephone, e-mail interviews and other forms of investigation, several thousand people were consulted directly. Since 2010, the results of the annual survey shows the satisfaction indexes have all exceeded 81%. The results of these surveys are depicted in Table 6.7.

If patent applicants in China are dissatisfied with the decision of the patent office, they can apply for review of the decision at the PRB and, if they fail again in their appeal, they can continue to appeal to the court in China. According to statistics over the last ten years, among every 10,000 patent examination cases (ECC) concluded by SIPO, only one or two will ultimately be appealed by patent applicants to the court (see Table 6.8).

Table 6.8 Review and appeals of patent examination outcomes (2008–2016)

Year	ECC	Review application	Review concluded	Appeal against the review decision (1st + 2nd instance)	Ratio of appeal/ECC (%)
2008	567,520	4360	3867	86	0.015
2009	846,403	9195	6697	125	0.014
2010	1,064,654	12,369	9005	169	0.015
2011	1,217,706	12,946	10,116	194	0.015
2012	1,355,000	17,320	11,427	316	0.023
2013	1,622,406	18,829	14,805	231	0.014
2014	1,890,000	24,452	20,393	207	0.010
2015	2,080,000	12,678	25,756	478	0.022
2016	2,310,000	13,197	17,623	460	0.019

Source Annual Report of SIPO. Some figures may be rounded

Table 6.9 Spot audits on the trademark quality by QMB (2008–2010)

Year	Number of inspections	Examiners and assistants involved	Cases of TM application preliminarily approved	Sampling ratio (%)	Qualified ratio (%)
2008	3	295	6,393	2–3	97–98
2009	6	220	15,468	2	98.3
2010	10	200	–	2	99

Source Annual Report on China's Trademark Development Strategy

Trademarks

In February 2008, China's Trademark Office decided to set up a professional quality management organization called the Quality Management Department (QMD). Interim Measures concerning Quality Management of Trademark Examination and Evaluation Standards on Quality of Trademark Examination were promulgated and implemented soon thereafter. These measures lay down the operation mechanisms, organizational structure, and principles and other measures for quality management. According to the measures, the China Trademark Office divided its management system into three levels, namely, the Work Leading Group, Quality Management Division, and Quality Inspection Group (Zhou 2010). Databases were also established to improve the efficiency and quality of examination such as the Database of Trademarks with Immoral Influence, and Database of Geographical Names Not Allowed as Trademarks. Annually, QMD conducts spot audits to oversee the quality of trademark examination Table 6.9.

In 2016, the Trademark Review Collaboration Center (the Center) received 3.07 million trademark applications, and preliminarily examined and publicized 2.03 mil-

Table 6.10 Typology of errors made by assistant trademark examiners at TMO in 2015

Types of error	Number of cases	Rate (%)
Made no reference to identical or highly similar trademarks	355	31.55
Wrongful deletion of similar goods or services	319	28.16
Made no reference to similar marks or made reference to distinguishable marks	135	11.92
The cited trademark is invalid, has a later filing date, or was held and filed by the same applicant on the same day	123	10.86
Obvious mistake in the title and classification	62	5.47
Did not apply the forbidden clause to reject the application	43	3.80
Wrongful application of provisions	30	2.65
Misrepresentation of the status of citation mark	24	2.12
Others	42	3.71

Source Data collected from Guan (2016)

lion trademarks. Among these applications, 58,800 oppositions were filed by third parties in 2016, which is a dissent rate of 2.9%, (0.4% lower than that of 2015). More than 1 million trademark applications were rejected by the Center and among them 120,000 reviews were rejected in 2016. The review rejection rate was 11.5%, which is lower than that of 2015 (12.2%) (Li 2016). In 2016, the TMO completed another inspection of trademark examination in 2015. During the inspection, 32,875 trademarks were sampled and around 1500 cases were found problematic, accounting for 4.86% of the sample. Among these problematic examinations, 1052 cases handled by assistant examiners had various errors as elaborated on in Table 6.10 (Guan 2016).

Although substantial efforts have been made to improve the quality of trademark examination and reduce the error rate in examination, the huge number of trademark applications in China poses significant challenges to TMO. Some errors made by assistant examiners are quite obvious such as "Made no reference to identical or highly similar trademarks" or "obvious mistake in the title" (see Table 6.10), and inferably can be corrected as these examiners become more experienced or are replaced.

Many of the problematic trademarks have been misused by their right holders in China to restrict commerce. For example, many trademarks without distinctiveness because they use a generic name of goods or services have still successfully passed the examination in China and have been used against businesses on e-commerce platform such as Alibaba's Taobao.com (Liu et al. 2017).

Similarly, "bad faith" trademarks are still being filed in China, which is of significant concern to industry, particularly foreign industry with well-established brands.[2] Bad faith trademarks are those filed/used elsewhere that are filed by another party

[2]For example, see https://www.gov.uk/government/publications/factsheet-on-bad-faith-trademarks-in-china.

Table 6.11 Number of trademark reviews requested and concluded (2009–2016)

	2009	2010	2011	2012	2013	2014	2015	2016
All review cases concluded	37,002	39,220	35,043	88,440	144,182	115,931	108,915	125,200
RR requested	50,572	61,887	55,298	56,524	58,491	77,390	99,557	130,600
RR concluded	28,594	29,985	26,840	42,778	108,301	86,000	88,900	104,200

Sources Annual Report on China's Trademark Development Strategy; China IPR Yearbook. Some figures may be rounded

without the consent of the owner, and can take other forms in China (see Chaps. 2 and 7 for more analysis about bad faith trademarks in China.).

When TMO rejects a trademark application, the applicant can file a request to the trademark review board (TRAB) to review the rejection (RR) decision of TMO. Table 6.11 shows the increasing number of RR cases requested and concluded at TRAB. However, in the absence of information regarding the final outcome of these disputes, it is not possible to further analyze the quality aspect of rejection decisions made by TMO.

6.2.3 *Efficiency and Quality of the Invalidation Process*

Patents

According to the information released by SIPO (see Table 6.12), as of the end of 2014, the Patent Reexamination Board (PRB) accepted a total of 118,000 patent review requests (PRRs) and concluded 91,000 PRRs; and accepted 38,000 patent invalidation requests (PIR), concluding 91,000. The average processing time of PRRs and PIRs were 14.6 and 7.2 months, respectively. According to our own consultations with reviewers of PRB, the average processing time for reviews of patent grant decisions is between 10 to 12 months.

According to SIPO statistics (see Table 6.12), the average patent grant decision appeal rate from 2009 to 2011 was about 20%. Available data indicate that the PRB has a high win rate at court with regards to disputes over its invalidation decisions—only 1.6% of PIR decisions made by PRB were overruled by the court (SIPO 2013b). This being said, as perhaps to be expected, our consultations with foreign firms in particular suggested that in some cases they strongly disagreed with the invalidation (or lack therefore) decisions by SIPO.

Table 6.12 Patent invalidation requests received and concluded at the PRB (2008–2016)

Year	PIR received	PIR concluded	Appeal (1st, 2nd instance)	Appeal rate	PRB win rate
2008	2038	2727	757 (undivided)	–	–
2009	2247	2310	858 (undivided)	–	98.4%
2010	2411	1946	706 (undivided)	–	
2011	2749	2567	770 (487+283)	18.97%	
2012	2941	2599	1026 (684+342)	26.31%	–
2013	2930	2313	794 (undivided)	–	–
2014	3422	2742	778 (undivided)	–	–
2015	3724	3652	1198 (undivided)	–	–
2016	3969	4100	1030 (undivided)	–	–

Sources Annual Report of SIPO; SIPO (2013b)

Table 6.13 Trademark DRT, IAR, and LAR cases received and concluded (2012–2015)

	2012	2013	2014	2015
DRT received	448	4121	–	–
DRT concluded	197	5042	–	–
RCRT received	4213	2156	2768	4430
RCRT concluded	2442	607	2033	3729
IAR received	–	–	5129	11,951
IAR concluded	–	–	4875	7465

Source Annual Report of China IPR Protection Status

Trademarks

According to statistics from the Annual Report released by SAIC (see Table 6.13), the average processing time for trademark invalidation cases at the TRAB has remained below 18 months for the last 6 years. TRAB is in charge of reviewing both the Trademark Office's decisions of trademark application and registered trademark disputes including disputes over registered trademarks—first called "DRT" then called the Invalid Announcement Review (IAR) after 2013)—and the Review of Cancellation of Registered Trademarks (RCRT).

Regarding the decisions made by TRAB, TRAB keeps data on cases disputing their decisions (see Table 6.14). For example, about 5% of all the trademark invalidation cases were concluded. Additionally, there was a high win rate in the courts, with more than 80% in the first instance won and almost 90% in the second instance.

Table 6.14 Figures on appeals of TRAB trademark decisions (2009–2016)

	2009	2010	2011	2012	2013	2014	2015	2016
1st instance case as defendant	1346	1815	2632[a]	2143	1760	7452	3700	5345
Winning rate of first instance	85.8%	80.1%	82.1%	82.4%	82.4%	84.6%	82.7%	–

Source Annual Report on China's Trademark Development Strategy ([a]This number includes cases of second instance and retrial)

6.2.4 Coordination Between Central-Level Bureaus and Provincial and Local Bureaus in Making IP Strategies and Administering IP Rights

China used to have a highly fragmented system of IP administration. SIPO, TMO (SAIC), NCA, MoA, MFA, the Ministry of Commerce (MOFCOM), the General Administration of Customs, AQSIQ, and many other government bodies—in fact of a whopping 28—were in charge of different aspects of governing IPR in China (Song et al. 2016). Some of their functions overlapped.

This "departmental administration" system is a product of China's planned economic system under which the state's decision-making locus has absolute power in state resource allocation and aims at cross-sectoral coordination. However, in China's present market economy, inefficient coordination among the many government bodies governing IPR poses a challenge to the state's ability to administer IPR effectively and efficiently. The excessive fragmentation is not suited to effectively manage the inner-connectivity between different types of IPRs, can create uncertainty and other confusion in the marketplace, and reduces administrative efficiency. More generally, the system often undermines the ability of China's IP regime to create an effective appropriability environment for innovation and entrepreneurship.

A number of important initiatives have been launched over the last decade to better coordinate governance of IP in China. To better address the problems caused by the fragmentation of IPR governance in China, the State Council promulgated the Outline of the National Intellectual Property Strategy on June 5, 2008, to better coordinate among state authorities tasked with IPR administration. Further to the 2008 National IP Strategy, the Inter-Ministerial Joint Conference System for the Implementation of the National IP Strategy was established. The joint conference is a highly important mechanism for coordinating across the many government authorities governing IP in China. At the outset, the head of the SIPO was the convener of this coordinating body of 28 agencies/ministries. Then, as of March 2016, the Inter-Ministerial Joint Conference System was upgraded in the state hierarchy and is now led by the State Council with 31 different administrative agencies as its members. However, the coordinating capacity and efficiency of these coordinating mechanisms remains debatable thus far.

Other coordination initiatives are worth mentioning. The Joint Ministerial Meeting to Promote the Use of Genuine Software was established in 2012, consisting of 15 members of different IP governmental bodies with its office located in NCA. In 2013, another coordination mechanism, the Leading Group of National Crackdown on IPR Infringements and Manufacture and Sale of Counterfeit was established with an office in SAIC.

Further, some measures have been taken by some Chinese state authorities to ease the challenges posed by decentralization of IP enforcement in particular. For example, MOFCOM established 50 complaint service centers nationwide for the protection of IPRs in 2007. These centers are open to the public to file reports and complaints about IPR infringements and offers consulting services regarding IPR protection to the general public. Yet other initiatives have been launched by SIPO and other authorities (see Chap. 7).

Another important initiative is the recent development of the Office of the Intellectual Property Leadership Working Group at the municipal/provincial level to strengthen the coordination of patent, trademark, copyright and other intellectual properties enforcement. Several important measures have already been formulated in response to this initiative. To name just a few listed in SIPO's website: in 2015, Wuhan adopted the Interim Measures for Joint Law Enforcement of IPRs in Great Light Valley Zone to establish a coordination mechanism to jointly enforce IPRs and better respond, handle, and mediate IP disputes; a joint enforcement mechanism for IPR was developed by the Hainan Provincial IPO jointly with the Industry and Commerce Bureau, Copyright Bureau, Haikou Customs and other departments in Haikou City to inspect supermarkets and crackdown on various IP infringement activities on April 20, 2016; Guangdong, Guangxi, and Hainan Provinces jointly carried out patent administrative law enforcement inspection on November 1, 2016; Xiamen city's Office of the Intellectual Property Leadership Working Group organized a joint enforcement of IP on April 21, 2017; and a cross-provincial enforcement of patent rights initiative called "Thunderbolt", which spanned 10 provinces and cities, was launched in August 2017.

As discussed in Chap. 2, in 2018 the structure of IP administration in China was overhauled through the establishment of a new government agency, SAMR. SAMR was established on April 10th 2018 to take over various IP administrative enforcement affairs which used to be separately governed by SAIC, AQSIQ, CFDA, and their local bureaus.

After the reform involving SAMR, SAIC, AQSIQ, and CFDA will be gradually absorbed into SAMR, and SIPO—with the new name CNIPA—will be an affiliate of SAMR. Meanwhile, the functions of the previous three antitrust agencies—i.e. merger review under the MOFCOM, price-related antitrust investigations under NDRC, and non-price related investigations under SAIC—have also been consolidated under SAMR. SAC, which helps govern standards involving IP, will also be consolidated under SAMR.

6.3 Summary

Since the 1980s, China has gradually established a complex and complete system for administering IP rights. Following China's accession to the WTO, one of the biggest challenges facing IP administration officials in China has been the rapid growth of IP applications and a shortage of IP examiners. This being said, China's government institutions for administering IP rights have, in general, become better managed over the years.

Still, some improvements can still be made to guarantee the efficiency and quality of administration of IP rights in China. Inefficient coordination among the many central, provincial, and local government bodies governing IPR in China poses a challenge to the state's ability to administer IPR effectively and efficiently to enable innovation and entrepreneurship. Some important initiatives have been developed to address these challenges, although it appears that further reforms could be useful. Specifically, the state should improve coordination of IP administration and enforcement (e.g., improve coordination/better streamline IP rights granting, for example for GIs, and other IP administration aspects among state bodies; and enhance oversight of sub-central-level IP policy-making/strategizing). Also, the state should expand the size and quality of China's IP administration infrastructure (e.g., by increasing quality staff and quality management in IP administrations). More specific recommendations are provided in Chap. 9.

References

Guan, M. 2016. 2015年审协中心商标审查质量显著提升 (The quality of Trademark examination was greatly improved in 2015) (in Chinese). *China Trademark* 7: 21–22.

He, Yuan Fang. 2011.《中国专利审查质量年度报告》(2010) 显示我国专利审查质量稳步提升 (The quality of Patent examination is steadily improved according to the Annual Report of the Quality of Patent Examination in China of 2010) (in Chinese) China IPR Daily, 22 Apr 2011.

IP5. 2013. 2012 IP5 statistics report, www.fiveipoffices.org/stats/statisticalreports/2012edition.htm.

Li, H. 2016. 超限退文两并降数量质量双提升—商标审查协作中心商标实质审查工作取得新进展 (Trademark review collaboration center made progress of its substantial examination work) (in Chinese), available at http://www.tdtm.com.cn/?newsxq/id/217/gzgtid/169.html.

Liang, M. 2012. Chinese patent quality: Running the numbers and possible remedies. *John Marshall Review of Intellectual Property Law* 11: 478–522.

Liu, X., T. Zhang, and H. Zhu. 2017. 借电商平台、行商标挟持:无显著性商标恶意投诉之现状与治理 (The regulation of malicious complaints of non-distinctive registered trademarks) (in Chinese). http://www.weixinso.com/document/064Jhc.html.

SAIC. 中国商标战略年度发展报告 (China Trademark Strategy Annual Report) (in Chinese). http://www.saic.gov.cn/sbj/tzgg/index_1.html.

SAIC. 2015. 地理标志和农产品商标 (GI and agricultural goods) (in Chinese). http://sbj.saic.gov.cn/ztbd/xsbfss/gzgl/201504/t20150422_231422.html.

Shen. C. 2017. 审查员达1.1万人堪称世界第一大局 (With 11 thousand examiners SIPO is now the biggest IP Office) (in Chinese). Legal Daily, http://www.legaldaily.com.cn/index/content/2017-04/25/content_7122448.htm.

SIPO. 中国知识产权年鉴 (China IPR Yearbooks) (in Chinese). IPR Press.

SIPO. 国家知识产权局年报 (Annual working reports) (in Chinese). http://www.sipo.gov.cn/gk/ndbg/.
SIPO. 中国知识产权保护状况 (Annual Reports of China IPR Protection Status) (in Chinese). http://www.sipo.gov.cn/gk/zscqbps/.
SIPO. 2013a. 国家知识产权局关于进一步提升专利申请质量的若干意见 (Several Opinions on Further Improving Quality of Patent Applications) (in Chinese), available at http://www.sipo.gov.cn/zscqgz/2013/201312/t20131225_891833.html.
SIPO. 2013b.《中华人民共和国专利法修订草案(送审稿)》说明 (Explanation of revision draft of the patent Law of PRC) (in Chinese).
Song, H., and Z. Li. 2014. Patent quality and the measuring indicator system: Comparison among Chinese provinces and key countries. In *Berkeley center for law & technology IP scholars conference*, 6–8 Aug 2014, Berkeley Law School. Available at https://www.law.berkeley.edu/files/Song_Hefa_IPSC_paper_2014.pdf.
Song, S., P. Zhang, and B. Ge. 2016. 中国知识产权体制演进与改革方向研究 (The developing regularity and reform direction of China's intellectual property administration system) (in Chinese). *Chinese Public Administration* 9: 34–41.
Xia, Y. 2003. 专利授权期的有效管理研究 (Research on effective management of patent authorization period) (in Chinese). Sichuan University Master Dissertation.
Zhou, Z. 2010. Overview on quality management of trademark examination, Beijing, 2010 (Presentation by the Deputy Director of the QMD of TMO of SAIC). www.ipkey.org/zh/component/flexicontent/download/2052/2181/23.

Chapter 7
IP Enforcement

7.1 Overview

An IP right affords its owner the ability to exclude others from exploiting their protected assets without consent. When IP rights are infringed, rights holders have the ability to take action against infringing conduct, i.e., to enforce their rights. IP enforcement is therefore critical for those reliant on IP to protect the returns from their investments in innovation. Without an effective and efficient IP enforcement mechanism, the value of IP is greatly undermined as is the ability of the IP system to promote innovation.

China has a globally unique dual-track system for IP enforcement. Aside from universal border protection by Customs, both courts and "local administrative enforcement" agencies (hereafter "administrative agencies") (i.e., government agencies at the local levels in China that can investigate and seize infringing products, among other IP enforcement activities) in China play a direct role in IP enforcement. To be clear, the enforcement handled by these local administrative enforcement bodies (who are typically, formally or informally, local affiliates of central-level government bodies governing patent, trademark, copyright, and other IPRs) is distinct from what is separately called "administrative litigation/cases" in most jurisdictions. (In administrative litigation/cases, complainants lodge cases against the official central-level state authorities that are assigned with administering the examination and grant of IP rights. In these cases, complainants bring cases regarding invalidation/not granting of IP rights (see Chap. 6 for a further discussion on the administrative governance of IP rights).)

Many improvements have been made to China's IP enforcement system over the past few decades. However, noteworthy challenges still remain: China could benefit from an even higher quality IP enforcement system that is more time and resource friendly to rights holders, transparent, and creates a stronger deterrent effect against IP infringement/misappropriation. This chapter will evaluate the efficiency and effectiveness of China's IP enforcement system, including how it may be influencing innovation, based on statistical analysis, literature review, and legal analysis.

D. Prud'homme and T. Zhang, *China's Intellectual Property Regime for Innovation*, https://doi.org/10.1007/978-3-030-10404-7_7

Although we have tried to collect data that is as rich as possible to perform this assessment, the explanatory power of the collected data and our statistical analysis in particular still faces several limitations. First, some of our data only covers only a limited number of courts and years. Second, we only use a basic descriptive approach to our analysis. Third, our analysis focuses primarily on data about enforcement of patents, trademarks, and copyrights. Less data is available about enforcement of trade secrets, GIs, and the other types of IP available in China. Yet maintaining an IP regime that allows the efficient and effective enforcement of trade secrets is critical to innovation, and firms have expressed serious concern about China's IP regime for enforcing trade secrets in recent years (also see Chaps. 2 and 4 on this subject). As such, further data collection is warranted about the enforcement of trade secrets in particular.

Statistics

IP right holders in China have many routes through which they can enforce their IPRs, but which route do they normally take? Findings from the Report of Chinese Patent Investigation Data (2015, 2016) provide some answers to this question. According to the 2016 report, 19.1% of 8389 enterprises surveyed claimed that their patents have been infringed (SIPO 2017). Several interesting trends emerge regarding Chinese entities approaches to enforcing IP (see Table 7.1).

Table 7.1 shows that 38.2% of Chinese patentees give up enforcement efforts entirely when their patents are infringed and only 8% of patentees use both administrative and judicial routes to enforce their patents. Also, possibly due to resources made available to them to enforce IP, universities are more likely to utilize both admin-

Table 7.1 Preferred enforcement approaches by Chinese patentees

Number IP enforcement routes	Entity type				
	Enterprise	University	Research unit	Individuals	Sum
	2036 (%)	60 (%)	83 (%)	98 (%)	2277 (%)
Administrative enforcement	11.5	30.3	5.6	16.9	13.8
Judicial enforcement	16.5	3.8	16.8	8.8	13.2
Both administrative and judicial enforcement	11.2	35.0	7.6	3.9	8.0
Doing nothing	32.9	15.7	35.3	45.1	38.2
Sending cease and desist letter via attorney	27.8	15.2	34.6	25.3	26.8
Sum	100	100	100	100	100

Source SIPO Survey on Chinese Patents (2015, 2016), calculations

Table 7.2 Preferred enforcement measures by Chinese patentees

Entity measures	Enterprise (%)	University (%)	Research unit (%)	Individual (%)	Sum (%)
Report to the administrative authority	44.6	48.8	40.3	46.6	45.7
Litigate in court	23.0	23.9	21.5	25.3	24.3
Ex official enforcement by administrative authority	62.8	57.1	58.4	58.6	60.4
Negotiation	29.2	37.3	34.8	23.6	26.2
Others	0.2	0.1	1.9	0.0	0.1
No preference	1.9	0.8	2.3	3.7	2.9

Source SIPO Survey on Chinese Patents, 2015, 2016. N > 8000 respondents. **Note* More than one option can be selected

istrative and judicial routes to enforce their patents. Enterprises, research units, and individuals prefer to send cease-and-desist letters to alleged infringers.

When polled about the optimal ways to enforce patents (where multiple options were provided), several trends emerge in Chinese patentees' responses. According to Table 7.2, Chinese patentees generally prefer cost-saving methods to enforce their patent. For example, ex officio enforcement by an administrative authority ranks first, accounting for 60.4% of preferences; administrative enforcement is second at 45.7%; and negotiation is third. Only about 24% of respondents consider litigation as a feasible method of IP enforcement (or as little as 20% considering the results in the prior table).

Although the aforementioned figures provide useful contextual information, China covers a vast territory with uneven development among regions, and therefore the nuances of IP enforcement in China are complex and difficult to describe with aggregated nationwide statistics. The remainder of this chapter will first examine geographical trends in IP enforcement in China and then assess the effectiveness and efficiency of each route of IP enforcement in China.

As mentioned in Chap. 1, we draw upon a very rich collection of Chinese language data sources to perform our assessment in this chapter, which should give it significant descriptive value. We attempted to cast a wide data net in order to limit overly narrow interpretation of statistics.

Geographical patterns of IP enforcement in China

Economic development levels dramatically vary across different regions in China. This impacts the level of IPR generation, commercialization, and enforcement in different regions in China. Likewise, IP protection, and enforcement in particular, can impact aspects of technological development in China, which can in turn act as a mediator variable for economic development. In other words, there is two-way and often deeply endogenous relationship between IP enforcement and development.

Various empirical studies show that differing levels of IPR protection across China impact the investment and technology transfer decisions of firms. For example, Han and Li (2005) develop a method to measure IPR enforcement levels across China's provinces using a variation of the Ginarte-Park index method (Ginarte and Park 1997). Yao and Rao (2009) further expand on Han and Li (2005)'s approach to measuring IP enforcement across Chinese provinces looking at data from 2001–2005 and find a significant correlation between more robust IPR enforcement in Chinese provinces and GDP/capita (although find a weak connection between IPR enforcement and R&D investments). Du et al. (2008) find that foreign firms (US ones in particular) prefer to invest in areas within China with better levels of IPR protection. Based on a variety of indicators on IPR protection across China,[1] Luo (2013) finds that IP strength in eastern China is twice that of western China, and that IP protection levels across China are positively correlated with GDP.

Ang et al. (2014) develops a unique index of IPR enforcement across different Chinese provinces based on two measures of IP protection: the winning rates of plaintiffs in IP cases based on a sample of several thousand civil litigation cases in the high-tech sector from 2001–2005, and an examination of the number of times official provincial-level Communist Party newspapers call for strengthening IP protection. Ang et al. (2014) then finds that better enforcement of IPR in Chinese provinces encourages more financing and investing in R&D, which allows firms to generate more invention patents and more sales from new products.

The Chinese Academy of Social Sciences (CASS) has created an annual IPR Index for different regions in China (up until 2012) based on thousands of survey responses about the length of time required for courts to resolve IP disputes, costs of resolving a dispute as a percentage of the value of IP under dispute, and perceptions about the fairness of court decisions in China. Fang et al. (2016) collect these indexes from 2001 to 2011 and find that a number of provinces in the East of China (e.g., Beijing and Shanghai) score the highest on the indexes; they also find that regions with better IPR protection create stronger incentives for innovation and that private firms are more sensitive to IPR protection than SOEs in China.

Hammer and Linton (2011, pp. 318–319) find that IP rights are best enforced in Beijing, Shanghai, and Guangzhou, yet, paradoxically, foreign firms also face some of the most significant challenges efficiently and effectively enforcing their rights in these regions. Our consultations with foreign and domestic Chinese firms operating in China also corroborate these findings—although we also find similar trends in Jiangsu, Zhejiang, and other provinces in the coastal region in eastern China. This paradox is likely partially explained by a causal chain where a significant

[1]Indicators were selected from the China Intellectual Property Index Report (2011) and include, for example, IP output per capita, number of well-known trademarks, total quantity of "China time-honored brands", total trademark quantity, index of total copyright quantity, as well as in terms of indicators of intellectual property transactions.

amount of economic activity is centered in these areas so they are more prone to IPR infringements in the first place, meanwhile high corresponding caseloads may sometimes slow the speed of IP enforcement. Also, given that businesses often have the most vested in these regions, a less-than-optimal enforcement outcome therein (whether owed to protectionism or other factors) can have a more pronounced impact than a similar outcome in a region in which less is vested.

Various Chinese government publications, including the Report on National IP Demonstration Cities, as well as the Annual Report of National Patent Status (全国专利实力状况年度报告) and the Annual Report of National IP Development Status (全国知识产权发展状况年度报告) explore different indicators of IP protection across China, including IP enforcement (e.g., by creating an IP administrative enforcement index, IP customs enforcement index, etc.). We draw on these reports and, as mentioned, a wide range of other official Chinese government reports, datasets, and scholarly research in our evaluation of China's IP enforcement environment in this chapter.

One useful and up-to-date index of IPR protection in China that we do not see used (or if it is, it is sparsely used) in existing scholarly literature is the China IPR Index Report. The China IPR Index Report 2016 tabulates an "IPR Index" (IPRI) that covers different aspect of IP, i.e., IP production, IP commercialization, IP "potential creativity", IP Comprehensive Performance, among other indicators. According to this index, the top ten Chinese provinces with the highest IP protection scores are (in descending order): Beijing, Jiangsu, Shanghai, Guangdong, Zhejiang, Shandong, Tianjin, Chongqing, Fujian and Anhui (China IPR Index Report 2016a, b). This list of top ten provinces with the highest IPR Index scores has remained almost the same since 2010. These index scores appear correlated with the GDP of these provinces.

With regards to IP enforcement specifically, the China IPR Index Report 2016 also provides a more disaggregated ranking of different provinces in China in the form of the IPR Protection Index (IPRPE) (see Table 7.3). The IPRPE covers the following sub-indexes and indicators: the (1) Patent Administrative Enforcement (PAE) Index and its two indicators: (a) Numbers of concluded patent infringement and other patent disputes, and (b) Numbers of concluded patent passing-off disputes; the (2) Trademark Administrative Enforcement (TAE) Index and its two indicators: (a) Numbers of concluded trademark cases and (b) Total amount of money involved in such cases; the (3) Administrative Enforcement Service Capacity (AESC) Index and its four indicators: (a) Quality of law enforcement officers, (b) Number of law enforcement officers, (c) Financial support for IP enforcement, and (d) Number of complaints or consultant telephone calls accepted; and a (4) Judicial Enforcement Capacity (JEC) Index which accounts for the number of first instance IP cases concluded.

Although the indexes depicted in Table 7.3 do not cover every aspect of the IPR enforcement landscape in China (for example, usage of the number of first instance IP cases concluded alone is an insufficient measure of judicial enforcement capacity), as a whole the indexes provide a broad perspective about the levels of IP protection in different regions in China. The top 10 provinces according to IPRI (mentioned earlier) is similar with the top ten provinces by IPRPEs except that Beijing and Shanghai are not in the same top three but fall to number nine and ten, respectively,

Table 7.3 Ranking of IPR protection levels across all provinces in China (2015)

Province	*IPRPE*		PAE		TAE		AESC		JEC	
	Index	Rank	Index	Rank	Index	Rank	Index	Rank	Index	Rank
Jiangsu	0.754	1	0.601	1	0.702	3	0.694	1	1.000	1
Zhejiang	0.618	2	0.560	2	0.833	2	0.120	21	0.961	2
Guangdong	0.582	3	0.404	5	0.936	1	0.299	6	0.687	4
Hunan	0.450	4	0.456	3	0.153	11	0.433	2	0.756	3
Shandong	0.348	5	0.406	4	0.156	10	0.157	15	0.674	5
Hubei	0.304	6	0.149	7	0.593	4	0.228	11	0.248	7
Fujian	0.278	7	0.147	8	0.349	6	0.371	4	0.244	8
Henan	0.241	8	0.192	6	0.339	7	0.111	22	0.322	6
Shanghai	0.191	9	**0.022**	**25**	0.354	5	0.348	5	**0.038**	**25**
Beijing	0.173	10	**0.056**	**17**	0.123	13	0.420	3	**0.094**	**17**
Sichuan	0.169	11	0.111	10	0.189	9	0.190	12	0.185	10
Guizhou	0.132	12	0.125	9	0.063	18	0.131	18	0.207	9
Anhui	0.115	13	0.054	18	0.210	8	0.105	24	0.091	18
Tianjin	0.104	14	0.053	19	0.044	24	0.231	9	0.088	19
Chongqing	0.102	15	0.041	22	0.045	23	0.252	8	0.070	22
Guangxi	0.100	16	0.043	21	0.138	12	0.147	16	0.072	21
Shanxi	0.098	17	0.068	12	0.081	16	0.178	13	0.067	23
Hebei	0.094	18	0.060	14	0.071	17	0.143	17	0.102	13
Liaoning	0.091	19	0.070	11	0.048	21	0.129	19	0.117	11
Jilin	0.086	20	0.017	26	0.028	26	0.268	7	0.029	26
Jiangxi	0.075	21	0.060	15	0.039	25	0.102	25	0.100	15
Inner Mongolia	0.073	22	0.062	13	0.008	30	0.120	20	0.102	14
Shanxi	0.070	23	0.002	29	0.046	22	0.231	10	0.003	29
Heilongjiang	0.069	24	0.058	16	0.013	28	0.110	23	0.096	16
Gansu	0.066	25	0.040	23	0.062	19	0.160	14	0.002	30
Xinjiang	0.060	26	0.052	20	0.091	15	0.096	26	0.000	31
Yunnan	0.056	27	0.025	24	0.097	14	0.061	28	0.041	24
Xizang	0.048	28	0.000	31	0.000	31	0.079	27	0.112	12
Ningxia	0.040	29	0.005	27	0.009	29	0.059	30	0.087	20
Hainan	0.033	30	0.005	28	0.056	20	0.061	29	0.009	27
Qinghai	0.015	31	0.001	30	0.016	27	0.036	31	0.008	28

Source China IPR Index Report 2016

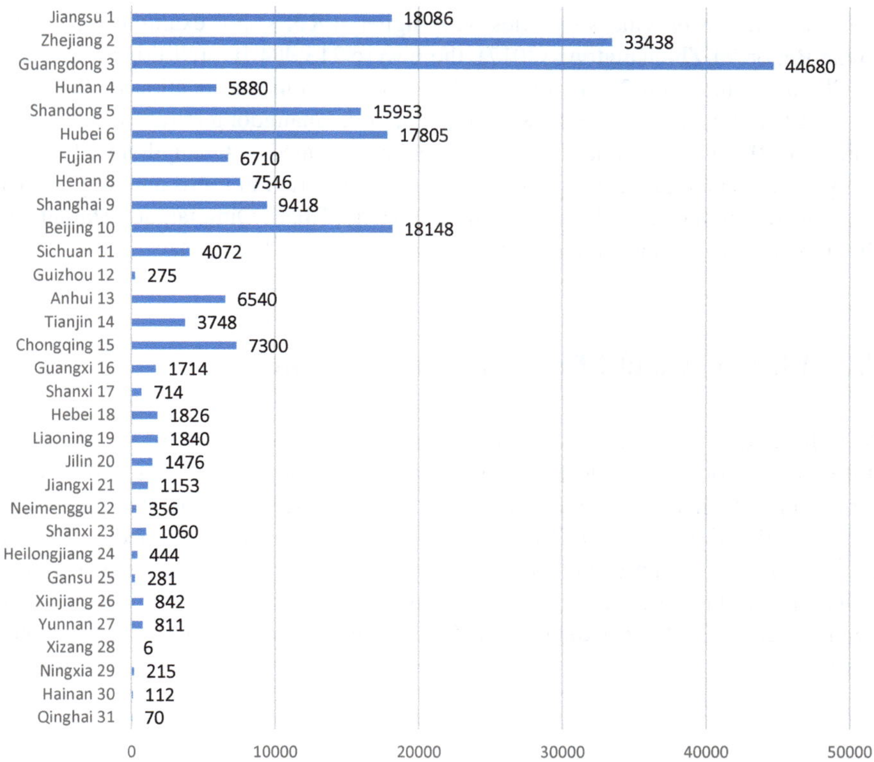

Fig. 7.1 Number of IP civil litigation in all Chinese Provinces (2014–2017) by IPRPE Rank (2016)

in the latter's list. These municipalities' low scores on the PAE and JEC in particular seem to be at fault for this discrepancy with their scores on the IPRPE. As mentioned, a comparison of the China IPR Index Report 2016 with previous ones reveals only a slight change of the ranking of the top and bottom ten provinces.

Local governments (those below the provincial level) also play important roles in IPR protection in China. IP protection matters at the local level for several reasons (Fang et al. 2016). First, there is very little forum shopping in China. Chinese law stipulates that plaintiffs can only file lawsuits either in the location of their domicile or where the violation occurred, i.e., the location of the defendant. Second, filing for international patent protection is still rare among Chinese firms. Finally, most of the firms operating in China are focused on the domestic market. Therefore, most IPR disputes are likely to be argued in the Chinese administrative and judicial system (Fang et al. 2016).

However, because of the spread of the Internet and the flow of goods across borders, IP right holders still have chances to enforce their IPR in areas with more IPR-friendly regimes or in ones that are otherwise better equipped with more competent IP enforcement personnel such as IP agents, attorneys or judges. Normally these areas are the top provinces or cities with higher IPRPEs. For example, according to the Report of Zhichangtong (2017), there were 213,984 IP civil litigation trialed in China's court from 2014 to mid-2017. Judging from the location of the court where IP civil cases were heard within this period, Guangdong attracted the largest number of IP civil litigation. The coastal areas represented by Guangdong, Zhejiang, Jiangsu, Shanghai and Beijing, as well as the central region represented by Hubei, were the major sites for IP civil litigation. Xizang (Tibet), Qinghai, and Hainan are the provinces with smallest number of IP civil litigation (Fig. 7.1).

7.2 Efficiency and Effectiveness of the Courts

IP right holders can enforce their IPR through the judicial system, i.e., courts in different locations and levels. However, different from the regimes in the UK and US, for example, China follows the German bifurcation model for judicial enforcement: i.e., IP invalidation cases and IP infringement cases are separately handled in different courts under different procedures. Therefore, ordinary Chinese courts have no power to handle validity cases involving trademark or patent validity. Only select courts, i.e., the Beijing 1st Intermediate People's Court and its higher courts, can hear such cases.

7.2.1 General Structure of the IP Court System

There are four levels of courts dealing with normal cases in China. At present, courts having the authority to hear IP cases are as follows: (1) One Supreme People's Court, located in Beijing, with a specialized IP chamber that hears IP appeals and is responsible for the drafting of judicial interpretation relating to IP matters; (2) 30 Higher People's courts located in each province, autonomous region, or directly controlled municipality; (3) 336 Intermediate People's courts; (4) 1376 basic-level (grass-root) People's courts. In addition, China has special courts handling only certain types of IP cases (see below) (Fig. 7.2).

Normally, each court is comprised of civil, criminal and administrative chambers. IP civil cases will be handled in the 3rd Civil Division, i.e., the IP Division. IP criminal cases will be handled in criminal chambers and administrative cases in administrative chambers. However, recent reforms combine the trial of these three kinds of IP cases together in one chamber (resulting in the so-called 3 in 1 model). However, most of the courts in China have not established a new IP chamber; instead, they organize judges from different chambers to form an interim panel for specific IP cases.

Disputes will only go through two instances of trials, and then a final decision will be handed down by courts of second instance. With regards to IP civil disputes, this means many cases will end at the High People's Court's level, because normally the first instance for IP civil cases will be handled by the Intermediate People's

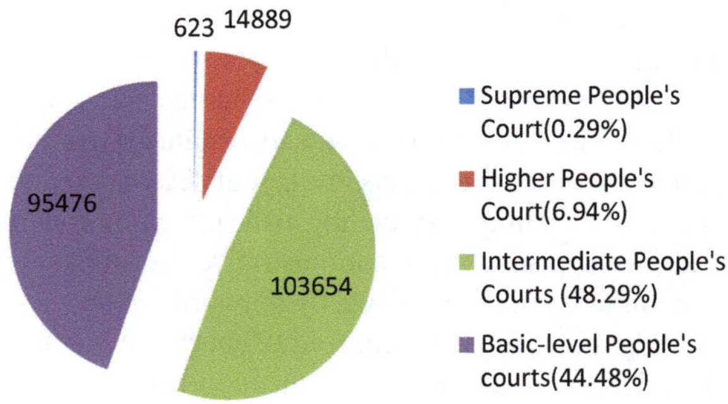

Fig. 7.2 Number of IP Civil Cases heard by different levels of Chinese Court (2014–2017). *Source* Judicial Big Data Research Institute 2017

Court—except in Beijing, Shanghai, or directly controlled municipalities where the Primary People's Courts have the authority to handle IP cases. However, the situation is changing because (1) an increasing number of basic-level People's Courts have been appointed by the Supreme People's Court to hear IP cases, even patent cases; and (2) cases with significant effect have been more frequently taken and reheard by Supreme People's Court after the second instance.[2]

Meanwhile, due to the complexity of patent and other cases, the first instance of civil case regarding patents, plant variety, and other high technologies will only be heard by a competent Intermediate People's Court or a limited number of basic-level People's Courts appointed by the Supreme People's Court. At present, there are more than 243 courts in China with authority to hear patent cases (this is due to the technical complexity of ruling appropriately on these cases).[3]

The establishment of specialized IP courts and IP tribunals

With the explosive growth of IP registrations in China and of IP disputes before Chinese courts, there is a strong demand for the judicial system to improve the efficiency, quality and unity of IPR judicial protection. In an effort to provide a more centralized system for, and otherwise more effective and efficient, IPR protection, the Chinese government recently decided to establish specialized IP courts to adjudicate IP cases.

On July 9, 2014, the Supreme People's Court issued the Fourth Five-Year Reform Outline of the Court (2014–2018) which proposed establishing specialized IP courts in areas with significant numbers of IP cases. On August 31, 2014, the Standing Committee of the National People's Congress ("NPC") passed the Decision of Establishing Intellectual Property Courts in Beijing, Shanghai and Guangzhou. On November

[2]The Supreme People's Court of China has a very active IP tribunal which heard and decided 623 IP civil cases from 2014 to mid-2017. Most of these cases are retrial cases [See Zhichantong (2017)]. It seems to us that the main role of the Supreme People's Court of China is different from that of Federal Supreme Court of U.S. whose philosophy is just to unify the application of law rather than correct the error of lower level courts.

[3]IP House's updated information about IP courts in China, available at https://v1.iphouse.cn/court/navigate.html?c=2.

3, 2014, the Supreme People's Court issued the Supreme Court's Regulations on Jurisdiction of Cases of the IP Courts in Beijing, Shanghai and Guangzhou.

The Supreme People's Court specified the scope of the Specialized IP Courts' exclusive jurisdiction: (i) civil and administrative litigation relating to patents, new plant varieties, trade secrets, the layout design of integrated circuit and computer software; (ii) civil litigation relating to the judicial recognition of well-known trademarks; and (iii) Appeals against administrative decisions involving copyrights, trademarks, and unfair competition made by ministries at and above the county level.

Judges in the new specialized IP courts are said to be more independent regarding their decision-making than in other courts in China. They are fully in charge of their cases and do not need to report extensively on their cases to an administrative director. The only exception to this is when the case is so complicated and important that it needs to be taken over by the Adjudication Committee of the IP Court. Meanwhile, the decision-making process of the Adjudication Committee in IP Courts seems to be becoming more transparent. In some cases, public hearings can be held by the Adjudication Committee before a ruling is reached.

In August and September 2017, the jurisdictional aspects of judicial enforcement of IP in China changed further. Many new IP Tribunals have been established—for example, in Chengdu, Wuhan, Hefei, Fuzhou, Nanjing, Suzhou, Jinan, Qingdao, Hangzhou, and Ningbo—in order to hear cross-regional patent cases within these respective provinces. This expansion of jurisdictional scope, including for appeals, may exert pressure to harmonize judicial patent enforcement in China.

To further harmonize the decisions of IP infringement cases made by different IP tribunals, it has recently been proposed to establish more specialized IP courts and a national appellate system of IP cases. Meanwhile, it has been suggested that less complex IP cases should be heard by one single IP judge to make IP trials more efficient and save judicial recourse (Supreme People Court's Working Report 2017a, b).

Specialized National-level Appeal Tribunal for high-tech IP/patent cases

On October 26th 2018, the Standing Committee of China's National People's Congress (NPC) issued a Decision to establish a new IP Tribunal of Appeals at the national level within the Supreme People's Court (SPC). This Decision came into effect on January 1st 2019.

China used to have a judicial system characterized by "four levels and two-instance of trials" according to which a patent case normally starts from an intermediate court (e.g., Shanghai IP Court) and the potential higher court that tries the appellate proceeding should be a higher court at the provincial level (e.g., Shanghai Higher People's Court). This is, however, no longer the case. According to SCNPC's decision, after the establishment the new IP Tribunal of Appeals within the SPC, a "leapfrog appeal mechanism" skipping the trial of the provincial higher court has been set up for patent and other technical cases such as cases involving technical know-how, plant breeder's right, computer software, etc. (She Hans 2018). In other words, for patent cases and other cases involving complex technology, the appellant may bypass the higher/highest court at the provincial level altogether and appeal the intermediate or IP court's ruling directly to the SPC.

More specifically, the newly established IP Appeal Tribunal has jurisdiction to handle: (1) all appeals against first instance civil judgments in technology-related IP cases such as cases regarding patents (with the exception of design patents), new varieties of plants, layout designs of integrated circuits, technical trade secrets, computer software and anti-trust cases; and (2) all appeals against administrative judgments issued by the Beijing IP Court regarding the decisions of Patent Review Board decisions.

The establishment of the specialized IP appellate tribunal (within the SPC) at the national-level, akin to the Court of Appeals for the Federal Circuit ("CAFC") in the United States, is a fundamental change to China's technical IP dispute appeal process and a groundbreaking event for the IP enforcement landscape of China. It is expected to "solve the problem of non-uniformity of the judgment standards, improving the quality and efficiency of IP trials, strengthening the judicial protection of intellectual property rights, and effectively improving the judicial credibility" (SPC 2018). However, given the fact that significant numbers of IP cases have actually been reheard by SPC after the second instance (i.e. "the third instance"), a new concern arises regarding how to handle the independence of, or relationship between, the specialized IP appellate tribunal and the SPC's IP Tribunal which still exists and continues to effectively govern the retrial of IP cases.

7.2.2 Challenges and Ongoing Judicial Reforms

The explosion of IP litigation in China has brought challenges to IP judicial enforcement in China. Besides, other aspects of Chinese IP judicial enforcement have often been criticized and are currently undergoing reform. Among them, the access to evidence, the admissibility of evidence, enforcement of judicial orders or judgments, and protectionism (see separate section on protectionism) are most frequently discussed.

Explosion of IP litigation in China and the potential threat of frivolous litigation by IP trolls

As mentioned before, there are currently more civil IP cases filed in China than anywhere else on earth (Wild 2010; Global IP Project 2014). From 2011 to 2016, there were 577,326 first-instance IP civil cases received by China's local courts with the number of cases growing annually within this period (see Fig. 7.3).

A comparison of the number of patent litigation filings also reflects the same phenomena. From 2010 to 2012, China ranked first in terms of the number of patent suits, i.e. 30,000, and had a much higher number than the United States (second on the list) (see Fig. 7.4 and Global IP Project 2014).

These figures for China are not particularly surprising. They reflect the significant amount of manufacturing taking place in China, the massive size of its population,

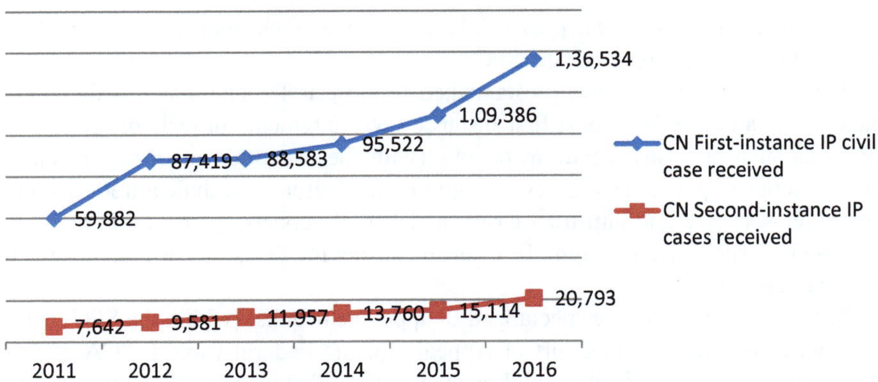

Fig. 7.3 Number of first and second-instance IP civil cases received by Chinese local courts. *Source* SIPO's China IPR Yearbook

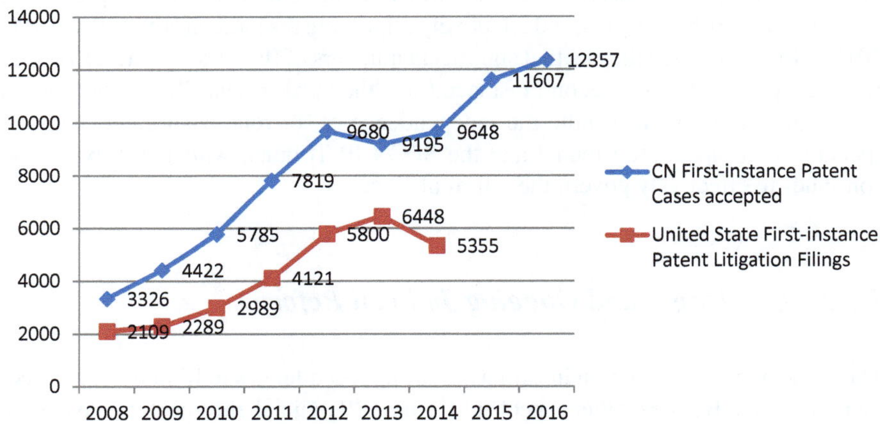

Fig. 7.4 Fist-instance patent case filings or acceptance in China and US. *Sources* Supreme People's Court, Annual Report on Judicial Protection of IPR in China; Global IP Project (2014)

the increasing number of IPR prosecuted and granted in recent year in China, and the enhanced awareness of enforcing or strategically making use of IPRs.

The majority of IP cases are litigated at courts in China's coastal area such as Beijing, Shanghai, Guangzhou, and Shenzhen. Certain economically developed cities in the inland such as Wuhan, and Chongqing also attract IP litigation (Zhichantong 2017; Love et al. 2016). The explosion of IP litigation in China could possibly effect the efficiency and effectiveness of IP enforcement in these areas and cities and become a challenge to the judicial system there. For example, with the piling up of pending cases and increasing applications, it becomes more difficult for the courts to receive new cases during the last three months of each year since they would increase the incompletion rate of the courts—thereby reflecting poorly on the performance evaluations of judges. The heavy backlog of cases and shortage of judges will also likely lead to the judicial propensity to apply statutory damages in order to avoid complicated and time-consuming calculation of real damages of the IP right holders, and to hesitancy to apply coercive measure to collect evidence outside the courtroom. Additionally, the duration of litigation could last longer.

To reduce the burden on Chinese courts associated with the explosion in IP litigation, mediation before and during litigation has been actively and sometimes strategically used by the judges and their assistants to reduce the number of cases entering into the final stage. The average mediation withdrawal rate was approximately 67% for first-instance IP cases in China from 2013 to 2016 and 28% for second-instance IP cases (Supreme People's Court, Annual Report on Judicial protection of IPR in China Court). Other measures and reforms have also been taken in recent years, including the establishment of specialized IP courts in Beijing, Shanghai, Shenzhen, and so on (see infra).

Although there are potential negative effects, the rise of IP litigation also helps build IP expertise in the court and amongst lawyers, and offers a learning opportunity to further reform China's IP laws. Also, the rise in IP litigation might cautiously be interpreted by some as an indicator of greater confidence—and therefore willingness to bring cases—in China's IP enforcement regime. Further, the negative effects of the rise in IP litigation in China should not be overestimated since the vast majority of IP litigation cases in China only involve small sums of money (Wild 2010). This means that individual cases normally have insignificant economic influence over the industry. Additionally, it may be heartening to foreign firms that the vast majority of IP lawsuits in China (over 98% according to some estimates) are between Chinese firms (Bloch et al. 2014; Wild 2010).

Another inter-related question is: Are frivolous lawsuits becoming more prevalent amidst the increase in IP litigation in China, and what implications does this have? One typical culprit of frivolous lawsuits is the so-called "patent troll" (i.e., an entity that profits from licensing/assigning and enforcing patents without actually producing corresponding products) and "trademark troll" (i.e., a trademark squatter who profits from enforcing their trademark especially on e-commerce platforms that might be illegally prosecuted).

When analyzing this problem, there are a few things to keep in mind. First, it is difficult to argue that more patent litigation, per se, significantly inhibits innovation. For example, the US and Germany are, respectively, the second and third most popular destinations for patent litigation in absolute terms and the first and second most popular destinations on a per capita basis,[4] and yet both remain highly innovative nations. Significant amounts of patent ligation in the US and Germany (and China) is not necessarily conducive to innovation. However, it is the type of litigation—not merely its quantity—that ultimately determines its deterrent impact on follow-on innovation. Second, as we detailed throughout Chap. 3 of this book, China has already accomplished a significant amount in just the last few years to improve patent quality (including revising its IP-conditioned incentives). This will help limit lawsuits based on low-quality patents. Third, the design of a country's legal system arguably plays

[4]Calculations based on population data from the World Bank and darts IP patent litigation data.

a more important role than the sheer number of patents in determining if frivolous IP lawsuits will be brought. For example, there is more "patent troll" activity in the US than in China. This is, to a large extent, due to the design of the US legal system in terms of consistently high damages awarded, extensive evidential discovery procedures, and availability of jury trials (e.g., Cotter 2016). These instruments do not really exist in China (Zhang 2014).

Access to evidence in IP litigation

There are several significant challenges facing those trying to assert their rights in IP lawsuits. Firstly, there are challenges in evidence collection. China does not have a "discovery" procedure in the common law sense. There is no general obligation on a party to disclose evidence that goes against his/her own case. Parties usually have had to obtain evidence by means of self-forensics, pretrial evidence exchange, and evidence preservation orders (Zhang and Zhang 2014). The Judicial Interpretation of Chinese Civil Procedure Law, newly revised in 2015, tries to introduce the concept of a document production order from the civil law system and institute it by the rule of obstruction of evidence (Article 112). Herein, the party with a burden to prove, by paying relevant costs, can apply to the court to request the opposite party to submit documentary evidence under his/her control. The court then determines the content of the document involved if the opposite party refuses without reasonable excuses. The document production order is the primary way for IP right holders to collect evidences from the opposite party and third parties in IP litigation in civil law countries. We expect Chinese courts can make the most of the instrument to help alleviate the difficulty of proof in IP cases.

Second, IP-related evidence preservation is also a significant concern of IP right holders. In practice, due to the difficulty of obtaining evidence, litigants increasingly apply evidence preservation orders to obtain key evidence in the litigation. However, there are negative factors which hinder the effective acquisition of these orders. First, because of the huge caseload and the unreasonable division of labor between the judges and executing staff, some judges are more prone to reject evidence preservation orders when exercising their discretionary power. Second, the rules governing evidence preservation are too principled and make no distinction between the pretrial and proceeding stage (Zhang and Zhang 2014).

Third, although the right of information is a valuable tool for IP enforcement, it is not afforded a central role in the Chinese system. Choosing not to institute suggestions in the TRIPs Agreement, Chinese IP laws and China's Civil Procedure Law do not offer the "right of information"[5] to IP right holders. However, they do impose certain disclosure obligations on distributors and users who claim a legitimate source defense of their alleged infringement.

Fourth, due to the difficulties of collecting evidence and acquiring infringer's information, the determination of damages in IP litigation also becomes a problem in

[5] According to Article 47 of TRIPS, members may provide that the judicial authorities shall have the authority to order the infringer to inform the IP right holder of the identity of third party involved in the production and distribution of the infringing goods or services and of their channels of distribution, unless this would be out of proportion to the seriousness of the infringement.

China's IP trial work. In judicial practice, the investigation of actual loss or the amount of profit of infringement has been replaced by adopting the statutory damages, which results in low damages that are inadequate for punishing infringement and offering remedies.

The admissibility of evidence

One problem with the rules surrounding admissibility of evidence in China is the compulsory notarization and certification of extraterritorial evidence. In accordance with Article 11 of the Evidence Regulation, extraterritorial evidence presented by the parties in IP litigation should be notarized and certificated. However, overemphasis on the notarization and certification of extraterritorial evidence may problematically lead to the court ignoring the relevance of reviewing the distinctions between evidence and facts and between different types of evidence, and instead result in a total reliance on notarization and certification rather than on the parties' testimony, cross-examination and court certifications (Zhang and Zhang 2014).

A second problem with the rules surrounding admissibility of evidence in China is that the efficiency of judicial technical appraisals and China's expert consulting system do not actually live up to their expectations. In practice, only a few judicial appraisals receive interrogations from litigants. This makes it difficult for their opinions to become a solid foundation of the judgment.

Mechanisms for enforcing court orders and judgments

According to the Chinese Civil Procedure Law, non-compliance with court orders and judgments will be met with mandatory measures imposed by the courts such as fines, detention and so on. In practice, however, Chinese judges usually hesitate to use coercive measures against non-compliance activities. According to a survey conducted by the Hunan Provincial Higher People's Court on the psychological preference of judges to apply the mandatory measures against contempt activities, 67.4% of nearly 100 judges surveyed did not want to use coercive measures (Deng et al. 2013). Among the five reasons listed in the questionnaire, the top reason selected was the worry about delaying the trial, followed by fear of the parties participating in a petition outside court and by fear of blocking the mediation of cases (Deng et al. 2013). All of these factors might, in one way or another, lead to a negative evaluation of a judge's trial work according to the evaluation criteria of the court—therefore perversely incentivizing judges to avoid such behavior (Zhang and Zhang 2014).

Ongoing reforms

In an effort to address the challenges described above, in 2007, the Supreme People's Court released the Opinions on Fully Strengthening IP Judicial Work to Provide Judicial Safeguard for building an Innovation-oriented Country. That set of opinions included the following guidelines: (1) appropriately reduce right holder's burden of proof concerning damages; (2) reduce the requirement of notarization and legalization formalities for certain extraterritorial publications; (3) temporary injunctions, advance execution, property preservation and evidence preservation sought by parties before or during the trial should be accepted actively, reviewed quickly, judged prudently, and executed immediately; (4) perfect the execution mechanism of IP judgments by coordinating police departments and prosecutors to prosecute those refuse to obey the binding judgment; and so on.[6]

In 2011, the Supreme People's Court released the Several Opinions on Sanctions against Behaviors Circumventing the Enforcement in Accordance with the Law. This measure suggested that courts should make full use of the civil and criminal sanctions to punish illegal practices of circumventing the enforcement of valid decisions, such as transferring property in bad faith.

Recent revisions to Chinese IP laws have attached great importance to improving provisions for determining damages. For example, Article 6, Sect. 7.2 of the newly revised Trademark Law stipulates that after a right holder has produced evidence to the best of his/her ability, the court can order the infringer to present accounting books and other materials relevant to the infringement under his/her control for the purpose of determining damages. If the infringer refuses to provide or falsely provides accounting books and other materials, the court can determine the damages vis-à-vis the claims of the right holders and related evidence. Article 61 Sect. 7.3 of the Fourth Amendment of Patent Law (Draft) also introduces similar provisions in an attempt to address the challenge of calculating damages. Present rules applied to evidence collection and disclosure related to calculating of damages in China are quite similar to the rules in the EU. Nevertheless, the key to effectively utilizing these rules lies in how to effectively carry out these rules.

In an attempt to improve provisions related to technical appraisal, Article 46 of the Outline of China's National Intellectual Property Strategy proposes that the Chinese government should improve the litigation system in the areas of judicial appraisal, expert witnesses, and technical investigations. The Amendment of the Civil Procedure Law (2012) requires judicial appraisals to be largely drawn from litigants. Article 123 of the Judicial Interpretation of the Civil Procedure Law also provides that the court and parties can interrogate technical experts in court. Additionally, experts brought by the parties in a lawsuit have the right of confrontation with regards to the technical facts of the case. By introducing a system requesting that the judicial authenticators and expert assistants involved appear in courts, the Civil Procedure Law and its judicial interpretations provide a safeguard for the right to interrogate the parties in IP lawsuits.

In an attempt to improve compliance with court judgments and decisions in China, the Supreme Court issued Some Opinions on Sanctioning Evasion of Enforcement in May 2011. The Opinions suggest that greater use be made of civil and criminal sanctions and their implementation in order to safeguard the authority of the court. The revised Civil Procedure Law further increases the intensity of punishments for violations of the law, including via increased fines and detention for up to 15 days.

---

[6]Opinions on Fully Strengthening IP Judicial Work to Provide Judicial Safeguard for building an Innovation-oriented Country, Supreme People's Court, 2007.

In January 2015, the Supreme People's Court recommended establishing a discovery system of IP litigation; allocating the burden of proof reasonably and properly; giving full play to the function of the evidence preservation system and evidence collection system to solve difficulties regarding evidence production; enhancing behavior preservation measures during or before litigation, and strengthening the enforcement of IP judgments to enhance the effectiveness of sanctions.[7] Further, in February 2015, the Supreme People's Court announced the Interpretations of Several Issues on the Review of the Legal Application Concerning Behavior Preservation in IP and Competition Disputes (draft), which stipulates the necessary factors to be considered before granting a behavior preservation order.

Additionally, in terms of other reforms, a policy that has been adopted in an attempt to deal with the costliness of the IP litigation in China (especially relative to potential damages awarded), is the development of state financing and insurance schemes to cover costs associated with such litigation. Although the requirements for such programs are changing, it would seem that such state support should focus on the most financially needy firms to whom IP is also critical for their businesses (e.g., technology start-ups).

Despite all of these reforms to China's IP enforcement system, the country still lacks unified rules at the statutory level to address the different problems these reforms attempt to tackle. The judicial application of some of these proposed reforms, therefore, still varies from court to court across China. Moreover, the newly revised Civil Procedure Law and the latest judicial interpretations have also failed to solve the challenges to IP enforcement mentioned in this section in their entirety (Zhang and Zhang 2014). Further, performance evaluations of judges in China still appear to be designed in a way that does not fully address the challenges mentioned (e.g., Zhang and Zhang 2014).

Other ongoing judicial reforms

To further harmonize the decisions of IP infringement cases made by different IP tribunals, a new proposal to establish more specialized IP courts and a national appellate system of IP cases was put forth in 2017. Meanwhile, simple IP cases are suggested to be heard by one single IP judge in order to make trials more efficient and save judicial resources (Supreme People Court's Working Report 2017a, b). In late October, 2018, China approved changes to litigation procedures in patent and other technical IP cases. And, as mentioned, a national-level IP appeals tribunal for these disputes has been established within the SPC to hear appeals directly from courts of the first instance.

Other reforms focus on, for example, the status of judges to make independent decisions without the interference of administrative officers, the introduction of technical investigation officers to assist in technical cases, the procedures for speeding up trials, and so on.

---

[7]Establish the evidentiary discovery system of IP litigation, Legal Daily, Jan 23, 2015. http://www.legaldaily.com.cn/rdlf/content/2015-01/23/content_5940154.htm?node=34013.

7.2.3 Statistical Analysis of Efficiency and Effectiveness of Sample IP Cases

7.2.3.1 Efficiency

We choose (i) case acceptance rates and (ii) the duration of trials (processing times) to reflect the efficiency of courts during IP trails. Data on these indicators is analyzed below.

(i) ***Efficiency: Case acceptance***

As to case acceptance rates, there is no available record showing how many IP cases have been denied. Therefore, we can only use data on case acceptance, completion and other information on case acceptance reform in China in our analysis. Figures 7.5, 7.6 and 7.7 present the trend using available data across these indicators.

Figure 7.5 shows that the number of IP civil cases accepted has grown rapidly in recent years. When too many cases are filed at the courts and it becomes clear that the courts cannot hear and conclude the cases within a reasonable time period, some courts will try to raise the standard of case acceptance and reject/refuse to hear certain cases merely to achieve a high concluded rate of cases. This of course poses a challenge to case acceptance, and has been the subject of various complaints from firms over the years. This phenomenon should also be considered when reviewing the statistics presented in Figs. 7.6 and 7.7 which show that, in the same period, the concluded rate of IP civil, criminal, administrative and retrial cases are normally higher than 90%.

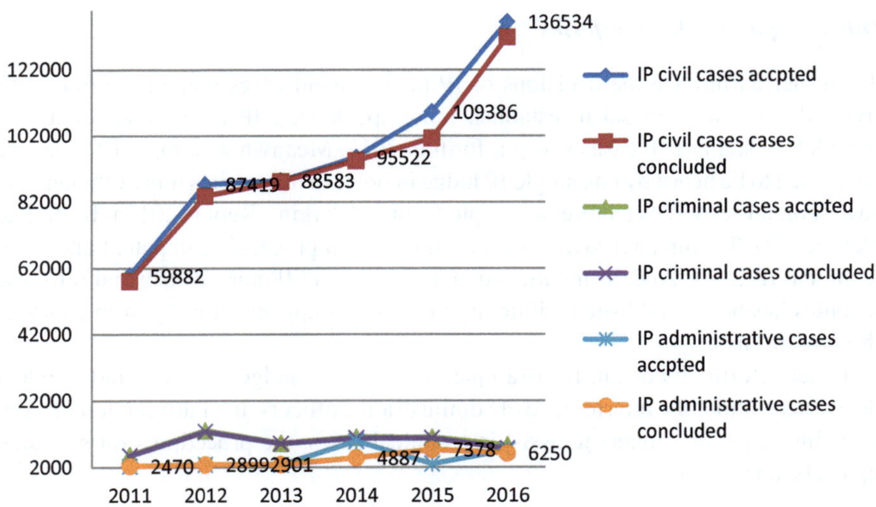

Fig. 7.5 First-instance IP cases accepted and concluded in China (2011–2016). *Source* Annual report issued by Supreme People's Court of China

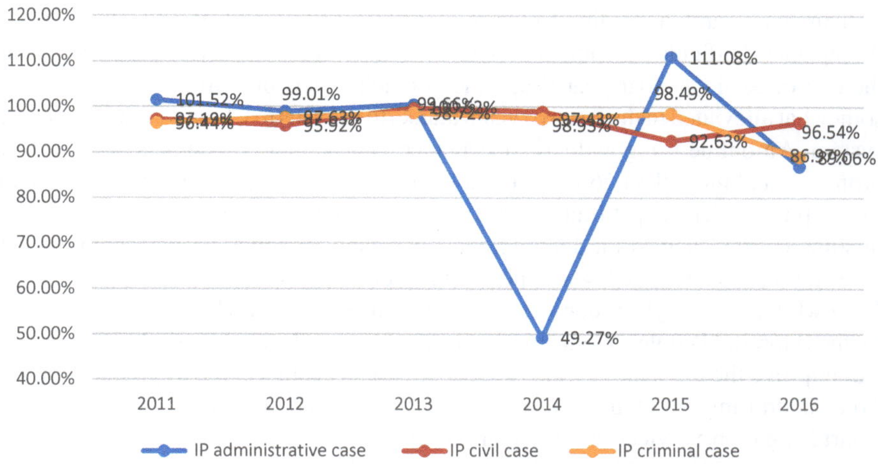

Fig. 7.6 Rate of IP cases concluded in China (2011–2016), by type. *Source* Annual report issued by Supreme People's Court of China. *Note* >100% rate owed to fact that more cases are sometimes concluded per calendar year than received in that year (therefore reducing backlog)

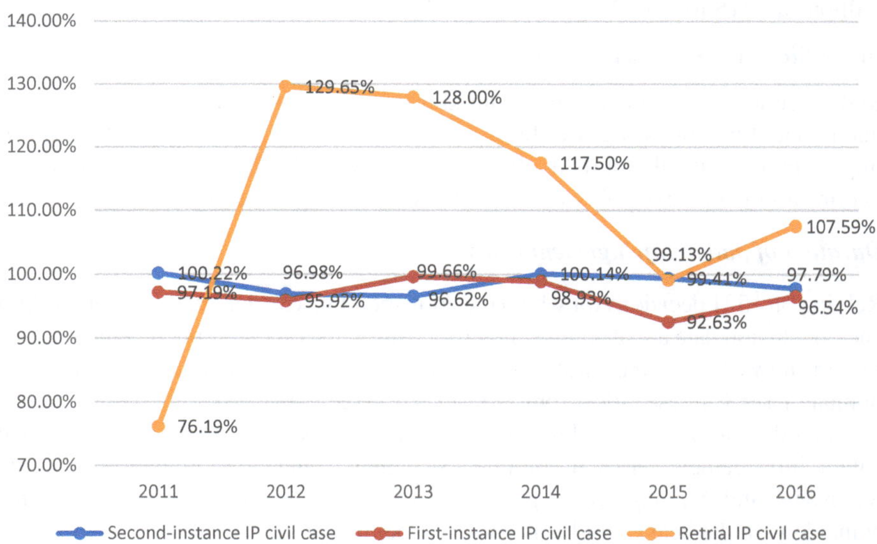

Fig. 7.7 IP civil cases concluded rate in China (2011–2016), by instance. *Source* Annual report issued by Supreme People's Court. *Note* >100% rate owed to fact that more cases are sometimes concluded per calendar year than received in that year (therefore reducing backlog)

This being said, according to the Supreme People's Court, the so-called "Case Acceptance Difficulty" problem (for IP and other types of cases) especially near the end of each calendar year (Supreme People's Court of China 2009)[8] has been somewhat alleviated in the last two years thanks to reforms to China's case acceptance system. An online filing and case acceptance management model has been widely promoted and more than 2605 courts in China provide an open online filing system to the public. Self-help filing has also become a new model for case acceptance in some courts, such as the Pudong court in Shanghai which has accepted 23,741 cases through scanning a "two-dimensional code on the spot" related to case filings. Meanwhile, seven higher courts and seven intermediate courts have been designated by the Supreme People's Court to accept cross-regional case filings. To standardize and improve the efficiency of the process of case acceptance, the Supreme People's Court is drafting the Online Case Acceptance Rules and Guidance of the People's Court Litigation Services and Judicial Assistance.

From May 2015 to March 2017, more than 31 million cases were accepted by Chinese courts, an increase of 33.92%. Among these cases, more than 95% were accepted on the spot. Jiangsu, Guangdong and Zhejiang each accepted more than 2 million cases in this period while nine other provinces each accepted more than 1 million cases (Supreme People's Court 2017a, b).

(ii) ***Efficiency: Processing times***

In this section, we first analyze the duration of patent case trials nationwide. Then, due to data limitations, we use Beijing (which is home to some of, if not the most, important and busy IP courts in all of China and state bodies which hear IP invalidation cases) as an example to evaluate trends in case processing times.

Duration of patent infringement trials

Relying on 1521 decisions for which the corresponding exact acceptance date (EAD) and conclusion date are available, the Processing Time of Patent Infringement Cases Report shows the average duration of first instance trials of patent infringement cases in many large Chinese cities from 2011 to 2015 (see Table 7.4).

According to the data in Table 7.4, the average processing time of first-instance patent infringement cases in Beijing, Shanghai, Hangzhou, Wuhan, Changsha, Shenyang, and Nanjing are longer than 180 days. To be expected, these figures coincide with the heavy caseloads known to be filed at these courts.

According to data in Table 7.5, invention cases normally last longer than utility model or design cases and are therefore more typically included in statistics of delayed cases. Given the comparative technical complexity of invention patents, this trend is to be expected.

[8]On March 10, 2009, the Supreme People's Court of China for the first time responded to the "case acceptance difficulty" problem by issuing a judicial opinion which clearly requires "People's Court shall not refuse to accept cases at the end of the year for raising the case concluded rate."—See the Supreme People's Court of China, 2009《关于进一步加强司法便民工作的若干意见》(Several Opinions on Further Strengthening the Work of Judicial Convenience) (in Chinese).

Table 7.4 Processing time of first-instance patent infringement cases (2011–2015) in China

Court name	Cases concluded	Decisions with EAD	Ratio in samples (%)	**Average time (day)**	Shortest time (day)	Longest time (day)
Beijing IP Court	229	161	70.3	**186**	8	352
Courts of BJ area	477	271	60.6	**171**	14	1331
SH IP Court	119	42	35.5	**196**	29	332
Courts of SH Area	911	376	41.3	**229**	24	2043
Guangzhou IP Court	296	22	7.4	**97**	78	175
Courts in Guangdong area	1522	203	13.3	**171**	14	1331
Shenzhen IC	418	24	5.0	**176**	29	366
Changsha IC	192	69	35.9	**233**	61	1060
Wuhan IC	125	29	23.2	**205**	61	678
Hangzhou IC	326	71	21.8	**264**	27	1242
Nanjing IC	319	45	14.1	**192**	65	567
Jinan IC	368	111	30.2	**165**	27	1164
Chengdu IC	198	81	40.9	**155**	28	669
Shenyang IC	54	16	29.6	**213**	17	417
Zhengzhou IC	299	0	0	**–**	–	–
Xi'an IC	67	0	0	**–**	–	–

Source Processing Time of Patent Infringement Cases Report. *IC* Intermediate Court. IP Court = Specialized IP Court

Within the data available in Table 7.6 (based on 5983 sample decisions), of the 1521 cases with an EAD, the number of cases with a trial duration over six months (i.e., "overdue cases") was 564, accounting for 37.1% of all cases. The average processing time of these overdue cases was about six to seven months, which is just a bit longer than the statutory six-month period. It is, therefore, difficult to argue that the delay in 1521 cases reflects a particularly significant institutional problem. However, it certainly could be a problem for the rights holders involved in those cases.

Table 7.5 Duration of trials of different types of patent infringement (2011–2015) in China

Court	Types of patent cases	Cases completed	Decisions with EAD	**Average time (day)**	Shortest time (day)	Longest time (day)
Beijing IP Court	Invention	51	42	**262**	53	352
	Utility	40	23	**125**	8	351
	Design	132	95	**169**	21	324
Courts of BJ area	Invention	95	74	**389**	47	1438
	Utility	74	40	**175**	17	1336
	Design	243	122	**135**	3	706
SH IP Court	Invention	15	5	**188**	29	325
	Utility	33	11	**212**	100	309
	Design	71	26	**191**	59	332
Courts of SH Area	Invention	255	105	**365**	24	2043
	Utility	222	69	**227**	34	771
	Design	431	202	**159**	31	603
Guangzhou IP Court	Invention	16	0	**–**	–	–
	Utility	200	0	**–**	–	–
	Design	212	21	**97**	78	175
Courts of Guangdong area	Invention	113	11	**213**	14	650
	Utility	326	20	**200**	14	607
	Design	1072	172	**166**	23	1331
Shenzhen IC	Invention	53	1	**29**	29	29
	Utility	104	5	**256**	105	366
	Design	320	18	**162**	59	356
Changsha IC	Invention	35	13	**286**	61	608
	Utility	35	18	**208**	100	527
	Design	119	38	**227**	77	1060
Wuhan IC	Invention	22	12	**226**	142	678
	Utility	30	2	**199**	61	337
	Design	72	15	**190**	147	382
Hangzhou IC	Invention	26	5	**137**	27	219
	Utility	86	29	**463**	28	1242
	Design	213	37	**124**	35	609
Nanjing IC	Invention	32	8	**219**	68	326
	Utility	62	7	**142**	106	171
	Design	221	30	**196**	65	567

(continued)

Table 7.5 (continued)

Court	Types of patent cases	Cases completed	Decisions with EAD	**Average time (day)**	Shortest time (day)	Longest time (day)
Jinan IC	Invention	29	18	**217**	89	808
	Utility	87	29	**217**	56	1164
	Design	167	64	**127**	27	402
Chengdu IC	Invention	19	13	**212**	58	621
	Utility	86	30	**142**	57	307
	Design	90	38	**146**	28	669
Shenyang IC	Invention	7	2	**71**	60	81
	Utility	26	10	**286**	37	417
	Design	17	3	**52**	17	103
Zhengzhou IC	Invention	104	0	–	–	–
	Utility	62	0	–	–	–
	Design	130	0	–	–	–
Xi'an IC	Invention	3	0	–	–	–
	Utility	8	0	–	–	–
	Design	36	0	–	–	–

Source Processing Time of Patent Infringement Cases Report. *IC* Intermediate Court. IP Court = Specialized IP Court

Further, the available data is only a sample of the full range of patent infringement cases, and therefore is subject to sample bias.

Suspension time for patent infringement cases due to invalidity challenges

Among the 5983 decisions analyzed in Table 7.5, there are 198 cases in which defendants raised an invalidation challenge in order to suspend the patent infringement litigation. The courts sampled in Table 7.5 suspended 74 of the sampled cases, accounting for 37.4% of the 198 cases (which is 3.3% of the 5983 cases in the total sample). Data on exact suspension time (EST) is available for only 38 of these 74 cases.

All of the 36 cases with EST data ended with the decision from the Patent Reexamination Board (PRB), and their average time of suspension was 199 days. The longest suspension time of these cases was 469 days, the shortest was 34 days. Only two cases with EST data went through the procedure of the PRB and the first instance of court. Their total suspension time was 565 and 1048 days respectively, including 206 and 231 days respectively in front of the PRB. Judging from this data—namely the mere 74 cases suspected due to an invalidation challenge, i.e. 1.2% of the 5983 case sample—it can be concluded that there are not many overdue trials because of invalidation challenges in China.

Table 7.6 Patent infringement cases with a duration beyond 180 days in the first instance (i.e., overdue cases), by region

Court	Decisions with EAD	Overdue cases	Ratio (%)
Beijing IP Court	161	86	53.4
Courts of BJ area	271	104	38.4
SH IP Court	42	26	61.9
Courts of SH area	376	157	41.8
Guangzhou IP Court	22	0	0.0
Courts of Guangdong area	203	56	27.6
Shenzhen IC	24	9	37.5
Changsha IC	69	26	37.7
Wuhan IC	29	10	34.5
Hangzhou IC	71	23	32.4
Nanjing IC	45	17	37.8
Jinan IC	111	25	22.5
Chengdu IC	81	17	21.0
Shenyang IC	16	8	50.0
Zhengzhou IC	0	0	0.0
Xi'an IC	0	0	0.0
Total	1521	564	37.1

Source Processing Time of Patent Infringement Cases Report. *IC* Intermediate Court. IP Court = Specialized IP Court

In sum, the sometime slow processing time of patent infringement cases in China might still be a problem for some patent holders trying to enforce their rights, especially when the cases involve invention patents and/or are accompanied by a corresponding invalidation challenge. This said, slow processing times do not seem to be an endemic problem in China faced by all rights holders, at least according to available data. As such, the system could still be improved in several ways.

Duration of patent invalidation cases

Patent invalidations are considered "administrative" cases in China because the institution (namely SIPO) that administers the IP examination and grant system in China also hears these cases in the first instance. Specifically, patent invalidation cases typically go through the Patent Reexamination Board (PRB) at SIPO, and if one party is unsatisfied with the decision reached by the PRB they can appeal to the courts. According to the Report on Patent Law Enforcement issued by the NPC Stand-

Table 7.7 Average duration of trials at Beijing Specialized IP Court

Type of trial	Nature of case	Average duration of trial in 2016 (days)	Average duration of trial in 2015 (days)
Patent administrative case	Retrial of rejection	325	179
	Announcement of invalidation	373	181

Source Analysis Report on Judicial Protection Data of Beijing IP Court (2016)

Table 7.8 Average duration of IP cases at Beijing Specialized IP Court, by type

Level of trial	Nature of case	Average duration of trial in 2016 (days)	Average duration of trial in 2015 (days)
First instance	Civil	351	251
	Administrative	167	132
Second instance	Civil	108	67

Source Analysis Report on Judicial Protection Data of Beijing Specialized IP Court (2015–2016)

ing Committee Law Enforcement Inspection Group in 2014, the following average durations could be observed in 2012: approximately 200 days for patent invalidation cases at the PRB; 195 days for the first instance in court; and 137 days for the second instance court. As such, a patent invalidation case in China can last several years when also factoring in the time needed to serve the judgments (and minding the statutory time limits on appealing rulings).

The Beijing Specialized IP Court, which was established in 2014, is now in charge of the first instance of patent invalidation cases. Table 7.7 shows the average processing times at the court, which is a measure of the efficiency of the court in the last two years.

According to the data in Table 7.7, the average duration of trial of cases at the Beijing IP Court in 2016 is longer than the duration experienced in 2015. This trend is due to many factors: (i) 2015 was the first year that the Beijing specialized IP Court was in operation; (ii) one-third of the cases concluded in 2016 were accepted before 2016; and (iii) amongst the cases concluded by Beijing Specialized IP Court in 2016, there were more than 1300 technical cases (patents, computer software and new varieties of plants), which is more than double the technical cases concluded in 2015. This is also the major factor affecting the average duration of trials.

Processing time of trademark cases and other IP cases: a focus on the Beijing IP Court

A survey of Beijing Specialized IP Court's trials in 2015 and 2016 reveal several trends regarding the processing time of cases at this court. IP civil cases in the first instance (see Table 7.8) and patent cases (Table 7.9) are more likely to have an overdue problem.

Table 7.9 Average duration of IP civil cases at Beijing Specialized IP Court, by right

Level of trial	Type of case	Average duration of trial in 2016 (days)	Average duration of trial in 2015 (days)
First instance	Trademark	331	169
	Patent	382	259
	Copyright	406	209
	Unfair-competition	493	–
	Monopoly	326	–
Second instance	Trademark	116	80
	Copyright	103	63
	Unfair-competition	167	–

Source Analysis Report on Judicial Protection Data of Beijing IP Court (2015–2016)

Table 7.10 Average duration of trademark administrative cases in Beijing Specialized IP Court

Type	Nature of case	Average duration of trial in 2016 (days)	Average duration of trial in 2015 (days)
Trademark	Review of rejection	109	104
	Review of dispute	393	179
	Review of no registration	125	–
	Review for announcement of Invalidation	273	166
	Retrial of revocation	283	192

Source Analysis Report on Judicial Protection Data of Beijing IP Court (2015–2016). *Note* "Retrial of no registration" refers to cases stipulated upon implementation of Trademark Law in 2014. Such cases did not appear in the cases concluded in 2015

Regarding trademark administrative cases, the average duration of trial of first instance trademark lawsuits at the Beijing Specialized IP Court in 2016 was 158 days compared to 128 days in 2015. Further data about the average duration of trademark trials based on different courses of action in trademark administrative cases are illustrated in Table 7.10. One important development for trademark cases heard by Beijing Specialized IP Court in 2016 is the establishment of a "speedy trial" group. Upon establishment of the speedy trial group, the average duration of trial of cases regarding review of rejected applications for trademark was reduced by 45.5%. As such, the efficiency of trademark cases in Beijing has witnessed significant improvement.

Comparison with other jurisdictions

According to the Global IP Project (2014), China is one of the fastest growing jurisdictions for patent litigation in the world. In 2012, the average duration for invention patent and utility patent infringement decisions in China was less than 1 year for almost all the reported courts in China. The average time for a validity decisions from SIPO in 2012 based on 1096 decisions was 8 months. By way of comparison, the average duration of infringement and validity proceedings in Germany in the same year is slightly less than 2 years. In the US, reported times for reaching IP infringement decisions were even longer than in Germany. These data show that IP infringement and validity proceedings in China are, on average, concluded twice as fast, if not faster, than in Germany and the US.

7.2.3.2 IP Court Effectiveness

We choose several indicators to evaluate the effectiveness of the Chinese judicial system: (i) the rate at which the court provides injunctions when requested, (ii) IP right holder's winning rate, (iii) the rate at which the court provides preliminary measures and remedies, and (iv) the ratio of requested damages to awarded damages.

(i) ***Rate of providing injunctions when requested***

At present, there are limited statistics revealing the rate of providing injunctions when requested in IP infringement cases in Chinese courts. Data on the rates of provision of injunctions when requested collected from the Beijing IP Litigation Report 2016 and Shanghai IP Litigation Report 2016 is illustrated in Fig. 7.8. It shows that Beijing has a higher award rate of injunctions in First-instance trademark and copyright cases than Shanghai but lower than that of Shanghai with respect to patent cases. However, Beijing has a much higher vacate rate of injunction award in second instance trademark cases (20.7%) and patent cases (89.0%) than those of Shanghai (11.5 and 5.2%).

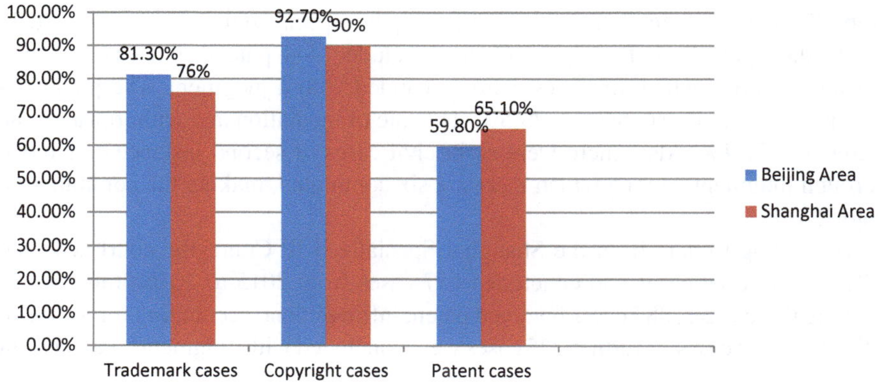

Fig. 7.8 Award rate of injunctions in First-instance IP civil cases concluded in Beijing and Shanghai (2013–2015). *Sources* Beijing IP Litigation Report 2016 and Shanghai IP Litigation Report 2016

(ii) ***IP right holders' winning rate***

Other statistics provide insights into IP right holders' "winning rates" in IP infringement cases in China. ("Winning rate" means the number of cases where the plaintiff's claims have been supported or partially supported relative to the number of cases concluded with a court judgment). For example, according to the Judicial Big Data Report, from 2015 to the end of 2016, plaintiffs of IP infringement cases of first instance received full support of their claims in 7.93% of cases and partial support in 84.90% of cases that were concluded with a judgment. This means the winning rate of IP right holders in China in the sample is more than 90%. This is a high winning rate.

However, several other facts need to be considered alongside these figures. Notably, only 27.86% of IP infringement cases in China were concluded with judgment from January 1, 2015 to December 31, 2016, while the majority of cases were concluded via withdrawal of the case (50.88%) or meditation (12.90%). However, among IP civil cases of first instance concluded by the Beijing IP Court in 2016, the winning rate is only 46.8%—much lower than that in 2015 (72.34%).

An international comparison of patentee winning rates in infringement cases and validity cases conducted by Global IP Project (2014) shows that the winning rate of IP right holders in China is higher than other countries (see Figs. 7.9 and 7.10). The average patentee winning rate in countries with bifurcated IP infringement adjudication systems is 49% compared to 39% in countries with unified IP infringement adjudication systems.[9] In China, the patentee winning rate between 2007 and 2013 was 68% for invention patents (231/340), 72% for utility model patents (381/531), and 86% for design patents (1093/1278).

However, according to the aforementioned report and its collected samples, the average patentee winning rate on validity issue in China is about 45.3%—lower than that of the U.S. and Canada, but higher than Germany (Federal Patent Court) and Brazil and on par with South Korea (see Fig. 7.10).

Patent Infringement Cases

Table 7.11 depicts trends in winning rates in the Specialized Beijing IP Court. In 2016, the Specialized Beijing IP Court concluded 444 patent civil cases of first instance, among which 88 cases were concluded with a judgment. The plaintiff's winning rate in these cases was 79.5%. The rate of mediation and withdrawal of the cases was 72.7%. Also, there were eight civil cases of second instance concluded through judgment, among which there are six commuted, making the commutation rate 75.0%.

According to data from the Shanghai Specialized IP Court, the court accepted 1011 patent civil cases and concluded 657 cases from 2015 to 2016 (Table 7.12). Among these cases, 887 cases involved patent infringement, accounting for 87.7% of all patent civil cases. A further 225 cases were concluded with judgments. Patent right

[9]For reference, the patentee winning rate in Duesseldorf Regional Court in Germany from 2009 to 2013 is 66% (534/812).

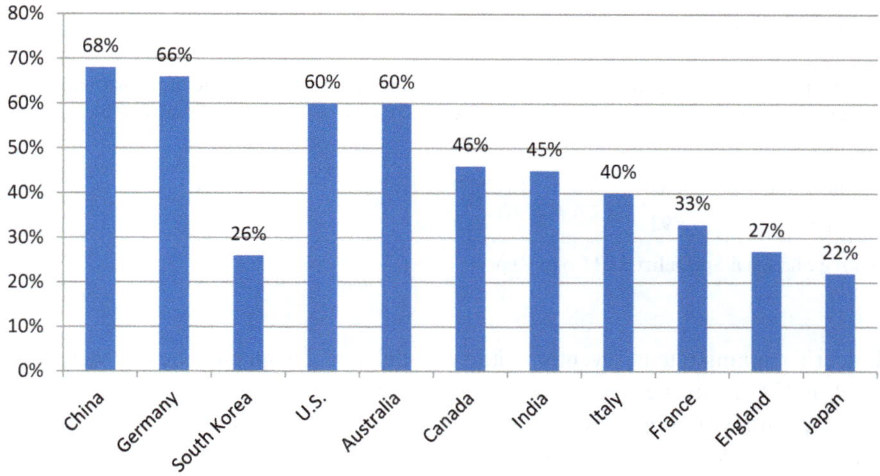

Fig. 7.9 Patent owner infringement win rates in first instance litigation (2006–2012). *Source* Global IP Project (2014), S-15

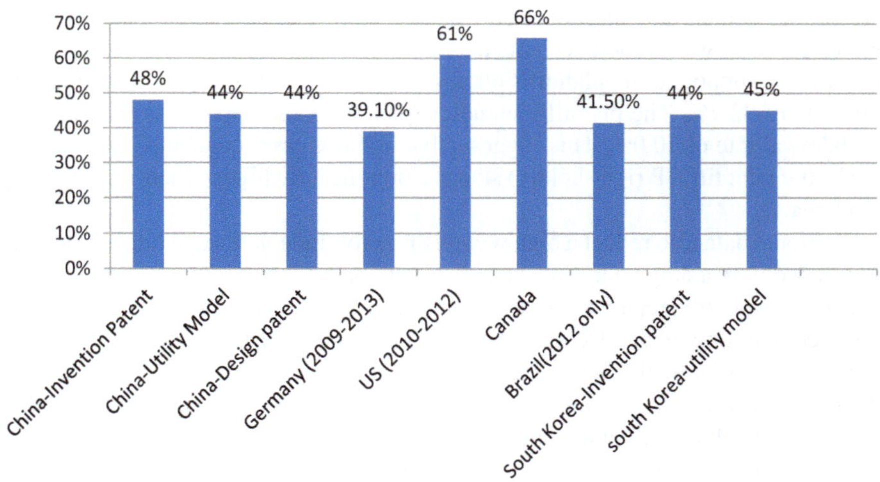

Fig. 7.10 Patentee win rate in validity cases in select countries. *Source* Global IP Project (2014), S-15

Table 7.11 Plaintiff's win rate in patent infringement cases at Beijing Specialized IP Court (2016)

Category of patent	Plaintiff's winning rate(%)	Rate of mediation and withdrawal (%)
Invention	70.4	82.5
Utility model	55.6	39.1
Design	93.2	63.2

Source Beijing IP Court Report

Table 7.12 Plaintiff's win rate in patent infringement cases at Shanghai Specialized IP Court (2015–2016)

Category of patent	Number of cases	Plaintiff's winning rate in concluded cases (%)	Rate of mediation and withdrawal (%)
Invention	212	62.2	52.8
Utility model	282	72.9	71.4
Design	393	76.2	56.8

Source Shanghai Specialized IP Court Report

holder's winning rate in invention, utility model, and design patent cases were 62.2, 72.9, and 76.2%, respectively. The Shanghai Specialized IP Court noted that, because of the complexity of understanding the technique and the difficulty of determining the protection scope of invention patents, right holders in invention patent cases are sometime more likely to have lower winning rates.

Trademark Infringement cases

According to the Trademark Lawsuit Report 2016,[10] among the first instance cases reviewed, 3228 were concluded with a judgment, among which the courts supported or partially supported the plaintiffs claims in 3024 cases. This equates to a plaintiff win rate of 93.7%. The plaintiffs withdrew their suits in 8050 cases, resulting in a withdrawal rate of 70.0%. This suggests that in those cases concluded with a judgment, the plaintiff (IP right-holder) stands a significantly higher chance of winning in China.

Regional data also reflect a high winning rate for trademark right holders in cases concluded with a judgment. For example, in 2016, the Beijing Specialized IP Court concluded 108 trademark civil cases. Of these, there were 26 civil cases of first instance, among which 14 cases were concluded with a judgment. The plaintiff's winning rate was 92.9% while the rate of mediation and withdrawal was 34.6%. Additionally, there were 80 civil cases of second instance, among which 53 cases were concluded through judgment, with the rate of vacate and remand and mediation and withdrawal being, respectively 10.0 and 32.5%. In the civil judgment of first instance, there were 11 cases with well-known trademarks affirmed resulting in a plaintiff winning rate of 90.9%.

In sum, judging from the many statistics reviewed in this section, IP right holders in China have a high winning rate (and can enjoy injunction remedies) in various IP infringement cases. Among them, trademark cases rank as having the highest winning rate with copyright cases ranking second.[11] Patent cases and unfair-competition

[10] Its statistics contain a total of 11,501 civil trademark lawsuits in the first instance, including 11,366 ownership and infringement-related cases and 135 contractual cases.

[11] In the Beijing area, the Beijing Specialized IP Court concluded 1090 copyright-related civil cases in 2016. The winning rate of the plaintiff in the cases involving software copyright was 84.9%.

Table 7.13 Trends in preliminary remedies in China

Year	Type of remedies	Number of applications	Number supported	Ratio of support (%)
2011	Preliminary injunction	130	128	98.23
	Preliminary preservation of evidence	186	174	93.42
	Preliminary preservation of property	20	20	100
2012	Preliminary injunction	27	22	83.33
	Preliminary preservation of evidence	320	310	96.73
	Preliminary preservation of property	74	70	94.67
2013	Preliminary injunction	11	9	77.78
	Preliminary preservation of evidence	173	169	97.63
	Preliminary preservation of property	47	46	96.97

Annual Working Reports issued by Supreme People's Court. Data from 2011–2013

cases[12] had the lowest winning rate. The technical and legal complexity of ruling appropriately in patent and unfair competition cases may help explain why win rates in these cases were low. Limitations of the data analyzed should also be kept in mind: much of the most readily available we could find was from some specialized IP courts, which are not necessarily reflective of other courts across China.

(iii) ***Rate of providing preliminary measures and remedies***

According to the Supreme People Court's Annual Working Reports, the ratio of providing preliminary remedies such as a preliminary injunction and preservation of evidence or property before a hearing in China is high (see Table 7.13). However, it can also be seen that only a very limited number of applications have been filed. The limited use of these remedies means that they are not common remedies to IP right holders in ordinary IP cases in China.

[12]In 2016, Beijing Specialized IP Court concluded 47 cases involving unfair competition. The plaintiff winning rate was 33.3%.

(iv) ***Support rate for damages awarded***
High ratio of statutory damages

The gap between the requested damages and awarded damages is a major concern of Chinese IP right holders when enforcing their IP rights (see Table 7.14). On the one hand, the statistics show the average damages awarded in China between 1995 and 2015 was only RMB 113,049—far below the average requested damages of RMB 355,490. Moreover, according to the Middlesouth Rewarded Damages Report (2014), the rewarded damages in more than 97% of trademark and patent infringement cases and 78% copyright infringement cases were decided using statutory damages with a notably low support ratio of requested damages to awarded damages (Table 7.14). This indicates that Chinese courts' preference of providing statutory damages instead of calculating actual damages or illegal profits is one of the main reasons for the observed gap between the requested and awarded damages.[13]

On the other hand, some judges point out that the preference for, and high rate of, statutory damages in IP cases in China is explained by the fact that: (i) IP rights holder themselves often request statutory damages; (ii) the plaintiffs fail to offer evidence of damage; and (iii) the majority of IP lawsuit defendants are local small stores or individuals. For example, plaintiffs directly claim statutory damages in 93.2% of the sample cases in Middlesouth Rewarded Damages Report (Chen 2015) while 98% of plaintiffs directly claim statutory damages in the sample cases provided in the Changsha Report (Jiang 2016a, b). Further, according to the Report *The trials of Patent Cases in Shanghai IP Court (2015–2016),* issued by Shanghai IP Court, among of the 182 patent infringement sample cases analyzed that were concluded with judgment and with specific damages, all determined damages by using statutory damages. In explaining this outcome, the Shanghai IP court pointed out that it had to apply the rule of statutory damages because rights holders could not submit any evidence with regard to their actual loss, the illegal gains of the infringer, or patent royalties.

To make changes to this situation, in one of its judicial policy issued on December 29, 2017, the Supreme People's Court reiterated that the judicial system shall enhance the damages of IP infringement to protect entrepreneur's IPR and try to establish new standards for damages based on the market value of IPR and assisted with punitive damages (Supreme People's Court 2017b). However, due to the reasons stated above, it is possible that the average damage award in China will remain small. Furthermore, it seems that injunctions rather than damages are the primary objective of most patent litigations in China. This is similar to the situation in Germany and many other countries while different from the U.S. (Global IP Project 2014). However, the awarded damages of IP civil cases in several Chinese cities has increased rapidly in recent years. For example, the average awarded damages in patent infringement cases

[13] Available statistics from the Guangzhou Intermediate and District Court in particular confirm this nationwide trend. Among 10,356 cases during the period 2008–2011 all district courts in Guangzhou applied the rule of statutory damages, and only less than 10 cases were decided by Intermediate Court preserved evidence to calculate the illegal profit of the defendants. Therefore, almost 100% of cases ended with statutory damages (Guangzhou Intermediate People's Court 2014).

Table 7.14 Trends in award of statutory IP damages versus requested damages across China

Type of cases	Statutory damages		Actual lost		Illegal profit		Average requested damages	Average supported damages	Ratio (%)
	Number of cases	Ratio (%)	Number of cases	Ratio	Number of cases	Ratio (%)			
Trademark	1071	97.63	15	1.37%	11	1	366,000	62,000	16.9
Patent	816	97.25	14	1.67	4	0.48	501,881	158,787	31.6
Copyright	1596	78.54	431	21.21%	5	0.25	77,000	15,000	19.4

Source Middlesouth Rewarded Damages Report

in the Specialized Beijing IP Court was 450,000 RMB in 2015 and 1,380,000 RMB in 2016—an annual increase of 206%. Additionally, many IP right holders in China receive the full amount of their claimed compensation. For example, among 54 IP infringement cases with fully and partially supported judgments, the Beijing IP Court fully awarded the whole claimed damages in 18.52% cases. For more information about compensation awarded in IP infringement cases in Beijing and Shanghai, see Annex A.

7.2.3.3 Summary

The statistics analyzed in the prior section are from many sources and cover different courts in different regions. Due to the shortage of data from many courts, we are unable to analyze the entirety of IP judicial enforcement in China. Meanwhile, hindered by the limited availability of nationwide statistics concerning IP judicial enforcement, this book has had to analyze statistics from some key areas for IP litigation in China, such as Beijing, Shanghai, Nanjing, and Changsha.

It should also be noted that all patent *invalidation* cases are litigated in Beijing and the data from Beijing can therefore accurately depict trends in IP administrative litigation in China. However, when it comes to IP civil cases, the data on the duration of trials and average damages collected from Beijing courts are not necessarily representative of those in other areas of China.[14]

Overall, the statistics in this section show that:

- A large portion of IP cases—either civil or administrative—are processed within a reasonable timeframe and, therefore, do not have an "overdue" problem. However, the overdue problem does exist in some IP cases. This is especially true when litigation suspension occurs because of IP invalidation or jurisdictional suspension. The procedure of IP litigation will become lengthy under these circumstances although the statistics that are readily available show that only a limited number of cases have been suspended because of these challenges.
- IP right holders' winning rates in IP infringement cases concluded via judgments in China is high—more than 90%. But the majority of cases, nearly 65%, end up with meditation or withdrawal being the method for concluding the cases.
- Preliminary measures are rarely used but supported at a high rate in China.
- High rates of statutory damages—almost 100% in a number of districts courts—are common in most Chinese courts. However, the preference of statutory damages is consistent with the reality that parties in IP lawsuits in China fail to offer evidence of damages given China's lack of serious evidential "discovery" and given that IP rights holders often request statutory damages themselves.

[14]There are several reasons why we make this statement: the Beijing IP Court receives many technical IP cases, which might lengthen the trial's duration; the Beijing IP Court tends to grant more damages to IP right holders than other courts in less economically developed areas; and the rising number of IP disputes at the Beijing IP Court also leads to some case 'overdue' problems and make the average duration of trials longer.

- The statistics also show that in most of the cases offering statutory damages, the damages granted are far below the ceiling set by the law. The reform of the rule of discovery of evidence and introduction of a higher evaluation of statutory damages against IP thefts could help change this situation.

7.2.4 *Cases Involving Foreign Parties and the Problem of Protectionism*

Cases involving foreign parties

According to the data collected from the Annual Report on Judicial Protection of IPR in China Court (see Table 7.15), the ratio of IP civil cases in China involving foreign parties is about 2% on average. In contrast, the ratio of IP administrative cases (those involving invalidation issues) involving foreign parties in China is 40%. This means that more foreign parties are involved in IP administrative litigation, namely the IP invalidation process.

Jin (2015) analyzes the win rates of IP cases involving foreign parties in China, covering only a limited sample of decisions. According to the study, foreign parties are more likely to be the plaintiffs than defendants in IP litigation in China and their winning rate (about 73%) is higher than the average winning rate of domestic plaintiffs in IP litigation (about 55%).

Tables 7.15 and 7.16 show the increasing number of IP litigation cases involving foreign parties in China. An increasing percentage of foreign firms as plaintiffs generally means that foreign parties more actively use the Chinese judicial system to enforce their IP rights. Whether or not this is in response to proportionately more infringement is another issue.

Table 7.15 Trends in IP civil and IP administrative cases involving foreign parties in China

	2010	2011	2012	2013	2014	2015	2016
First instance civil cases concluded	41,718	58,201	83,850	88,286	94,501	101,324	131,813
Involving foreign parties	1647	1956	2042	2180	2142	1714	2797
Ratio	3.95%	3.36%	2.43%	2.47%	2.26%	1.69%	2.12%
First instance administrative cases concluded	2391	2470	2899	2901	4887	10,926	6250
Involving foreign parties	1004	1237	1349	1312	2237	4928	2394
Ratio	41.99%	50.08%	46.53%	45.23%	45.7%	45.1%	38.3%

Source Annual Report on Judicial Protection of IPR in China Court

Table 7.16 Win rates for foreign parties in IP litigation in China

Cases involving foreign parties	Winning	Failure	Sum	Rate of winning
As plaintiffs	22	7	29	73%
As defendants	2	2	4	
Sum	24	9	33	

Source Jin (2015), collected from Gazette of the Supreme People's Court

The statistics also indicate that foreigners are generally more likely to be plaintiffs and have a higher winning rate in IP litigation in China than domestic parties. For example, there is only a very limited number of cases in which foreigners have been charged with IP infringement. Further, according to the statistics in the tables, among the eight patent cases in Beijing involving foreign plaintiffs, seven ended with supporting plaintiffs (87.5% win rate) (Beijing IP Litigation Report 2016). Further, according to the statistics, among the 19 patent cases in Shanghai, 16 cases ended with supporting plaintiffs (84.2% win rate) (Shanghai IP Litigation Report 2016). These trends are partly because foreign plaintiffs, more so than domestic ones, are normally more cautious about bringing litigation and when they do they like to ensure they are sufficiently prepared for the case.

So far, there are no official statistics discussing the different treatment between Chinese parties and foreign parties in judicial IP enforcement. Some studies have tried to explore this topic. For example, Zhang and Ke (2002) in their study of 620 sample decisions of economic law related cases decided by one Beijing district court find that local plaintiffs have a higher winning rate (39%) than that of non-local plaintiffs (25.9%). Long and Wang (2014) analyze over 102 IP cases published by Supreme People's Court Gazette from 1985 to 2010 and 449 sample decisions from five provinces. They also note that there is a positive relationship between local domicile of plaintiffs and their winning rate in the first instance; however, there is no such relationship in the second instance, which means that justice is better served at the appeal level. Long and Wang (2015) reach similar conclusions.

Other studies show that, generally speaking, there is no clear evidence of protectionism or discrimination against foreign parties in IP judicial enforcements in China. For example, Sepetys and Cox (2009), in their study of damages awarded by Chinese courts using a sample of 179 IP cases between 2002 and 2008, find that the median award in the cases is no different when a Chinese firm and foreign firm are opponents in a lawsuit, regardless of which firm is the plaintiff. Love et al. (2016) also come to a similar conclusion, stating that "*our findings on litigation outcomes [in China] bear little evidence of protectionism. Foreign patent owners brought over 10% of Chinese patent infringement actions in our database and won over 70% of those cases*."[15] Although there is limited data about appeal level IP cases, some

[15]Regarding damages, the study finds that "*Successful foreign patentees received a median damages award of 100,000 RMB in suits against private Chinese firms, exactly the same amount that private Chinese patentees received when they sued private domestic parties*". They also find that "*Chinese*

research shows that there is a 30% case overturn rate on appeal by foreign entities, compared to a 17% rate for domestic plaintiffs (Cohen 2016).

These findings are consistent with the other data collected and discussed throughout this section. Foreign companies often win IP lawsuits and receive higher damages when they do in China because they cautiously select cases they are more likely to win, and also because they often have more assets at their disposal and are better prepared for litigation than Chinese parties.

However, there is an important caveat to keep in mind that can easily be lost in aggregate statistics. Our consultations with foreign and Chinese firms indicate that there are IP cases in China in which the state intervenes in a judgement, rulings or acceptances of cases appear intentionally delayed, or a judgment is otherwise made that is inappropriate (or even downright wrong) according to the law and facts at hand. This type of protectionism can favor domestic firms against foreign firms, or one local domestic Chinese firm over another. In other words, protectionism sometimes exists in China (as in other countries). However, it simply does not appear to be reflected at a significant level in the more often-studied *aggregate statistics*. But even a handful of significant protectionist judgements can completely block out the market for some innovative firms.

Further, there is empirical evidence that geographic factors do indeed play a role in IP enforcement protectionism in China. Local plaintiffs do have a better chance of winning IP litigation than non-local plaintiffs, either domestic or foreign (Zhang and Ke 2002; Long and Wang 2014, 2015). Although second instance judgments seem to be less protectionist, the possible negative impact of protectionism in the first instance restrains the incentive to innovate by imposing inappropriate costs on innovators who seek to enforce their IP rights.

Unfair court rulings intent on protecting local firms undermine the sense of fairness in China's IP judicial system. Because of this, measures should be taken to lessen the propensity for local protectionism. It is important to enhance the transparency of litigation procedures, including fairly applying rules of evidence. Also, given that appeal courts are more likely to offer fairer decisions than lower level courts [see Long and Wang (2015) for a discussion about this dynamic], China's IP enforcement system should ensure that appeal of court rulings is a viable option so that higher level courts can address unfair rulings by lower courts. Under special circumstances where the local government has great interest in an IP lawsuit, cross-jurisdiction trials or appeals should also be considered to guarantee fair trials and judgments (Fang 2008). Although the newly established Specialized IP Courts in China may partly serve as an instrument for cross-regional appeals, a general rule on cross-regional appeals still should be introduced into China's Civil Procedure Law to better enable cross-jurisdiction trials and appeals against protectionism.

---

patentees received 20% less in suits against foreign companies and 60% more in suits against state monopolies. Similarly, foreign patentees received a permanent injunction in every case they won, while victorious domestic patentees were denied injunctions 5–10% of the time" (Love et al. 2016).

7.3 Efficiency and Effectiveness of Criminal Enforcement

Introduction to the system

China's IP laws are frequently updated by judicial interpretations, administrative provisions, and notices. In general, according to the Chinese Criminal Code, IP-related crimes are crimes that endanger the socialist market order. At present, there are seven specific IP crimes listed in the Criminal Code which can be categorized into four types: (i) patent-related crimes (Art 216, Crime of patent passing off); (ii) trademark-related crimes (Art. 213, crime of counterfeiting the registered trademark; Art. 214, crime of selling commodities bearing counterfeit registered trademarks; Art. 215, crime of illegal manufacturing registered trademarks or selling the said illegal manufactured trademark); (iii) copyright-related crimes (Art 217, crime of infringing copyright, Art. 218 crime of selling infringed reproduction); and (iv) crimes of infringing trade secrets (Art. 219). Meanwhile, other provisions on crimes might also have some relationship with IP crimes such as the crime of producing or selling fake and shoddy commodities (Art. 140), the crime of illegal operation (Art. 225), and others.

According to the Chinese Criminal Code and Criminal Procedure, all IP criminal cases in China should be dealt with by the Public Security Bureau (PSB, the police), the prosecutor, and the criminal courts. Two internal divisions within the PSB—the Social Order Department and the Economic Crimes Department have the authority of detecting, filing, and investigating IP criminal cases. Administrative agencies are required to transfer IP infringements reaching criminal thresholds to the PSB. The PSB will review the case to decide whether to get the arrest warrant from the prosecution agency and whether to transfer the case to the prosecution agency. The prosecution agency will further review the case to decide whether to prosecute in court. In addition, the victim of an IP crime can also file charges directly with the criminal court if there is ample evidence to potentially prove the case. The vast majority of criminal IP cases are tried by judges in criminal tribunals in regular local or higher-level courts. Recently, specialized IP courts and judges also started handling IP criminal cases, along with IP civil and administrative lawsuits.

Statistical analysis

To show the efficiency and effectiveness of IP criminal enforcement in China, we collected data on the following aspects of the criminal enforcement mechanism: (i) the number of IP criminal cases of first instance accepted (CA) and cases concluded (CC), Number of defendants (NOD) and Number of defendants convicted (NODC) involved; and (ii) the number of suspects PSBs request to arrest (NOSRTA), the number of suspects arrested (NOSA); the number of suspects prosecuted (NOSP) by prosecution agencies; and the number of suspects convicted (NOSC) by courts. The latter group of data is collected to reflect the efficiency and effectiveness of different stages of procedure in IP criminal enforcement.

Judging from the statistics, it can be seen that the caseload of IP crimes concluded in China has grown over the last ten years but decreased slightly in the last three

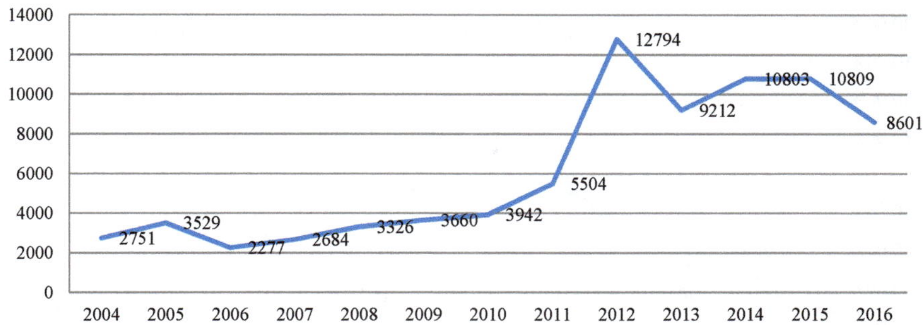

Fig. 7.11 Growth of IP criminal cases concluded in China (2004–2016). *Source* Annual Working Reports issued by Supreme People's Court; Annual Report of China IPR Protection Status

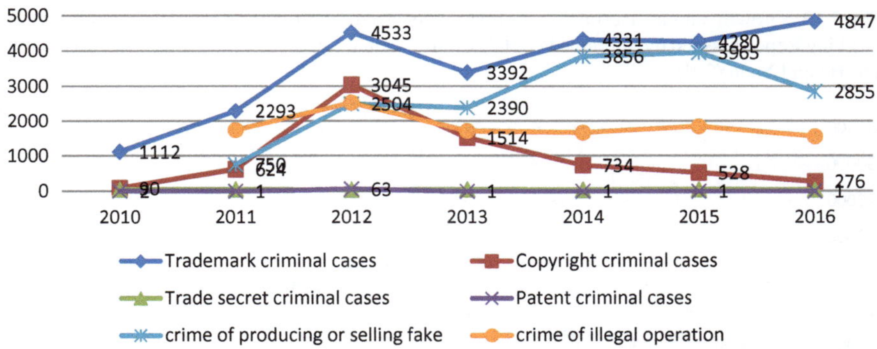

Fig. 7.12 IP criminal cases of first-instance (by right) and other relevant crimes concluded in China. *Source* Annual Working Report by Supreme People's Court; Annual Report of China IPR Protection Status

years (Fig. 7.11). The number of defendants and convicted defendants of IP Crime and relevant Crimes share a similar trend (Fig. 7.12). Meanwhile, there was a slight increase of cases in 2005 and then a drop in 2006, and a sizeable increase of cases in 2011–2012 and then a sharp drop in cases in 2013 (see Fig. 7.11). This likely reflects the impact of the two national campaigns launched by the State Council to crack down on IP between 2004–2015 and 2010–2011.

Trademark-related crime ranks first among various IP crimes and has continued to grow moderately over the last three years. Patent-related crime is on the bottom, with only 70 total occurring between 2010 and 2016. The number of copyright-related crimes reached its peak in 2012 and has declined annually since then. Crime of producing or selling fake and shoddy commodities ranks second in Fig. 7.12, however, there are no further data to tell how many of these are related to unqualified rather than fake goods.

Judging from the statistics, it can be seen that the growth rate of IP crime cases is much higher than that of other crimes (Fig. 7.13). This could represent an increase in resources devoted to IP criminal enforcement in China or a rapid growth of IP crimes,

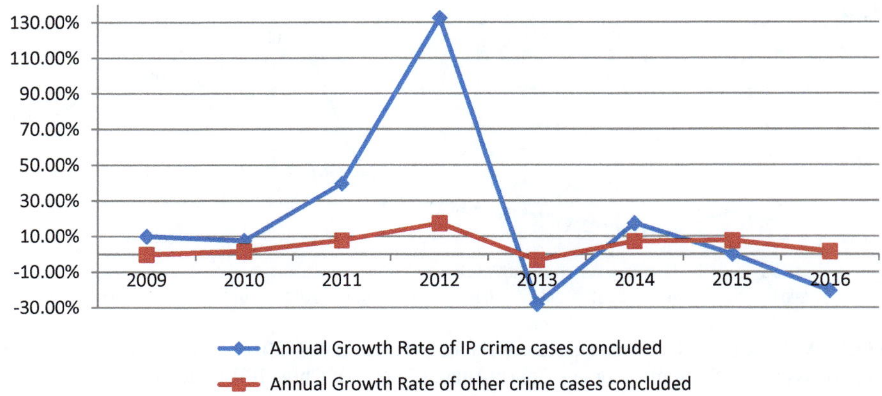

Fig. 7.13 Growth rates of IP crime cases versus other crimes in China (2009–2016). *Source* Annual Working Reports issued by Supreme People's Court; Annual Report of China IPR Protection Status; and He and Yuan (2015)

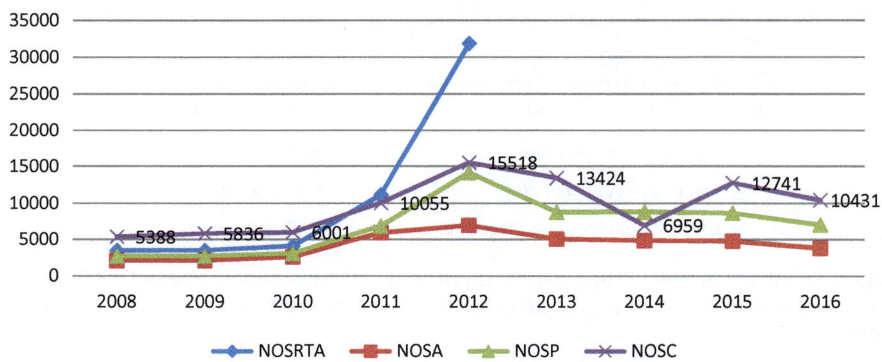

Fig. 7.14 Number of suspected in different stage of IP criminal enforcement procedure in China (2008–2016). *Source* Annual Working Report by Supreme People's Court; Annual Report of China IPR Protection Status; and He and Yuan (2015). *The number of suspects PSBs request to arrest (NOSRTA), the number of suspects arrested (NOSA); the number of suspects prosecuted (NOSP) by prosecution agencies; the number of suspects convicted (NOSC) by courts

especially due to the boom of Internet-intensive industries. Compared with the growth rate of other crimes, growth rate of IP crime is more unstable which suggests it is greatly affected by IP enforcement campaigns launched by governments (Fig. 7.14).

The rates of NOSA/NOSRTA, NOSA/NOSP, and NOSA/NOSC in IP crime cases have been gradually declining in recent years. This is consistent with the situation of other crimes (see Tables 7.17). One the one hand, the increase of input by PSB has led to growth in the number of NOSRTA; on the other hand, the less strict policy held by prosecutors and judges in recent years might explain the decrease of NOSP and NOSC. In December 2006, the Supreme People's Procuratorate promulgated Several Opinions on the Implementation of the "Loose and Harsh Coexistent Criminal Justice

Table 7.17 Efficiency and effectiveness of adjudicating IP criminal cases versus other cases in China

Year	IP criminal cases			Other criminal cases		
	NOSA/NOSRTA[a] (%)	NOSA/NOSP[a] (%)	NOSA/NOSC[a] (%)	NOSA/NOSRTA[a] (%)	NOSA/NOSP[a] (%)	NOSA/NOSC[a] (%)
2008	60.51	78.12	39.11	81.16	83.28	94.57
2009	60.23	78.63	36.31	/	82.96	94.39
2010	63.39	85.23	43.54	77.76	79.78	91.04
2011	53.40	86.64	59.19	73.24	75.66	86.47
2012	21.93	49.42	45.08	/	/	/
2013	/	57.73	37.85	63.95	66.43	75.98
2014	/	55.00	69.82	/	63.23	74.29
2015	/	55.08	37.45	/	62.77	70.87
2016	/	53.83	36.40	/	59.08	67.92

Source Annual Working Report by Supreme People's Court; Annual Report of China IPR Protection Status; and He and Yuan (2015) [a]Number of IP criminal cases of first instance accepted (CA) and cases concluded (CC), Number of defendants (NOD) and Number of defendants convicted (NODC) involved. And (ii) The number of suspects PSBs request to arrest (NOSRTA), the number of suspects arrested (NOSA); the number of suspects prosecuted (NOSP) by prosecution agencies; the number of suspects convicted (NOSC) by courts

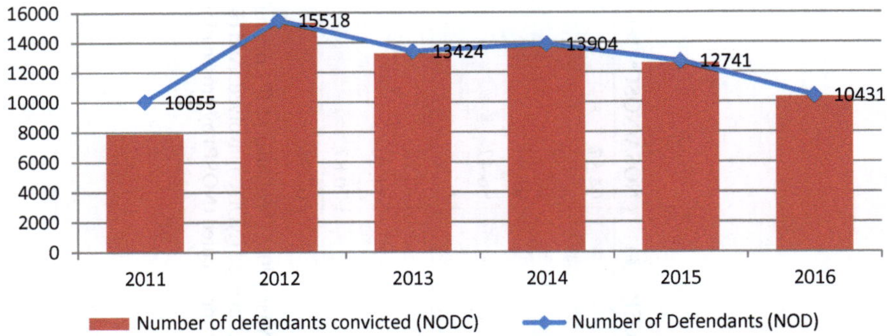

Fig. 7.15 Number of defendants and convicted defendants of IP Crime and relevant Crimes (2011–2016). *Source* Annual Working Report by Supreme People's Court; Annual Report of China IPR Protection Status

Policy" in Prosecution. The change of judicial policy makes the prosecutors more cautious with arrest and prosecution measures.

Meanwhile, the rates of NOSA/NOSRTA, NOSA/NOSP, and NOSA/NOSC in IP crime cases are lower than those in other crime cases. This could mean that China's PSB, prosecutors, and judges may have a bigger gap of understanding about the criminal threshold of IP crimes than that of ordinary crimes, or the prosecutors maintain a stricter and higher standard to arrest and prosecute IP infringement suspects.

However, at the end of this procedure, the conviction rate ("NOD/NODC") reflecting the understanding of Chinese prosecutors and judges about the IP crime threshold, is very high (near 99%) (Fig. 7.15), which could mean that approaches to prosecution are very cautious and there is a high prosecution standard to avoid failure of the litigation brought by the government.

Other commentary

Liu (2010a) provides a comparative study showing the victim characteristics between Chinese and US criminal IP cases. The samples it collects cover a dataset of the summary judgments of criminal IP cases in China from 1994–2009 and IP criminal cases in the US from 2002 to 2010. According to the study, most victims are companies "carrying top brands or copyrights of such products as home electronics, computer parts, personal care products, as well as foreign software, movies, and TV series on optical disks".

It is obvious that only a small proportion of IP infringements end up in China's criminal courts. This is mainly due to the fact that Chinese IP criminal law requires that only IP infringements with serious consequences can be prosecuted and convicted. Moreover, a decade ago, a private investigator further estimated that only about ten percent of those reaching criminal thresholds were charged criminally with the rest being handled administratively (Mertha 2005).

There are several factors behind this phenomenon and some of them are still working. First, local PSBs are overloaded with other criminal cases and, partly due to the cultural influence, IP cases are often considered "civil" matters and hardly the priority of the police force. Second, the Chinese PSB and prosecutors will not bring cases to the criminal court unless there is a very high chance of winning. Failing to convict a suspect will lead to a "wrong case" and result in negative evaluation of their performance. Meanwhile, there is no motivational measure to encourage the transferring of cases to PSB (Mertha 2005). Additionally, for local administrative agencies, especially local AICs, putting counterfeiters in jail will normally cut off an important source of revenue from business registration fees, regulation charges and fines imposed on counterfeiters (Dimitrov 2004).

Subsequent to the publication of the aforementioned research, numerous efforts have been made to directly address some of the challenges to effective criminal IP enforcement in China. For example, many campaigns have been launched to raise public and local PSB's IP awareness. The number of IP criminal cases handled by PSB, prosecution agencies and courts has increased sharply after such campaigns. Additionally, many joint meetings, information exchanges, collaborative enforcement campaigns, and other large-scale cooperative efforts have been initiated by the PSB, the prosecutors, and the relevant administrative agencies to ease the bureaucratic incentive issues (Liu 2010a, b).

7.4 Efficiency and Effectiveness of Customs

Customs IP protection focuses on border protection of IPRs. It is one of the essential ways to protect IPR in China. In order to accede to the WTO, China began to carry out border protection of IPRs in September 1994 and passed its first enactment of the Regulations for Intellectual Property Rights Customs Protection (The Customs Protection) in October 1995. Since then, China has gradually established an IPR border protection system in line with the rules of the WTO. At present, China Customs has set up a complete IP enforcement system including inspection of documents and goods, detention and investigation of infringing goods, imposition of penalties for illegal importation and exportation, and disposal of infringing goods, amongst other border initiatives.

China's Customs protection of IPRs can be divided into two models: (i) the "Protection on request/passive protection" model, and (ii) the "Protection ex officio/active protection" model. Under the "Protection on request" model, whenever IP right holders discern that alleged infringing goods are going to be imported or exported they can file applications to the Customs to take measures to detain suspected infringing goods. However, Customs will not investigate the goods and right holders should bring the case to the court without undue delay (see Art. 12, 13 and 14 of the Customs Protection Regulation).

Under the "Protection ex officio/active protection" model, if the Customs suspect that the imported and exported goods have infringed the IPRs registered at the General Administration of Customs in China, the Customs should ex officio suspend the cross-border transit, notify the relevant IP right holders, and detain suspected goods upon

Table 7.18 Goods investigated and seized by Chinese Customs during IP enforcement (2014–2016)

Year		Model		Import/Export		Independent IPRs held by domestic enterprises
		Protection ex officio	Protection on request	Import	Export	
2016	SGS[a]	17,433	50	667	16,828	–
	Ratio	99.7%	0.3%	3.8%	96.2%	–
	NGS[a]	38,557,800	3,500,400	441,421	41,616,795	7,578,500
	Ratio	91.67%	8.33%	1.05%	98.95%	–
2015	SGS[a]	*23,192*	68	22,000	22,000	1939
	Ratio	*99.71%*	*0.29%*	96.76%	96.76%	–
	NGS[a]	45,558,879	24,214,246	69,440,000	69,440,000	6,694,780
	Ratio	65.30%	34.70%	99.53%	99.53%	–
2014	SGS[a]	23,817	43	23,000	23,000	514
	Ratio	99.82%	0.18%	96.5%	96.5%	–
	NGS[a]	90,331,038	1,634,510	91,000,000	91,000,000	12,000,000
	Ratio	98.22%	1.78%	99.6%	99.6%	–

Source China Customs IP Protection Status; China IPR Yearbooks. [a]Shipments of goods seized (SGS), Number of Goods Seized (NGS)

the request of the IP right holders. Customs might also actively investigate the case and punish the infringing parties. To take advantage of the "Protection ex officio" model, IP right holders in China need to register their IPRs at the IP Protection Office of General Administration of Customs in advance.[16]

According to the official data disclosed in the China Customs IP Protection Status (2016) report by the General Administration of Customs, within the period 2014–2016, China Customs took measures more than 19,500 times to protect IPRs, resulting in total "shipments of goods seized" (SGS) in excess of 17,400 and involving more than 42,058,200 pieces of infringing goods (Number of Goods Seized, NGS) (Table 7.18).

Nearly all shipment detentions happen under the "Protection ex officio" model (see Table 7.18). In 2016, 99.7% of SGS happened under the "Protection ex officio/active protection" model, involving 91.67% of suspended infringing goods. Although only 50 SGS occurred because of active IP enforcement by right holders, they accounted for 8.33% of suspended infringing goods for the whole year. The status in 2014 and 2015 is similar. This means, to some degree, that if the right holders have registered their IPR, especially registered trademarks at the IP Protection Office of General

[16]This is important for several reasons. First, the recording procedure is cost-free, straightforward and ultimately saves time. Second, without prior recording and in case of interception of infringing goods by Customs upon request of the IP right holders, China customs may detain the goods for a limited period of time but do not have the authority to establish the existence of an infringement. The IP right holder will then have to file a lawsuit with the court.

Table 7.19 Scale of IP infringement in Customs enforcement in China (2014–2016), by IPR

Types of IPR cases	Item	2014	2015	2016
Registered TMs	Ratio	96.86%	98.23%	98.56%
	NGS[a]	89,075,040	68,539,932	41,456,410
Copyrights	Ratio	1.20%	0.37%	0.14%
	NGS[a]	1,100,857	258,460	57,193
Patents	Ratio	1.94%	1.38%	1.28%
	NGS[a]	1,786,551	965,533	538,613
The Olympic logo	Ratio	0.01%	0.01%	0.01%
	NGS[a]	3100	9200	6000

Source China Customs IP Protection Status; China IPR Yearbooks. [a]Number of Goods Seized (NGS)

Administration of Customs in advance, China Customs normally can actively and effectively take action against the infringing activities.

The majority of IP cases enforced at China Customs involve trademark infringement (Table 7.19). In 2016, more than 98% of goods seized (NGS) were goods allegedly infringing a registered trademark. The number of patent cases continued to grow compared with previous years, involving 538,613 allegedly infringing goods, but this only accounted for more than 1% of the NGS. Other IPRs accounted for a very small portion of the total number. The situation in 2014 and 2015 was similar. One decisive factor explaining the high ratio of trademark cases enforced at Customs in China is that passing-off and trademark infringement is easier to discover and determine than infringement of other rights. This also means that Customs protection is a very efficient and effective way to protect registered trademarks.

The majority of allegedly infringing goods were seized under export control (see Table 7.18). In 2016, China Customs detained more than 16,600 SGS under export control, accounting for 96.20% of total batches of detainees that year. The number involving suspected goods was 416,167,000, accounting for 98.95% of the total number of detained goods. Meanwhile, standard postal services were used to send approximately 80% of all seized batches of counterfeit products out of China. The status in 2014 and 2015 is similar.

The ratio of SGS and NGS from important control at China Customs is much lower than for export control (see Table 7.18). One possible reason behind this phenomenon is that most IP infringing goods crossing the Chinese border were manufactured in China. Another reason might be that goods imported from foreign countries normally have less chance of infringing on Chinese IPRs, especially trademarks that are registered in advance with China Customs.

Nearly all seized goods were intended for sea transport. Of the total amount of seized counterfeit units, 96% were en route to being shipped overseas. Hong Kong (as a transit/trans-shipment hub), the US, and several developing countries such as Iran and Brazil are top destinations for seized counterfeit products.

Table 7.20 Origin of IP rights' holders protected at China Customs (2014–2015)

Country or region	Year	Number of Rights	Ratio	Quality [Piece/Pair]	Ratio	Amounts of value involved	Ratio
China	2014	514	7.38	11,961,097	13.01	74,243,420	25.74
	2015	381	6.22	6,622,922	9.51	55897996.97	25.01
HK, TW, Macao	2014	59	0.85	890,630	0.97	11,774,685	4.08
	2015	27	0.44	110,742	0.16	885283.78	0.40
US	2014	2266	34.65	13,850,107	15.07	78,962,480	27.38
	2015	1822	29.77	30,522,032	43.84	57327802.19	25.65
EU	2014	3121	44.84	52,483,633	57.10	78,626,841	27.26
	2015	3030	49.50	28,536,928	40.99	51891967.81	23.22
Others	2014	1000	14.37	12,734,985	13.85	44,815,476	15.54
	2015	861	14.07	3,834,522	5.50	57462685.56	25.72

Source China IPR Statistical Yearbooks

Foreign IP right holders are more active than their Chinese counterparts at enforcing their IPR at China Customs (see Table 7.20). More than 70% of IP rights enforced at Customs were claimed by right holders from the US and EU, accounting more than 50% of the value of the seizures in 2014 and 2015. Only 7% of IP rights were claimed by right holders from China, but accounted for about 25% of the value of the seizures in 2014 and 2015.

Coordination efforts between China Customs and customs officials and other enforcement bodies in the main destination markets for counterfeit goods can be an effective strategy and should be regularly examined. China Customs has now established cooperation with more than 130 countries and regions in the world. Joint enforcement of IPR can be conducted under more than 170 bilateral administrative mutual aid agreements. For example, in March and April 2016, China Customs and the US Customs jointly carried out IP enforcement actions to combat Sino-US infringing trade: more than 1400 cases were investigated, more than 2 million pieces of allegedly infringing goods were detained (Guangming Daily 2016). Meanwhile, the Chinese government is considering a proposal to allow those holding exclusive IP licensees (not those just holding full ownership of IP rights) to register their rights and claim the corresponding protection (Zhou 2009).

In sum, it is obvious that much progress has been made by Chinese Customs with regard to IP cross-border protection in recent years. However, the data in this section also shows the continuing challenge of a high level of exports of counterfeit goods from China and the difficulties in enforcing patent rights in particular at Customs.

7.5 Efficiency and Effectiveness of Local IP Offices in Administrative Enforcement

Introduction to the system

As is stated in the previous section, IP administrative enforcement is presently the main way to enforce IPR in China. On the one hand, this is largely due to "its proactive nature, low cost, and relatively efficient procedures with ample space for discretion, administrative sanctions, especially fines" (Liu 2010a, b). On the other hand, judicial enforcement is generally complicated and it is difficult to collect evidence in China given the nature of the law and court procedures, which may sometimes lead to lengthy trials and a "cost-reward" problem.

There is no single and harmonized authority for IP administrative enforcement in China. As such, how to choose a suitable IP enforcement agency is often a problem for Chinese IP right holders. Aside from Customs, mentioned above, different authorities are in charge of IP enforcement of different types of IPRs in China. And China has a unique system of local IP "administrative" enforcement.

In this system, SIPO and the local IP offices (IPOs) (broadly affiliated with SIPO) throughout China deal only with patent infringement disputes and investigate the acts of patent passing-off. The administrations for industry and commerce (AICs) affiliated with SAIC at all levels across China are responsible for enforcement of anti-monopolistic behavior, unfair competition and trademark infringement. They also have comprehensive authority to protect enterprise names, famous packages, decorations of goods, and business secrets. Among these, acts of infringement involving business secrets should be determined and dealt with by AICs at or above the county level.

The Copyright Protection Center of China (CPCC), directly under the General Press and Publication Administration (GPPA), is responsible for copyright registration. The local press and publication bureaus (copyright bureaus) throughout China are responsible for handling copyright (software excluded) registration work under their governance. The National Copyright Administration of China (NCAC) assumes the responsibility for investigating, handling and organizing the investigation of copyright infringement cases. Therefore, the local press and publication bureaus, and copyright and cultural bureaus in various locations normally belong to one department.

As to new plant varieties rights, the Office of Protection of New Varieties of Agricultural Plants under the MoA and the Office of Protection of New Varieties of Forest Plants under SFA are respectively responsible for the receipt and examination of applications for rights in new varieties of agricultural plants and forest plants. Local administrative departments of agriculture and forestry of the people's governments in China at or above the county level assume the responsibility to handle infringement cases involving new plant varieties, enjoin the counterfeiting act, impose a fine, and confiscate illegal gains and propagation material of the plant variety.

The Quality and Technical Supervision Bureaus (QTSBs), local divisions of the AQSIQ, is also a competent authority for investigating and handling counterfeit and inferior commodities. The local QTSBs throughout the country focus their work on the crack down on the manufacture of counterfeit and inferior products, which involves overlapping of power with the AICs enforcement combating counterfeit trademarks. In the event that an IP right holder cannot collect sufficient evidence to pursue administrative or civil action against an infringer, it may still be possible to apply to QTSB to impound the infringing goods on the grounds of breaching quality or safety standards.

Regarding enforcement of domain name rights, the competent authority to take care its registration is the China Internet Network Information Center (CNNIC), founded upon approval of the Ministry of Information Industry (MII). Disputes regarding domain names must also be filed and resolved by institutions authorized by CNNIC.

Not every authority in the IP enforcement mechanism in China has equally competent power to enforce IPR. For example, AICs are very powerful because there are five levels of AICs corresponding with the five levels of government in China. Their enforcement teams are spread throughout the country and are well equipped with large staff There are 24,000 local AICs at the lowest level of government, equipped with more than 450,000 personnel (which is almost twice the number of judges in China) (He and Yuan 2015).

In contrast, most local IPOs (dealing with patent matters) have limited staff and are located in large and medium-sized cities in China. And only a handful of IPOs are located in cities at the county level. Therefore, patent enforcement via local IPOs in China is comparatively more difficult than trademark enforcement, for example.

The fragmentation of the IPR administrative enforcement system in China undermines the efficiency of the system. Cross-sectoral coordination within the system, therefore, has become the focus of the reform. Many "Office of the Intellectual Property Leadership Working Groups" have been established at the municipal/provincial level in China in recent years to strengthen the coordination of enforcement of various IPRs.

An increasingly harmonized approach to IP administrative enforcement in China can be found in many FTZs (Free Trade Zone). Table 7.21 explores ongoing initiatives in the Shanghai FTZ in this area (see Table 7.21), although other interesting initiatives are occurring in other places (e.g., the Xiamen FTZ, Chongqing FTZ, and Guangzhou FTZ).

Additionally, following SIPO's strategy to establish an "IP Fast-track Enforcement" mechanism to meet the development needs of certain regions in which major industrial activities have concentrated, many cities have established the so-called "IP Fast-track Enforcement Center" to expedite the enforcement of patents. A non-exhaustive list of these is as follows: Zhongshan (lighting industry), Nantong (home textiles industry), Beijing Chaoyang (design service industry), Hangzhou (pen manufacture industry), Dongguan (furniture industry), and Shunde (home appliances industry). This IP Fast-track Enforcement Center model combines resources of local IP Offices and other local governmental bodies. For example, the Zhongshan Center and Zhongshan City People's Court established a pre-mediation mechanism that

Table 7.21 Harmonizing IP administrative enforcement in China—approaches in the Shanghai Free Trade Zone

The Shanghai FTZ is one of the first to start the "three-in-one" model to enforce patent, trademark, and copyrights in one administrative unit. In 2013, the Shanghai Municipal Government promulgated the Management Measures of China (Shanghai) Free Trade Pilot Zone which allots patent and copyright enforcement power to the Free Trade Zone Administrative Committee (Art. 6). The authority to enforce trademark rights, however, is still technically in the hands of local AICs (Art. 8 of the measures). But in 2015, the Pudong IP Administration (PIPA) (an administration governing IP in the Shanghai FTZ) was established to experiment with the "three-in-one" model
PIPA has taken many other measures to improve IP administrative enforcement in the Shanghai FTZ. It accepts various IP infringement complaints; sets up a rapid-response mechanism to investigate and punish IP infringement; and established a diverse alternative dispute-settlement resolution (ADR) mechanism that includes forms of mediation to solve IP disputes. According to the information released by PIPA in September 2017, it received more than 700 IPR complaints and most of them have been fairly disposed of to date. From January to June 2017, it resolved 102 IP disputes via ADRs, an increase of 325% from the prior year
Despite these successes, because PIPA lacks sufficient enforcement personnel, limited official data has been collected to document the administration's successes. So far there are only 27 official staff in PIPA, although it has an IP Help Center with 77 persons. Nonetheless, PIPA's model has been widely adopted or is being adopted by the other FTZs in China at present, including the FTZs in Guangdong, Tianjin, Fujian, Chongqing, Sichuan, and other places

Source The authors

recognizes evidence discovered in this procedure; this mechanism reduces processing times in patent infringement cases by one month. By way of any example, the Beijing Chaoyang Center established a platform for sharing information to facilitate cooperation between various IP administrative bodies.

As mentioned in prior chapters, on April 10th 2018, SAMR was established to take over various IP administrative enforcement affairs which were previously dispersed across SIPO, SAIC, AQSIQ, and CFDA. Local AMRs were also gradually set up on the basis of local AICs and IPOs. Meanwhile, the functions of the previous three antitrust agencies (MOFCOM, NDRC, and SAIC) have also been consolidated into SAMR. It is still uncertain, however, how long this transitional period will last.

Statistical analysis

To evaluate the efficiency and effectiveness of the administrative enforcement efforts of local IP offices in China, we collect information on (i) the number of IP administrative cases and enforcement measures, (ii) the number of cases that administrative agents transfer to the PSB for criminal prosecution, and (iii) the originality of right holders (Note: The processing time of IP administrative cases is normally short and seldom becomes a problem for IP right holders. We therefore skip it in our evaluation.).

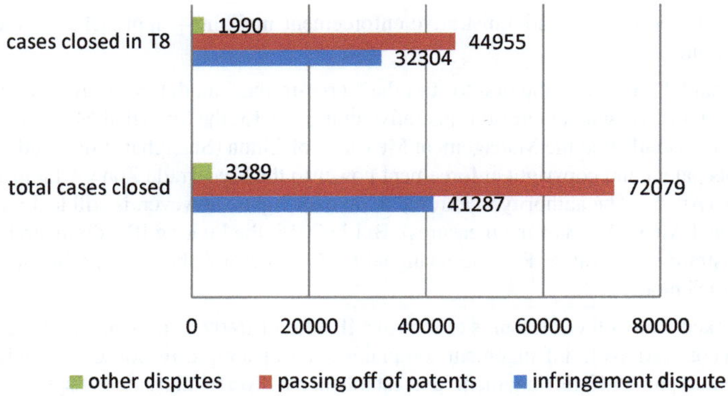

Fig. 7.16 Patent enforcement by local IPOs in China (1985–2015). *Source* SIPO, Annual Report of Chinese Patent Investigation Data (2015)

(i) ***Number of cases and measures***

Figure 7.16 shows the patent dispute numbers enforced by all local IPOs in China from 1985 (the year China's first Patent Law was introduced) to 2015, compared with that of 8 provinces (Zhejiang, Guangdong, Shandong, Jiangsu, Henan, Hubei, Hunan, and Sichuan). It shows that more than 75% of the administrative enforcement of patents is conducted by local IPOs in areas possessing better manufacturing ability.

Several trends emerge in the figures. Considering the data in Fig. 7.16, the development of IP protection in different regions in China is uneven. Also, there is a general trend that IP administrative enforcement has been more often utilized since 2000. The number of administrative enforcement cases for trademarks and copyrights as well as the relevant cases transferred to the PSB in China appears to have peaked in two periods: 2003–2005 and 2010–2012 (see Figs. 7.17 and 7.18). This coincides with major IP enforcement campaigns launched by the State Council during these times.

When examining Figs. 7.17 and 7.18, one can also find that trademark cases accounts for the majority of IP administrative cases in China. This trend may be somewhat due to the efficiency and effectiveness of the administrative enforcement mechanism for trademarks (although this in not certain from the statistics alone), as well as the propensity for commercial reasons for businesses to use the mechanism and the relative technical ease with which such cases can be investigated and dealt with relative to more sophisticated cases involving patents, for example. Meanwhile, during trademark administrative enforcement, many trademark-related criminal activities have been discovered and transferred to the PSB, making it a very important platform to bridge the divide between administrative enforcement and criminal punishment.

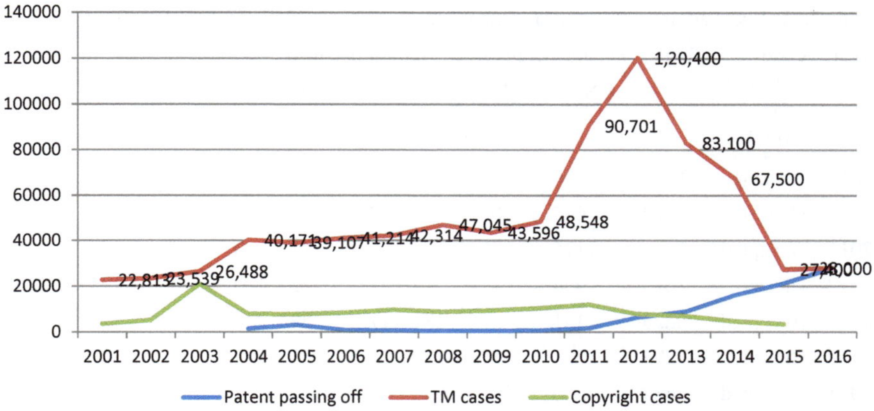

Fig. 7.17 Number of patent passing-off cases, trademark cases, and copyright cases enforced respectively by IPOs, TMOs, and copyright enforcement agents from 2001 to 2016. *Sources* Patent Annual Report from SIPO, China IPR Yearbook, Annual Report of China's IPR Protection Status

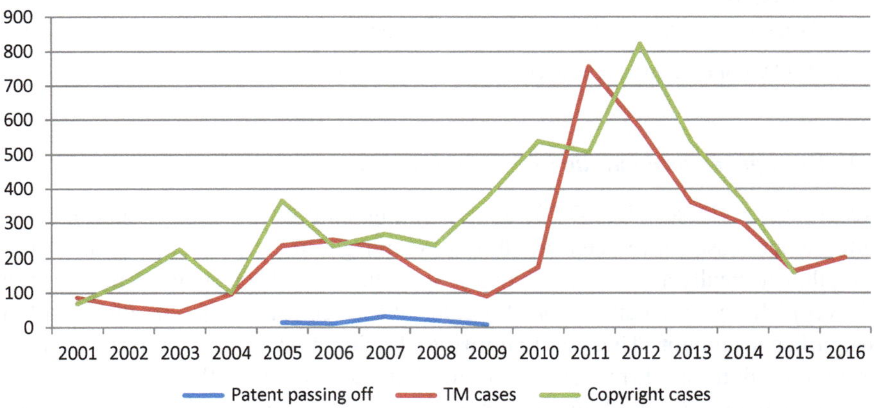

Fig. 7.18 Number of cases transferred to the PSB respectively by IPOs, TMOs, and copyright enforcement agents from 2001 to 2016. *Sources* Patent Annual Report from SIPO, China IPR Yearbook, Annual Report of China's IPR Protection Status

The complexity of determining IP infringement as well as the lack of administrative staff at local IPOs may explain the low number of patent enforcement cases in China in the early periods in which this enforcement was available. However, the number of administrative enforcements in patent cases has increased notably since 2010 (e.g., see Fig. 7.17). This may reflect the improvement of the efficiency and effectiveness of local IPOs in administering IPOs (although this in not certain from the statistics alone), and the relative propensity for rights holders to use local administrative enforcement for patents in China. More data about local governmental offices' administration enforcement of IP are available in Annex B.

Table 7.22 Local administrative enforcement against patent infringement (2010–2015)

Year	Cases accepted and closed	Total	Country/region of origin of patentee								
			CN	US	JP	GB	DE	KR	HK	TW	Others
2010	Accepted	1077	986	8	11	2	0	4	1	15	50
	Closed	712	634	10	8	2	2	3	3	20	30
2011	Accepted	1286	1176	10	16	3	25	0	8	9	39
	Closed	1019	936	7	7	2	22	0	6	12	27
2012	Accepted	2225	2141	3	8	17	29	2	5	2	18
	Closed	1294	1203	5	13	10	33	3	11	8	8
2013	Accepted	4684	4366	56	60	22	12	4	3	6	155
	Closed	3536	3270	48	44	25	10	3	3	1	132
2014	Accepted	7671	7157	62	58	18	109	7	11	13	236
	Closed	7640	7128	63	77	17	93	4	5	13	240
2015	Accepted	35,844	35,099	119	129	22	60	90	4	28	293
	Closed	35,654	34,917	120	125	23	74	85	10	29	271

Source SIPO, Annual Report of Chinese Patent Investigation Data (2010–2015)

(ii) ***Foreign versus domestic users of the system***

According to Tables 7.22–7.23, an increasing number of patent administrative enforcement cases have been raised by foreign right holders in recent years. However, they normally account less than 5% of all the cases. Then again, as a proportion of overall IP enforcement actions brought by foreign firms in China this is not an insignificant amount. The vast majority of IP litigation in the courts in China is brought by domestic firms rather than foreign ones (Wild 2010). Further, our consultations with large, medium, and small-sized foreign firms in China confirm that sometimes they indeed make use of local administrative patent enforcement in China, especially in regions where they have confidence in the authorities and their ability the provide sound investigations (e.g., in Shanghai).

In 2014 and 2015, there was a decline in the number of both trademark infringement and counterfeiting (TIC) and other trademark offenses (TO) (see Table 7.24). Nevertheless, the ratio of trademark infringement cases brought by foreign parties has continued to grow since 2012 and reached 23.59% of all cases in 2015. Judging from these figures, it appears that foreign right holders are more willing to use the local administrative IP enforcement mechanism to enforce their trademark rights in China. Further, as mentioned in the above section on patents, these figures should be considered alongside the fact that the vast majority of IP litigation in the courts in China is brought by domestic firms rather than foreign ones (see Wild 2010). Therefore, as a proportion of overall IP enforcement actions brought by foreign firms in China, these administrative-enforcement-specific figures on trademark usage reflect notable use of the local IP administrative enforcement by foreign rights holders. Further, our

Table 7.23 Local IP enforcement against patent passing-off (2010–2015)

Year	Number	Type of patentee[a]											
		A	B	C	**D**	**E**	**F**	G	H	I	J	**K**	L
2010	728	65	442	3	**19**	**28**	**40**	6	0	0	75	**0**	50
2011	1704	28	1256	26	**34**	**18**	**41**	1	0	0	134	**38**	128
2012	6521	52	4774	76	**206**	**103**	**237**	15	13	0	783	**7**	246
2013	11,171	803	6442	649	**346**	**348**	**734**	6	0	0	1088	**28**	827
2014	16,259	798	11,058	164	**406**	**213**	**424**	14	6	2	1806	**7**	1361
2015	21,237	763	14,280	47	**592**	**545**	**393**	5	2	24	2418	**0**	2168

Source SIPO, Annual Report of Chinese Patent Investigation Data (2010–2015). *Legend* A: state-owned enterprises; B: private enterprises; C: collective enterprises; D: foreign sole-funded enterprises; E: enterprises with sole funds from Hong Kong, Macao and Taiwan; F: joint-venture enterprises; G: institutions; H: universities; I: non-governmental organizations; J: individuals; K: foreign enterprises or organizations; L: others

Table 7.24 Figures on common trademark offenses and infringement cases in China handled by local IP administrative authorities in China

Year	Total number of cases (TO)		Among number of foreign-related cases		Total number of cases (TIC)		Among number of foreign-related cases	
	Total	Complaint cases	Subtotal	Complaint cases	Total	Complaint cases	Subtotal	Complaint cases
2012	7142	1402	258	26	59,085	14,239	14,033	4579
2013	6896	1114	99	29	49,971	13,656	11,636	4434
2014	5231	856	208	55	37,219	11,477	9636	3851
2015	3373	531	85	23	27,379	8984	6460	2764

Source China IP Statistic Yearbook. *TO* trademark offense, *TIC* trademark infringement and counterfeiting. Data from 2014 and 2015

consultations with large, medium, and small-sized foreign firms in China confirm that they often indeed make heavy use of local administrative trademark enforcement in China, especially in regions where they have confidence in the authorities and their ability the provide sound investigations.

Other commentary

China's system of IP administrative enforcement has been criticized by scholars (e.g., Torremans 2007) and foreign governments (e.g., Office of the U.S. Trade representative 2007) as being weak and incapable of discouraging IP infringement. However, the reality today is that the mechanism is working to some extent to discourage IP infringement. The previously reviewed data shows that administrative enforcement has been increasingly used in China. Further, the recent revision to China's Trademark Law, the Anti-Unfair Competition Law the Implementing Regulation of Copyright Law, and the ongoing drafting of the fourth Revision of Patent law all enhance the level of punishment against IP infringements, including the amount that local administrative IP authorities can themselves administer.

As discussed in Chap. 2, the fourth draft of the Patent Law proposes to give more power to local authorities to enforcement patents, such as the ability to punish those that resist the local IP office's evidence collection efforts, grant damages to patent right holders, and impose putative damages against intentional infringers. However, as discussed in further detail in Chap. 2, there are concerns that expansion of local administrative power is not within international norms and therefore could be problematic, and that it could increase the complexity of patent enforcement in China (Zhang 2013). As such, SIPO's attempt to expand the powers of local administrative enforcement authorities has somewhat changed during the drafting of the fourth revision to the patent law. In later drafts, due to the concerns expressed about the significantly expanded powers given to local administrative authorities in prior drafts of the law, SIPO suggested limiting the expansion of powers for local authorities to mainly the ability to confiscate infringement-related accounting documents among other materials and impose higher fines for infringement, especially on those repeated, group, and intentional infringers.

Another concern about administrative enforcement in China involves its protectionist tendencies. However, judging from the number of cases enforced by local administrative agents, especially the increasing number of foreign rights holders using this system, it is unfair to say protectionism significantly hampers the effectiveness of the administrative enforcement system. Concerns about protectionism could be alleviated via joint enforcement activities among different departments and regions in China as well as by supervision via the judicial review. At the same time, it is rare to have protectionist decisions in administration enforcement of complex infringement cases because administrative agents at present have no real power to grant damages and IP right holders normally do not rely on the administrative route to stop the infringing activities in complex cases (rather they primarily use the route for more straightforward cases).

A very important aspect of IP administrative enforcement in China often ignored by observers is that it plays an essential role in bridging the IP administrative enforcement and criminal enforcement. Therefore, it may greatly affect the efficiency and effectiveness of IP criminal enforcement in China. The involvement of professional IP staff during the administrative investigation of IP infringement can also be a cost-saving way to support IP criminal enforcement in later stages of a case, especially given the fact that most judges in criminal tribunals in China are not skilled hearing IP cases in particular.

Another significant concern of both domestic and foreign IP right holders in China regards local protectionism. It is difficult to discern blatant protectionism from available data on local IP administrative enforcement in China. However, our consultations suggest that it is indeed a problem. As with judicial IP protectionism, mentioned previously, IP administrative enforcement protectionism in China can take the form of intentionally delayed action or inappropriate decisions. In fact, it is a problem that has attracted the attention of Chinese legislators. Deputies of National People's Congress have proposed to eliminate local protectionism in IP enforcement by establishing a national enforcement system and enforcement supervision mechanism to quickly response to and harmonize the standard of administrative IP enforcement across China (Qiao 2009).

Further to this initiative, the Central Committee of the Communist Party of China (CCCPA) and the State Council issued a high-profile policy statement on protection of property rights in November 2016 entitled the Opinions of the CPC Central Committee and the State Council on Perfecting Property Right Protection System to Protect Property Rights according to Law. According to this statement, the following administrative measures will be introduced to strengthen China's system for IP protection and enforcement: (i) establish a credit blacklist against those willful infringers; (ii) collect information of counterfeit's origin and publicize the information of administrative punishments; (iii) strengthen the connection between administrative enforcement and criminal enforcement across China; and (iv) improve the IP enforcement mechanism relating to foreign interests in China.

In addition to this 2016 statement, a lower level statement on implementing the IP strategy was issued by The Joint Working Office of State Council for IP Strategy Implementation on June 23, 2017. The Implementation Plan reiterates the need to strengthen IP protection by revising various IP related laws and regulations including Patent Law, Copyright Law, the New Plant Variety Regulation and so on. It also assigns specific tasks for further reform to different governmental agents. For example, the Organization Department of the CPC Central Committee should work with other agents to formulate examination rules for party and government leading cadres, reflecting the relevant content and requirements of IP protection; and the Ministry of Science and Technology and SIPO should revise the rules related to national science and technology plans and IP management system of major special projects.

7.6 Efficiency and Effectiveness of Arbitration and Mediation

Introduction to the system

Aside from judicial and administrative IP enforcement, IP right holders in China can try ADR such as arbitration and mediation to protect their interests. ADR has many advantages over litigation: it offers a chance to resolve, in a single procedure, a dispute in a number of different countries; it offers greater control over the way the dispute is resolved; its proceedings are private; among other benefits.

China's IP laws clearly recognize mediation and arbitration as a legal way to solve IP disputes and many policies have been passed to encourage the use of them. For example, in June 2016, the Supreme People's Court issued two important documents to highlight the importance of ADR and mediation: (i) Opinions on Further Deepening the Reform of the Diversified Dispute Settlement Mechanism by People's Courts; and (ii) Provisions on Mediation Invited by People's Courts. In March 2017, SIPO issued the Notice on Carrying out the Pilot Project of Arbitration and Mediation of Intellectual Property Disputes.

Despite these initiatives, the development and popularity of IP mediation and arbitration in China are quite different. As to mediation, China has a very strong tradition in this field and develops a flexible mechanism to mediate disputes. This leads to the popularity of mediation in various dispute solution processes. In stark contrast to this, however, the development of the arbitration system in China is unsatisfactory.

Before 1995, China's arbitration system was like that of most East European Countries (Peng and Wu 2009) and had only a limited number of organizations to arbitrate disputes relating to labor, economic contracts and international affairs. Since the implementation of its Arbitration Law in 1995, China has gradually developed its arbitration system. According to Supreme People's Court, there were 251 arbitration organizations nationwide in China at the end of 2015. They received a total of 136,924 cases, 100 times the rate in 1995. However, the usage rate of arbitration in China is still relatively low. According to available statistics, the number of cases received by Chinese arbitration organizations as well as the value involved in such cases in 2014 is only about 1% of those by Chinese courts. These rates are quite low compared to trends in arbitration in some foreign countries (Jiang 2016a, b). Partly because of the low usage rate of the arbitration and the litigation explosion in China across many areas of law, the reform of China's present arbitration system is now undergoing a review and should be an important area in which future reforms should be made.

To be sure, IPR arbitration in particular in China is under-developed. In December 2000, the Domain Name Dispute Settlement Center of CIETAC was established and began operations in 2005 under the name of the Internet Disputes Settlement Center. In 2007, China established its first five IP arbitration organizations in Xiamen, Wuhan, Tianjin, Xi'an, and Guangzhou. In 2008, Shanghai Arbitration Court of IP was established within Shanghai Arbitration Commission. After the establishment of FTZ, certain IP Arbitration Courts or Centers have also been set up to assist IP dispute resolution. Despite these initiatives, IPR arbitration in China remains at a stage of infancy and continues to face many challenges (Zhang and Zhang 2014).

Statistical analysis

(i) ***Mediation***

According to the Annual Report on Judicial Protection of IPR in China Court, from 2002 to 2006, the average mediation and the withdrawal rate (M&W Rate) of IP civil cases of first instance was 52.57%. The M&W Rate for the most recent five years for which data is available (2012–2016) is higher (Table 7.25).

Many IP disputes enforced via administrative enforcement have been resolved in the form of mediation. For example, statistics from the Guangzhou IP Office show that the M&W Rate of cases in 2005, 2006, and 2007 were 87.04, 84.21, and 85.71%, respectively (Xu 2008).

(ii) ***Arbitration***

As alluded to previously, there is not a significant number of IP arbitration disputes in China. Taking the Shanghai IP Arbitration Tribunal as an example (see Table 7.26),

Table 7.25 Mediation and withdrawal (M&W) rate of IP civil cases in China

Type	2009	2010	2011	2012	2013	2014	2015	2016
A	61.08	66.76	72.72	67.3	68.45	65.96	63.78	64.21
B	–	–	–	–	–	29.28	–	27.44

Source Annual Report on Judicial Protection of IPR in China Court; Annual Working Report by the Supreme People's Court; Judicial Big Data Report (A = M&W Rate of IP Civil cases of First instance; B = M&W Rate of second instance)

Table 7.26 Caseload and case types at Shanghai IP Arbitration Tribunal

Type of cases	2014	2015	2016
Franchise contract	82	35	77
Technical service contracts	18	29	37
Technology development contract	11	17	27
Technology transfer contract cases	2	0	2
Technical consultation contract	2	0	0
copyright contract	1	3	0
Publication contract	1	0	0
Patent licensing	0	2	0
Trademark contract	0	1	5
Cooperation contract	0	1	2
Service contract	0	18	6
Sale contract	0	1	0
Assignment contract	0	4	0
Sum of case number	117	111	155
Sum of value involved	–	99,638,246	108,223,643

Source Shanghai IP Arbitration Tribunal

that tribunal receives an average of 116 cases per year. All of the disputes are contract disputes and most of them are franchise contract and technical service disputes (accounting for 80% the total value at stake in the cases). These figures are consistent with the commonly-held understanding that arbitration is more likely to be an alternative to solve disputes when the parties involved have a previous contractual relationship. To our knowledge, parties involved in IP infringement disputes in China very rarely, if ever, choose arbitration to solve their disputes.

Commentary

The high M&W Rate in IP disputes in China can be at least partially attributed to the mediation-friendly culture and policies in China. In our experience, Chinese courts often adhere to the principle of "mediation has priority" and "Combination of trial and mediation". Various types of mediation mechanism such as mediators, lawyer mediators, professional mediators, and specially invited mediators have been introduced before and during the litigation to alleviate the pressure from litigation explosion. Many IP-specialized "people mediation" organizations have also been established to assist the mediation work outside the courtroom (Li 2017).

Compared to the relatively vibrant mediation system in China, there are many limitations and deficiencies of China's current Arbitration Law. The law has long been criticized by lawyers and scholars for not fully respecting the autonomy of the parties in disputes and limiting the freedom of the parties' choice, which goes against the general rules and tendency of international business arbitration such as the UNCITRAL Model Law. For example, institutional arbitration is the only form of arbitration accepted by the current Chinese Arbitration Law, while ad hoc arbitration is not (Lai 2015). In terms of the selection of arbitrators, parties in China cannot choose their arbitrators from outside the list provided by the arbitration institution (Art. 13, Arbitration Law). Further, the current arbitration procedure in China borrows many rules from civil procedure and makes it a quasi-litigation proceeding. From the acceptance of request, formation of tribunal, and trial to rules of evidence, there is virtually no difference between these two procedures (Jiang and Liao 2008).

This low level of autonomy in arbitration cases for the parties involved decreases the convenience and flexibility of China's arbitration system. The over-reliance on judicature also adversely affects the efficiency and effectiveness of arbitration in China. Moreover, because the current arbitration mechanisms in China are not in accordance with international practices (generally speaking), arbitration services in China are usually not the first choice for parties involved in international business disputes. This, in turn, has a negative effect on the specialization of the Chinese arbitration system and weakens the international competence and credibility of Chinese arbitration organizations (Zhang and Zhang 2014).

Some reforms have been made to China's arbitration system, many of which are concentrated in certain FTZs. On April 8, 2014, the Shanghai International Arbitration Center issued the China (Shanghai) FTZ Arbitration Rules. Under the rule, the state should respect the autonomy of parties engaged in disputes related to commerce in the FTZ and the rules are generally in accordance with internationally-accepted arbitration practices (Zhang and Zhang 2014). For example, the rules allow parties to choose arbitrators outside the list of registered arbitrators (Art. 27). The rules also propose varied rules of evidence (Art. 44) and allow consolidation of arbitration and joining of third parties to the arbitration (Art. 38). An amicable arbitration system (Art. 56), emergency tribunal (Art. 21) and small dispute application (Art. 11) are also permissible. The rules also grant arbitration tribunals and emergency tribunals the authority to determine interim measures, the scope of which covers preservation of property, and evidence and act preservation (Art. 18). Foreign arbitrators can also be invited to arbitrate cases.

7.7 Summary

China's IP enforcement environment is extremely complex. The country has a unique model for IP enforcement in which many local administrative agencies are used in addition to those state bodies often used in other countries for enforcing IPR (e.g., the judiciary and customs). Coordination across this massive system has been challenging.

There are significant differences in the strength of enforcement of IP rights available in different provinces in China. Quantitative and qualitative research finds that provinces in the eastern coastal region of China tend to more strongly enforce IP rights. However, paradoxically, these areas are often also cited as hotspots for problematic IP enforcement. This paradox is likely partially explained by a causal chain where a significant amount of economic activity is centered in these areas so they are more prone to IPR infringements in the first place, meanwhile high corresponding caseloads may sometimes slow the speed of IP enforcement. Also, given that businesses often have the most vested in these regions, a less-than-optimal enforcement outcome therein (whether owed to protectionism or other factors) can have a more pronounced impact than a similar outcome in a region in which less is vested.

Based upon our quantitative and qualitative research, we find that, generally speaking, the courts in China handling IP disputes are more efficient and effective today than in the past. Most IP cases today do not face the "acceptance difficulty" and "overdue problem" that once plagued IP rights holders in the past. This being said, if litigation suspension occurs because of a corresponding IP invalidation case or from jurisdictional suspension issues, IP litigation procedures can still be lengthy in China. The win rate for plaintiffs in IP infringement cases in China, especially for foreign firms, is high. This being said, the majority of IP lawsuits in China end up ultimately being dealt with by meditation or are withdrawn.

Despite these positive developments in IP enforcement in China, the effectiveness of judicial IP enforcement remains undermined by the low damages traditionally awarded in IP cases. Suboptimal IP infringement deterrence in China can, to a great extent, be attributed to the fact that Chinese judges rely on statutory damages rather than other methods of calculating damages afforded by the law. Moreover, the statutory damages granted in most IP cases in China are far below the cap specified in the law. Although these problems are relatively well known, there is limited research properly investigating the real reasons why judges behave this way. We argue that the propensity to rely on statutory damages in IP cases in China reflects the reality that many parties in IP lawsuits in China fail to offer adequate evidence of damages, and given that IP rights holders themselves often request statutory damages. Further, and importantly, these trends are explained by the less-than-optimal design of some judges' performance evaluation criteria and the lack of discovery procedures and other insufficient procedures for challenging evidence in China. The state has made some recent attempts to address some of these issues.

Further, there is empirical evidence that local plaintiffs have a better chance of winning IP disputes in China than ones originally registered in different areas. Also, although not commonly reflected in available aggregate statistics, our consultations identify cases where the authorities intervened in IP judgements, rulings or acceptance of cases appeared intentionally delayed, and IP judgments were otherwise inappropriate according to the law and facts at hand. This type of protectionism can favor domestic firms over foreign firms, or one local domestic Chinese firm over another. Protectionism is always problematic because even a handful of significant protectionist judgements can completely block innovative firms out of the market. And, more generally, unfair court rulings intent on protecting local firms undermine the sense of fairness in China's IP judicial system which can ultimately restrain innovation investments. The state has recently launched some initiatives in an attempt to deal with this issue.

Only a small proportion of IP infringements in China end up in criminal courts. However, our quantitative and qualitative analysis finds that more IP criminal cases have been brought to the police, prosecutors, and courts in China in recent years, and the number of suspects convicted is also growing. Then again, in order to further disincentivize criminal IP infringements in China, more cooperation is needed between relevant administrative agencies, the police, and the prosecutors; and the performance evaluations of some of these authorities should be revised.

Improvements have been made to local IP administrative enforcement in China in recent years, although there is still a debate about how to best improve this type of enforcement. The number of disputes handled by local IP administrative enforcement authorities in China has risen rapidly in recent years. Measures for more severely punishing and otherwise enforcing IP rights, including by local IP administrative enforcement authorities, have been recently introduced in various Chinese IP laws. However, there is an ongoing debate about the extent to which the power of local patent administrative enforcement authorities in particular should be expanded given that patent matters that are quite technically complex and therefore require exceptionally well-trained experts to administer. Also, there continue to be cases of local protectionism by local IP administrative enforcement authorities—although some recent reforms have been proposed to help address this issue.

Several reforms should be instituted to address the aforementioned challenges to IP enforcement in China. First, the state should expand the size and quality of China's IP enforcement infrastructure (e.g., by increasing numbers of quality staff in courts and establishing more specialized IP courts). Second, the state should strengthen procedures and practices to make judicial IP enforcement more of a deterrent to IP infringement (e.g., in terms of procedures to deter local protectionism; access to and admissibility of evidence; enforcement of judicial orders and judgments, and fines and sanctions for noncompliance; and increasing damages typically awarded in practice). Third, the state should improve coordination of IP enforcement (e.g., better coordinate among local administrative enforcement bodies; and improve coordination of civil, administrative enforcement, and criminal procedures).

References

Ang, J., Y. Cheng, and C. Wu. 2014. Does enforcement of intellectual property rights matter in China? Evidence from financing and investment choices in the high-tech industry. *Review of Economics and Statistics* 96: 332–348.

Bloch, D., G. Chan, and E. Taylor. 2014. Chinese intellectual property litigation: Theories and remedies. In Doing business in China, ed. M. Moser and F. Yu. New York: Juris Publishers.

Changsha Intermediate People's Court. 2016a. Report on Damages Decisions in IP Civil Cases heard by Intermediate People's Court. http://www.weixinnu.com/tag/article/2244248386.

Changsha Intermediate People's Court. 2016. 知识产权民事案件损害赔偿额判定状况 (2011–2015) (Report on damages decisions in IP civil cases heard by Changsha intermediate people's court 2011–2015) (in Chinese). http://www.weixinnu.com/tag/article/2244248386#10006-weixin-1-52626-6b3bffd01fdde4900130bc5a2751b6d1.

Chen, Z. 2015. 积极提赔偿证据 客观看赔偿数额 (Actively offer evidence of damages, objectively treat the granted damages) (in Chinese). http://www.nipso.cn/onews.asp?id=22789.

China IP Index Report Research Team. 2016a. 北京知识产权诉讼报告 (Beijing IP Litigation Report 2016) (in Chinese), China IPR Index Report 2016, China Finance and Economics Press.

China IP Index Report, 2016b. 上海知识产权诉讼报告 (Shanghai IP Litigation Report 2016) (in Chinese), at China IPR Index Report 2016, China Finance and Economics press.

Cohen, M. 2016b. Patent litigation, local protectionism and empiricism: Data sources and data critiques. China IPR, available at https://chinaipr.com/2016/03/10/patent-litigation-local-protectionism-and-empiricism-data-sources-and-data-critiques/.

Cotter, T. 2016. A comparative law and economics analysis of damages for patent infringement. In *Comparative law and economics*, ed. T. Eisenberg and G. Ramello, 262–281. Cheltenham, UK: Edward Elgar.

Deng, Z., P. Zhang, and H. Wen. 2013. Dislocation and return: Analysis and regulation of adverse selection of coercive measures in civil action—based on 784 related cases in certain provinces in central China (in Chinese). The Collected Awarded Papers of National Court on the 25th Academic Seminar: Impartial Judiciary and Implementation of Administrative Law.

Dimitrov, M. 2004. *Administrative decentralization, legal fragmentation, and the rule of law: The enforcement of intellectual property rights laws in China, Russia, Taiwan, and the Czech Republic*. Doctoral Dissertation, Stanford University, Palo Alto, California.

Du, J., Y. Lu, and Z. Tao. 2008. Economic Institutions and FDI location choice: Evidence of US multinationals in China. *Journal of Comparative Economics* 36: 412–429.

Fang, L., J. Lerner, C. Wu. 2016. *Intellectual property rights protection, ownership, and innovation: Evidence from China*. NBER Working Paper, available at http://www.nber.org/papers/w22685.

Fang, X., 2008. 关于设立民事管辖回避制度的思考 (Suggestion to establish civil jurisdiction challenge system) (in Chinese). *People Judiciary* 13.

General Administration of Customs. 中国海关知识产权保护状况 (The China Customs IP Protection Status) (in Chinese). http://www.customs.gov.cn/publish/portal0/tab49564/info846639.htm.

Ginarte, J., and W.G. Park. 1997. Determinants of patent rights: A cross-national study. *Research Policy* 26: 283–301.

Global IP Project. 2014. Global patent litigation report. Darts IP/Bureau National Affairs, available at https://www.dartsip.com/newsletter/201508/AnnualGlobalPatentLitigationReport2014.pdf).

Guangming Daily. 2016. 海关加强知识产权国际联合执法 (China Customs strengthen international joint IP enforcement) (in Chinese). http://news.xinhuanet.com/politics/2016-11/23/c_129374258.htm.

Guangzhou Intermediate People's Court. 2014. 模糊的边界: 知识产权赔偿问题的实务困境与对策 (The vague boundary: Dilemma and policy about damages in IP cases) (in Chinese). *Rule of Law Forum* 3: 157–176.

Hammer, A., and K. Linton. 2011. China: Effects of intellectual property infringement and indigenous innovation policies on the U.S. economy. USITC Publication 4226.

Han, Y., and H. Li. 2005. Quantitative analysis of intellectual property protection levels in China (in Chinese). *Studies in Science of Science* 6.

He, Z., and Y. Yuan. 2015. 知识产权刑事司法—中国特色实证研究 (Intellectual property criminal judiciary: Empirical study on Chinese characteristic) (in Chinese). Peking University Press.

IP Center of Middlesouth University of Financial and Political Science. 2014. 知识产权侵权损害赔偿案例实证研究报告 (The research report of rewarded damages in IP infringement cases) (in Chinese). http://www.chinacourt.org/article/detail/2013/04/id/948907.shtml.

IP House. 2016. 北京知识产权法院2015年度司法数据分析报告 [Analysis report on judicial protection data of Beijing IP court (2015)] (in Chinese). http://www.iphouse.cn/report.html.

IP House. 2017a. 北京知识产权法院2015年度司法数据分析报告 [Analysis report on judicial protection data of Beijing IP court (2016)] (in Chinese). http://www.iphouse.cn/report.html.

IP House. 2017b. 专利侵权诉讼周期分析报告 (Report about the processing time of patent infringement cases) (in Chinese). http://www.sohu.com/a/134589714_221481.

IP House. 2017c. 2016年中国法院商标案件诉讼数据分析报告 (Data analysis of trademark Lawsuits in Chinese courts in 2016) (in Chinese). http://www.iphouse.cn/report.html.

Jiang, H. 2016.《仲裁法》二十周年回望: 民商事仲裁危机与重塑 (Arbitration law over 20 years: Crisis and reconstruction of civil and commercial arbitration) (in Chinese) *Law Research* 7, 94–100.

Jiang, Song. 2016b. 知识产权损害赔偿问题探讨:以实证分析为视角 (Discussion on compensation for intellectual property damage: From the perspective of empirical analysis) (in Chinese). *Intellectual Property* 5: 10–19.

Jiang, X., and Liao, Y. 2008. 重构我国仲裁证据制度之探析 (Explore and analyze the reconstruction of arbitration evidence system in China) (in Chinese). Seeker 5.

Jin, H.J. 2015. 我国知识产权经典案例统计分析—以《最高人民法院公报》(1985–2014)为据 (Statistical analysis of China's classical IP cases based on the Bulletin of Supreme People's Court 1985-2014) (in Chinese). *Intellectual Property* 6: 31–40.

Judicial Big Data Research Institute. 2017. 司法大数据专题报告: 知识产权侵权 (Judicial Big Data Report of IP Infringement) (in Chinese). http://www.gdcourts.gov.cn/web/content/37708-?lmdm=2000.

Lai, Z. 2015. 我国商事仲裁制度的阙如: 以临时仲裁在上海自贸区的试构建为视角 (On the vacancy of commercial arbitration system: From the perspective of establishment on temporary arbitration in Shanghai FTZ) (in Chinese). *Hebei Law Science* 2: 156–165.

Li, S. 2017. 最高人民法院多元化纠纷解决机制改革意见和特邀调解规定的理解和适用 (Understanding and application of Supreme People's Court's Opinion of ADR Mechanism Reform and Rule of Special Invited Mediation) (in Chinese). People's Court Press, 2017.

Liu, H., 2010a. The policy and targets of criminal enforcement of intellectual property rights in china and the United States, Washington International Law Journal. 24(1).

Liu, H. 2010b. The criminal enforcement of intellectual property rights in China: Recent developments and implications. *Asian Criminology* 5: 137–156.

Long, C.X., and J. Wang. 2014. 中国司法地方保护主义: 基于知识产权案例的研究 (Judicial protectionism in China: research on IP cases) (in Chinese). *China Economic Studies* 3: 3–18.

Long, C.X., and J. Wang. 2015. Judicial local protectionism in China: An empirical study of IP cases. *International Review of Law and Economics* 42: 48–59.

Love, B., C. Helmers, M. Eberhardt. 2016. Patent litigation in China: Protecting rights or the local economy? *Vanderbilt Journal of Entertainment & Technology Law* 18.

Luo, X. 2013. Regional differences and economic performance analysis on China's intellectual property rights index (in Chinese). *Science and Technology Management Research*, available at http://en.cnki.com.cn/Article_en/CJFDTotal-KJGL201321024.htm.

Mertha, A. 2005. *The politics of piracy*. Ithaca, NY: Cornell University Press.

Nanjing Railway & Transportation Court. 知识产权侵权诉讼成本与效率分析—基于南京法院案件的实证研究 (Report on litigation cost and efficient analysis of IP infringement—An Empirical Study based on cases in Nanjing area) (in Chinese), available at http://www.360doc7.net/articlenew/556527148.html.

NPC. 2014. The report of the law enforcement inspection group of the standing committee of national people's congress on the inspection of the patent law's implementation (in Chinese).
Office of the U.S. Trade representative. 2007. Special 301 report. https://ustr.gov/sites/default/files/2007%20Special%20301%20Report.pdf.
Peng, S., and F. Wu. 2009. Solutions for disputes over intellectual property between Taiwan and China—Analyzing arbitration. *Barry Law Review* 13: Iss. 1, Article 5. http://lawpublications.barry.edu/barrylrev/vol13/iss1/5.
Qiao, T. 2009. 关于消除知识产权执法中地方保护的建议(Proposal for the elimination of local protection in enforcement of intellectual property rights) (in Chinese). (Deputies of National People's Congress) http://money.163.com/09/0306/10/53NF5VMG0025388Q.html#from=keyscan.
SAIC. 中国商标战略年度发展报告 (China trademark strategy annual report) (in Chinese). http://www.saic.gov.cn/sbj/tzgg/index_1.html.
Sepetys, K., and A. Cox. 2009. Intellectual property rights protection in China: Trends in litigation and economic damages. NERA Consulting, available at http://www.ipeg.com/blog/wp-content/uploads/NERA-IP-Protection_China_2009.pdf.
Shanghai IP Court. 上海知识产权法院专利案件审判情况 (2015–2016年) (The trials of patent cases in Shanghai IP court (2015–2016) (in Chinese), available at https://www.sohu.com/a/134717939_726435.
She Hans. 2018. China mulls "leapfrog appeal" for patent and other technical cases, available at https://www.linkedin.com/wukong-web/articleShare/6460141770821943296?trk=wukong-web_wecaht-share_message&from=singlemessage.
SIPO. 中国知识产权年鉴 (China IPR Yearbooks) (in Chinese). IPR Press.
SIPO. 国家知识产权局年报 (Annual working reports) (in Chinese), available at http://www.sipo.gov.cn/gk/ndbg/.
SIPO. 中国知识产权保护状况 (Annual reports of China IPR protection status) (in Chinese). available at http://www.sipo.gov.cn/gk/zscqbps/.
SIPO. 2015. SIPO Survey on Chinese patents, available at http://www.sipo.gov.cn/tjxx/yjcg_tjxx/1052502.htm.
SIPO. 2016a. SIPO Survey on Chinese patents, available at http://www.gov.cn/xinwen/2017-07/01/content_5207170.htm.
SIPO, 2016b. 2015年中国专利调查数据报告. (Report of Chinese Patent Investigation Data 2015) (in Chinese) http://www.sipo.gov.cn/tjxx/yjcg/201607/t20160701_1277842.html.
SIPO. 2017. 2016年中国专利调查数据报告 (Report of Chinese Patent Investigation Data 2016) (in Chinese) http://www.gov.cn/xinwen/2017-07/01/content_5207170.htm.
Supreme People's Court. 2009. 关于进一步加强司法便民工作的若干意见 (Several opinions on further strengthening the work of judicial convenience) (in Chinese).
Supreme People's Court. 2010, 2011, 2012, 2013, 2014. 中国法院知识产权司法保护状况 (Annual report(s) on judicial protection of IPR in China court) (in Chinese), available at http://www.court.gov.cn/search.html?content=知识产权司法保护状况.
Supreme People's Court. 2015. 人民法院工作年度报告 (Annual working report of people's court) (in Chinese), available at http://www.court.gov.cn/zixun-xiangqing-13842.html.
Supreme People's Court. 2017a. 人民法院工作年度报告 (Annual working report of people's court) (in Chinese), available at http://m.thepaper.cn/newsDetail_forward_1778177?from=singlemessage&isappinstalled=0.
Supreme People's Court. 2017b. 最高人民法院关于充分发挥审判职能作用为企业家创新创业营造良好法治环境的通知 (Notice of the supreme people's court on giving full play to the role of trial functions to create a good legal environment for entrepreneur innovation) (in Chinese).
Torremans, P. et al. 2007. Intellectual property and TRIPS compliance in China: Chinese and European perspectives. Edward Elgar Publishing.
USPTO. 2011. Report on patent enforcement in China, Prepared by the U.S. patent and trademark office, available at http://www.uspto.gov/learning-and-resources/ip-policy/enforcement/report-patent-enforcement-china.

Wild, J. 2010. There is more IP litigation in China than anywhere else on earth. *Intellectual Assessment Management*, available at http://www.iam-media.com/blog/detail.aspx?g=3a9c9c06-dd4f-4adc-8e2f-5a6eadc847c1.

Yao, L., and Y. Rao. 2009. The measurement and regional differences of intellectual property rights protection in China. *International Business Research* 2: 108–114.

Xu, Y. 2008. 知识产权仲裁的理论与实践 (Theory and practice of intellectual property arbitration) (in Chinese). *Research on Arbitration* 01: 57–67.

Zhang, T. 2013. 有关专利法第四次修订的几点意见 (Comment on the Four Revision of Chinese Patent Law) (in Chinese), http://blog.sina.com.cn/s/blog_4d7d20930101a2xf.html.

Zhang, T. 2014. "专利流氓"威胁论:先见之明,抑或杞人忧天? (The threat of patent trll in China: A foresight or a fuss?) (in Chinese). *IP and Competition Law Review* 2 (IPR Press, Beijing).

Zhang, T., and W. J. Zhang. 2014. The improvement of intellectual property arbitration, mediation, and court procedures in the Shanghai Pilot Free Trade Zone. Report for EU-China IP Key project, available at www.ipkey.org/en/ip-law-document/download/2682/3396/23.

Zhang, W., and R. Ke. 2002. 诉讼过程中的逆向选择及其解释—以契约纠纷的基层法院判决书为例的经验研究 (Reverse choice in litigation and an explanation: Empirical research on the judgment of contract disputes in Chinese district courts) (in Chinese). *China Social Science* 2, 31–43.

Zhichantong. 2017. 2014–2017 年知识产权诉讼报告:权属侵权纠纷占93%,沿海地区成主战场 (2017年). Report on IP Litigation from 2014 to 2017 (in Chinese), available at http://mp.weixin.qq.com/s/9G3RL8vnEIIid1uyEp8ihw.

Zhou, Y. 2009. 试论我国知识产权海关保护制度的完善—以知识产权权利人与保护客体为视角 (Improvement on China's customs IP protection: from the perspective of IP right holders and subject matters) (in Chinese). *WTO Focus* 8, 10–15.

Chapter 8
Implications for Businesses

As illustrated throughout this book, although China's current IP regime poses a range of risks to various actors participating in the country's NIS, firms are often most directly and significantly impacted. In this chapter, we set-forth several basic tools that firms can use to manage these risks. We first discuss a few novel frameworks that integrate risk management tools with IP management concepts. We then discuss general best practices for managing IP in China.

8.1 Risk Management Tools for Managing IP in China

Perhaps surprisingly, there is relatively sparse literature integrating formal tools from the discipline of risk management with concepts from the discipline of IP management. However, doing so provides one useful framing to manage the range of hazards and costs that an IP regime can pose to firms. In this section, we attempt to develop several basic frameworks that bridge these two streams of literature while ensuring that the tools we generate are relevant for managing risks stemming from China's IP regime in particular.

The classic risk management process requires several steps: risk identification, risk analysis, prioritizing and planning for risk, managing risk, and monitoring and evaluating (M&E) risks and responses to them. Figure 8.1 depicts the interaction between these different steps. We discuss each of these steps and how they can be applied in the context of managing IP in China.

8.1.1 Identification of Risks from the IP Regime

The first step in the risk management process is to identify the risks a firm might face when doing business. Various checklists (e.g., Miller 1992) and frameworks are available to aid this process, such as SWOT, PESTLE, and SPECTRES (e.g., Clayton

D. Prud'homme and T. Zhang, *China's Intellectual Property Regime for Innovation*, https://doi.org/10.1007/978-3-030-10404-7_8

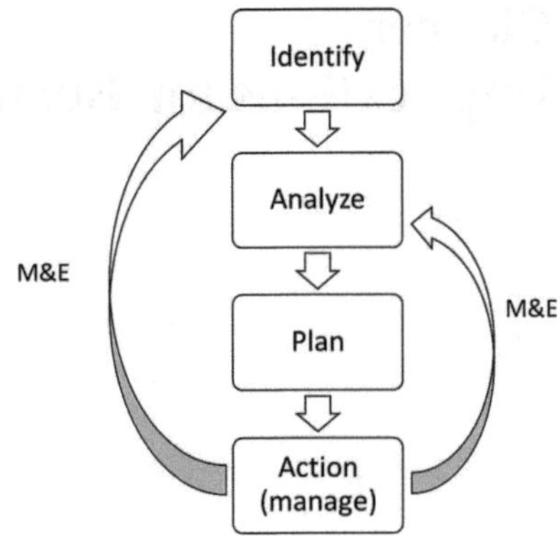

Fig. 8.1 Risk management process

2011; Olson 2016; Hopkin 2017). Some of these methods could be applied to help identify some risks that an IP regime poses. However, the framework developed in Prud'homme (2019) for determining the foreign business-friendliness/unfriendliness of an IP regime is more tailored to IP risk management. Although originally designed to assess the risks and costs that an IP regime poses to foreign firms, it in fact can be used to determine the risks that an IP regime poses to both foreign and domestic firms. The framework, which is depicted in Table 8.1, is grounded in theories about appropriability hazards, transaction costs, and entrepreneurial opportunities.

The framework is best applied by scanning the entirety of the IP regime (China's in our case) and identifying if any of the risks listed in the sub-indicators exist. The risks identified should then be written out next to each corresponding sub-indictor. This process can be completed by the IP and strategy managers, and potentially others, in a firm. The process can also be followed by more 'neutral' third parties (e.g., external legal and management scholars and practitioners). It can be helpful to break-down the IP regime into different components during this process in order to allow more granular analysis of each component. The chapter-based categorization of different IP regime components discussed throughout this book could be used, or a more general categorization relevant to China could be used (i.e., statutory IP laws, IP regulations and all other IP-related measures/policies, IP administration, and IP enforcement). The specific risks discussed throughout this book would of course be prime candidates to be identified in this process, although may be less relevant as China's IP regime evolves in the future.

It is risk management best practice to assign every identified risk a unique risk identification number ("Risk ID"). This ID and a short description of the risk can be inserted in a "Risk Register", which is a framework that allows managers to easily keep track of risks and how they are ultimately managed. A longer description of the risk can also be provided in the Risk Register or in a separate document linked to the Risk Register. An example of part of the risk register for identifying risks from the IP regime is depicted in Table 8.2. Within the Risk Register, each risk can further be categorized according to certain attributes, for example which type of IP is involved, which component of the IP regime is involved, and/or what type of

Table 8.1 Framework for measuring the risks from an IP regime

Indicator[a]	Sub-indicator[a]
Appropriability constraints on foreign MNCs	Suboptimal restrictions on breadth of IP rights (e.g., scope of patentable subject matter and number and scope of claims)
	Suboptimal restrictions on length of IP rights (duration)
	Suboptimal restrictions on maintaining/renewing IP rights
	Suboptimal restrictions on usage of one IP right alongside another IP right
	Suboptimal restrictions imposed on exploitation (i.e., licensing, assignment, and all other uses) of IP assets and related technology
	Suboptimal constraints imposed by state measures/practices, or lack thereof, on the ability to legally enforce (i.e., ensure compliance with) IP rights
Transaction costs[b] imposed on foreign MNCs	Excessive searching, screening, and bargaining costs to apply for and receive IP rights from the state (Excessiveness due to overly strict requirements for actually meeting IP eligibility (e.g., patentability) criteria, discrimination leading to delayed IP examination and granting, inefficiency leading to delayed IP examination and granting, discrimination leading to unfounded rejections/non-granting of IP rights, and/or opaque examination and granting procedures.)
	Excessive searching and screening costs to identify IP rights to invalidate, and excessive bargaining, decision-making, and monitoring and enforcement costs of invalidating IP rights (Excessiveness due to sheer quantity of rights in a technological field, quantity of low-quality rights in particular, and/or inadequate mechanisms to readily invalidate rights.)
	Excessive searching and screening costs to identify IP rights to in-license, and excessive bargaining, decision-making, servicing, and monitoring and enforcement costs of in-licensing others' IP rights or out-licensing own IP rights (Excessiveness due to sheer quantity of rights in a technological field, quantity of low-quality rights in particular, inadequate mechanisms to readily identify rights, excessive or insufficient legal appropriability offered by rights, and/or state restrictions on terms for licensing or assigning rights.)
	Excessive searching and screening costs to identify IP infringements, and excessive costs of enforcing (ensuring compliance with) IP rights (Excessiveness due to inadequate mechanisms deterring/dis-incentivizing IP infringement in the first place, overly burdensome requirements related to initiating IP enforcement actions, and/or due to intentional or unintentional lack of efficiency or effectiveness when determining and punishing IP infringements.)
	Excessive costs of switching suppliers, other alliance partners, technologies, and other business activities related to IP (Excessiveness due to insufficient legal appropriability offered by IP rights, inadequate mechanisms deterring/dis-incentivizing IP infringement in the first place, overly burdensome requirements related to initiating IP enforcement actions, and/or intentional or unintentional lack of efficiency or effectiveness when determining and punishing IP infringements.)

(continued)

Table 8.1 (continued)

Indicator[a]	Sub-indicator[a]
Entrepreneurial opportunity constraints imposed on foreign MNCs	Suboptimal limits on legal appropriability afforded by IP regime that indirectly dis-incentivizes entrepreneurial aspirations
	Suboptimal limits on legal appropriability that more directly dis-incentivizes entrepreneurial opportunities
	IP regime design limits IP-owners' entrepreneurial opportunities by raising the cost of delegating market development to an external party
	IP regime design imposes regulatory hurdles to pursuing innovation-based (rather than merely imitation-based) entrepreneurship opportunities

Source Adapted from Prud'homme (2019)
Note some indicators are inter-related
[a]The greater the constraint or cost described in the indicator/sub-indicator (in terms of frequency of occurrence and/or magnitude), the generally more *business-unfriendly* (less friendly) the IP regime. The lesser the constraints and costs (in terms of frequency of occurrence and/or magnitude), the *relatively more business-friendly* (less unfriendly) the IP regime
[b]The terms "transaction costs" and "costs" hereafter specifically refer to *excessive* transaction costs.

Table 8.2 IP regime risk identification part of Risk Register (example)

Risk ID	Category of risk	Short description of risk
...	...	...

risks are involved (e.g., drawing from Table 8.1), among other attributes. Although unnecessary complexity should be avoided, more than one level of categorization (i.e., categorization and subcategorization(s)) could be used.

8.1.2 Analyzing Risks from the IP Regime

The process for analyzing risks is commonly divided into two parts: assessing the likelihood of risks and assessing the impact of those risks if they were to materialize. Monte Carlo modelling is one of the more sophisticated methods for determining the likelihood of risks (Clayton 2011; Hopkin 2017). Yet several basic methods, namely qualitative indicators and numerical indicators, are also helpful to analyze the likelihood of risks (Clayton 2011; Hopkin 2017). When thinking about the likelihood of IP regime risks, managers should consider each risk identified and placed in the Risk Register and ask themselves: How likely are we to face this particular risk from the IP regime? There are numerous ways one could go about answering this question, each of which is best selected on a case-by-case basis. But most of these approaches will involve determination of the likelihood that the firm will engage *in the particular type of business activity at the heart of each risk* included in the Risk Register. This enables arrival at a very crude estimate of the likelihood of encountering the corresponding risk, and a more refined assessment can be conducted based upon that estimate. Table 8.3 provides some examples of basic approaches to thinking about how to determine the likelihood of encountering IP regime risks.

The assessment of the impact of IP regime risks should vary depending on the nature of the risk. Therefore, as with the risk likelihood assessment, impacts should be determined on a case-by-case basis. However, some generic guidance can be provided. For example, per every risk identified in the Risk Register, firm managers may want to carefully evaluate the specific corresponding aspects of the IP regime (e.g., X law, Y policy), and more disaggregated aspects therein (e.g., A, B, C, D provisions in X law; A, B, C, D provisions in Y policy). Such evaluation could take the form of a qualitative rating or numerical (Likert scale) rating of the perceived degree of risk/hazard and costs presented. Table 8.4 provides some examples of basic labels that could be associated with these assessments across financial, technological, strategic, and other dimensions.

Several tools can improve the thoroughness of the aforementioned approaches to risk analysis. First, an analysis could be conducted about the pre-existing root cause and/or trigger of each risk. Standard tools such as the Fishbone Diagram, Five Whys, and/or 5W2H could be used during this process (e.g., Clayton 2011; Olson 2016; Hopkin 2017). While the triggers of many of the risks from China's IP regime

Table 8.3 IP regime risk likelihood assessment (examples of approaches)[a]

Unit of analysis	Scale (less likely → more likely)		
Years	Once every ten years	Once every five years	Once a year
Qualitative label	Low probability	Medium probability	High probability
Quantitative label	1	2	3
Probability (%)	<33	34–66	>66

[a]Illustrative, non-exhaustive examples. Different approaches should be tailored to individual circumstances

Table 8.4 IP regime risk impact assessment (examples of approaches)[a]

Unit of analysis	Scale (lower impact → greater impact)		
Direct financial costs[b]	<2000 USD	>2000 USD <10,000 USD	>10,000 USD
Indirect costs[b]	<2000 USD	>2000 USD <10,000 USD	>10,000 USD
Technological lead-time advantage in existing segment	Low erosion	Medium erosion	High erosion
Weakened brand recognition	Low	Medium	High
Strategic importance of lost entrepreneurial opportunity	Low	Medium	High
Generic quantitative label	1	2	3

[a]Illustrative, non-exhaustive examples. Different approaches should be tailored to individual circumstances

[b]These costs can include expenditures on in-house or external human resources to mitigate risks (e.g., hours spent per staff X hours spent), direct litigation costs, among various other types of costs

may be obvious, the actual root causes may sometimes be less clear. Understanding both the triggers and root causes can help managers understand important conditions determining both the likelihood and impact of the risk, as well as help them formulate smart responses. Second, the proximity (closeness) of a risk, in terms of the time frame within which it could be faced and/or geographic region in which it will be faced can also be delineated. Third, more broadly, structured information-gathering approaches can be taken to identify risk likelihood and risk analysis. These can include the formal Delphi Technique or less-structured approaches capitalizing on both individual and group evaluations while minimizing the dangers of group-think (e.g., Clayton 2011; Hopkin 2017). All this being said, managers should be aware that there are assumptions and other limitations to every approach to evaluate the likelihood and impact of risks, and therefore this analysis should be cautiously considered.

The generic guidance provided thus far is applicable to analyses of the many types of risks an IP regime poses. Another tool, which is particularly useful for assessing the impact of FTT policies on firms (discussed in Chap. 4), is the FTT Strategy and Risk Forecasting Matrix developed in Prud'homme et al. (2018). This matrix is depicted in Table 8.5. The matrix requires users to first identify if the state is using the strategies described per each of the seven leverage conditions (denoted with a "√" or "Y" if being used, and a "0" or "X" if not). Users of the matrix can then tally these sub-scores to calculate the "total leverage" of an FTT policy. As mentioned in Chap. 4, FTT policy "leverage" is the ability of the policy to shift bargaining power in foreign-domestic technology transfer arrangements to favor domestic firms; in other words, leverage is tantamount to the ability of the state to pressure (what some would call "force") technology transfer. A more frequent occurrence of the strategies in the matrix generally indicates the policies will likely exert higher leverage.

8.1.3 Prioritizing and Planning for Risks from the IP Regime

After identifying and analyzing risks from the IP regime, these risks should be prioritized. Prioritization can provide firms a useful reference point for managing risks, including what resources should ultimately be devoted to managing a given risk. Prioritization can be approached in several ways. One of the easiest ways is to simply chart the impact versus likelihood scores of each risk in a matrix and/or to multiply these scores (if numerical) by each other. This approach results in a rough grouping of risks which can be color coded green (for low priority risks), yellow (for medium priority risks), or red (for high priority risks). Figure 8.2 provides one graphical example of the result of this approach. These same prioritization labels can be inserted into the Risk Register alongside each risk. Yet other approaches to risk prioritization can be used.

Table 8.5 Forced Technology-Transfer Strategy and Risk Forecasting Matrix (FTT Leverage Forecasting Matrix)

Conditions impacting FTT policy leverage	State strategies for maximizing leverage of FTT policies	Sub-score[a]
1. Strong state support for industrial growth	Market demand, production, and necessary infrastructure investments are supported in the industry in which the policy is deployed. Such support is at least provided in the short term until returns on investment increase and market-based demand matures	√ or 0
2. Oligopoly competition	Policy is deployed in an industry with an oligopoly of foreign firms. And these firms will want to benefit from significant government purchasing for new technology, obtain a license to manufacture and sell products or services integrating new technology, or receive other state-governed benefits or market access conditioned on compliance with the policy.[b] The state may also facilitate transfer of frontier technology from a foreign SME(s) to local firms, because SMEs are theoretically more likely to out-license technology than larger firms; the state may then capitalize on this competitive dynamic in combination with the aforementioned bargaining chips to pressure the few large-sized industry leaders to form more significant technology collaborations with local firms	√ or 0
3. Other policies closely complementing FTT policies	Environmental protection-related policies (e.g., restrictions on CO_2 emissions or renewable energy consumption targets) or certain other substantive policies (e.g., tariffs) are deployed alongside the FTT policy. These policies "complement" the FTT policy in the sense that they interact with the FTT policy to exert additional pressure on foreign firms to transfer technology to local counterparts	√ or 0
4. Degree of technological uncertainty in targeted industries	Policy is deployed in industrial segments that are technologically uncertain	√ or 0
5. Policy mode of operation offering basic appropriability and tailored to industrial structure	Policy operates via JVs in an emerging industry segment organized to make JVs conducive to technology transfer, or policy operates via licensing (or FDI) modes in industry organized to be more conducive to licensing (or FDI) than JVs. The policy does not dramatically reduce appropriability without allowing sufficient offsetting benefits	√ or 0
	The policy does not primarily operate via the "no choice" mode (for example, via blatantly unfair court rulings in IP civil litigation)	Y or X

(continued)

Table 8.5 (continued)

Conditions impacting FTT policy leverage	State strategies for maximizing leverage of FTT policies	Sub-score[a]
6. Reform avoidance by the state	Government avoids or delays policy reform, including exhibiting the veneer of reform but not fully committing to it, to buy time for domestic firms to benefit from the policy. And an environment may be created where firms fear reprisal if they dispute the policy[b]	√ or 0
7. Stringent policy compliance mechanisms	Stringent compliance mechanisms are instituted so that the policy is abided by as drafted rather than skirted	√ or 0
Total score		Tally of # of √, 0, and Y/X markers

Source Prud'homme et al. (2018). Working classification of levels of FTT policy leverage: five or more "√" marks = high leverage; five or more "0" marks = low leverage; an "X" = potential leverage in the short-term but low leverage and likely discouragement of frontier technology transfer in the mid or longer term; roughly equal mix of "√" marks and "0" marks, and a "Y" mark = medium leverage. Alternative ranges can be assigned by users of the matrix.

[a]√ or Y markers indicates strategy is in place, 0 or X markers indicates it is not

[b]Denotes optional supplementary strategy to exploit the corresponding condition

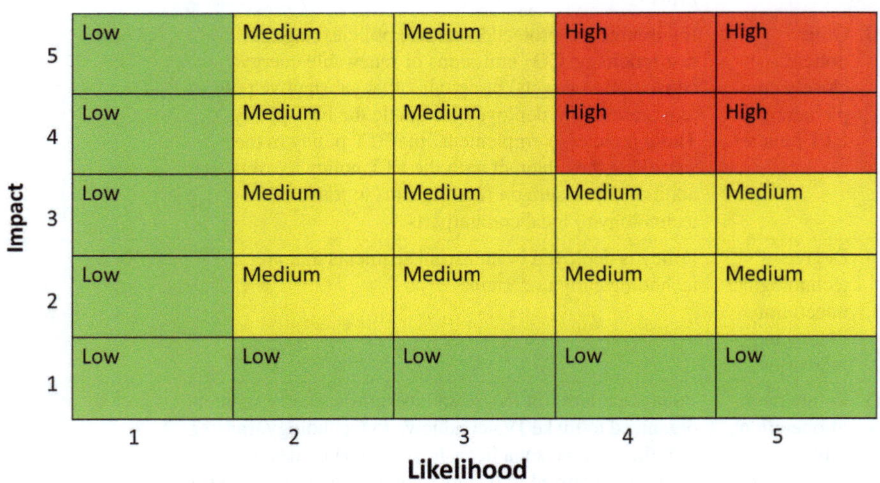

Fig. 8.2 Risk prioritization matrix (example) (Illustrative, non-exhaustive example. Different approaches should be tailored to individual circumstances)

The ultimate prioritization of risks, even for the same type of risk, can differ among firms depending on their "appetite" for risk (i.e., willingness and capability to respond to risks). And, as with the approaches to analyzing risks, managers should be aware that there are assumptions and other limitations of every approach to prioritizing risks.

After identifying, analyzing, and prioritizing risks from the IP regime, a plan can be formulated to respond to these risks. One the first steps in this process is to determine what generic planning approach the firm should adopt in response to the risk. Generic approaches include to (1) remove the risk (i.e., avoid the activity/activities leading to the risk), (2) reduce the risk (i.e., various actions to reduce the likelihood or impact of the risk), (3) develop a contingency plan (i.e., a course of action to take if and when the risk materializes), (4) transfer the risk (usually via contractual obligations including guarantees, indemnity, disclaimers or waivers; and various form of formal insurance instruments), or to (5) accept the risk (i.e., allow it to happen) (Clayton 2011; Hopkin 2017). It is beyond the scope of this chapter to discuss the specific situations in which these generic approaches should be used. But they must be considered on a case-by-case basis considering the details of the risk analysis conducted by the firm and the firm's appetite for risk and resources to respond to those risks.

In addition to specifying the generic risk planning approach per each risk, several other items need to be specified in a formal Risk Response Plan. These items include the risk owner (the person in the firm designated to oversee management of the risk), timing under which the risk should be managed, resources needed to manage the risk (in terms of people, assets, and materials), specific responsibilities of staff when managing the risk, communication processes when addressing the risk, the process for reporting on results of risk management, and the financial budget allotted to managing the risk. Table 8.6 depicts these elements, and others, in an example plan for responding to IP regime risks.

8.1.4 Managing and M&E of Risks from the IP Regime

Efficiently and effectively managing risks from the IP regime requires putting the details of the Risk Response Plan into action. Smart organizational approaches are needed to make this happen. Although different functional units in a firm may be assigned specific roles in risk management, it is important to avoid silos, especially when dealing with risks as dynamic as those derived from China's IP regime (Prud'homme and von Zedtwtiz 2018). Cross-departmental coordination (e.g., among the legal, R&D, strategy, and marketing departments) can help in this regard. It is also essential to establish smart routines. Regular meetings should be scheduled to review the status of risks derived from the IP regime, discuss strategies to address the risks, and chart actual progress of executing risk management plans. Lastly, a robust M&E process should be in place that includes formal monitoring and reporting, and cross-cutting risk assurance procedures and stakeholder engagement strategies.

Table 8.6 IP regime Risk Response Plan (example)

Section 1: The Risk	• Risk title • Unique risk ID • Risk description • Business activities impacted
Section 2: Risk Analysis	• Root cause • Trigger • Likelihood • Impact • Proximity (time scale) • Proximity (geographic) • Score/Priority
Section 3: Risk Response	• Risk owner • Generic risk planning approach • Specific actions to address risk • Timing/schedule • Resources (people, assets, materials) • Specific responsibilities of staff in carrying out actions • Communication process when addressing risk • Reporting process on results • Financial budget spreadsheet
Section 4: Residual risk	• Residual risk • Monitoring processes • Contingency arrangements
Section 5: Authorization	• Sign-off • Version control

8.2 General Best Practices for Managing IP in China

The academic literature provides helpful guidance to firms seeking to smartly manage their IP in China, including in response to some of the specific risks we identified in this book (e.g., Yang 2003; Yang et al. 2004, 2008; Keupp et al. 2009, 2010; Gassmann et al. 2012; Schotter and Teagarden 2014; Prud'homme and von Zedtwitz 2018, 2019). The practitioner literature also provides helpful advice. In the remainder of this chapter we reproduce, with some updates and other changes, a guide that the USCBC compiled of best practices to managing intellectual property in China entitled "USCBC Best Practices for Intellectual Property Protection".[1] The guide is by no means exhaustive, but is concise and provides a solid overview of some of the fundamental strategies needed to smartly manage IP in China. The recommendations reflect that not only traditional IP management strategies are needed to respond to risks from China's IP regime, but so are non-market strategies. Yet other strategies, including but not limited to those related to R&D and innovation (Prud'homme and von Zedtwitz 2018) can also be adopted.

[1] Special thanks to Erin Ennis of USCBC for authorizing reproduction of the guide and to Ryan Ong (formerly of USCBC) for facilitating communication about the matter.

8.2.1 Craft and Implement a Corporate IP Strategy in China

- Conduct an initial audit of the company's China operations to determine IP assets, IP risks, and assign appropriate levels of protection to those assets based on the risk of infringement.
- Review the company's internal IP controls to determine whether they provide sufficient protection. Make adjustments based on the IP audit, and dedicate resources in alliance with the company's IP protection goals.
- Classify IP-relevant information according to its level of sensitivity, and integrate that classification into information control and operational procedures.
- Make IP protection a core responsibility of the entire China management team, not merely a function of the legal or brand protection teams, and adjust internal information flows and reporting structures to reflect those responsibilities. Regularly communicate the value of IP protection—and the appropriate ways to handle IP—to key stakeholders, including government officials, employees, contract manufacturers, business partners, and customers. While the level of IP consciousness among Chinese citizens is growing, regular communication of the importance of IP is critical to instill a sense of ownership of company IP among key stakeholders.
- Take clear steps to document company IP protection policies and efforts as such documentation can play an important part in infringement disputes, particularly in areas like trade secrets.

8.2.2 Understand the IP Law and Policy Landscape

- Review not only China's core IP laws and regulations, but the growing body of other laws and regulations—as well as policies—that impact China's IP environment.
- Ensure that the legal protection the company is seeking for its IP in China is available.
- Monitor laws, regulations, and judicial interpretations to ensure that the company's IP enforcement strategies are valid under Chinese law. Examples of areas that may require scrutiny include employment contracts, IP licensing arrangements, and evidence collection procedures.

8.2.3 Adopt Preventive Measures to Protect IP

8.2.3.1 Register IP in China

- Companies should understand the requirements for the full range of IP they might file in China.

- If a company does not file its patents and (with some rare exceptions) trademarks in China, its IP has no formal protection there. Companies should register (or record) these and other IP rights in China as early as possible.
- Patents—Companies should file applications with CNIPA for IP that they view as valuable to their business for both core and peripheral technologies. Companies should ensure that their patents are properly translated before filing. Filing can be done directly with CNIPA or via international patent arrangements such as the Patent Cooperation Treaty. China offers three types of patents: invention patents, utility models, and designs.
- Trademarks—Companies should broadly register their core trademarks with CNIPA, including the English name, Chinese character name, and Chinese pinyin name for core brands. When filing, companies should carefully select the product categories and sub-categories in which to file, and check China's online trademark database for similar trademarks filed by competitors and infringers, including marks filed in categories outside a company's core products. Many companies have experienced challenges in which a local competitor registers a very similar trademark in a different product category, a practice allowed under the Trademark Law.
- Copyrights—Though registration is not required, entities should consider registering their works with the copyright authorities, since registration provides a public record and can serve as useful prima facie evidence in copyright disputes.
- Other types of IP rights—Companies should familiarize themselves with the requirements for maintaining trade secrets and obtaining plant variety protection, geographical indications, and integrated circuits layout protection in China.

8.2.3.2 Balance Global IP Protection Needs with China Market Opportunities in Transferring or Licensing IP

- Conduct a realistic assessment of the business risks and benefits of transferring IP to China. For many companies, this means keeping vital designs and latest-generation technologies overseas while bringing to China IP that supports their business in-country.
- Negotiate clauses in technology transfer and licensing contracts to address company needs on royalty rates and ownership of improvements. Companies should recognize differences in how China's legal framework treats ownership of improvements and liability, and that negotiated royalty rates in China are frequently lower than in other markets.
- Register technology licensing and transfer contracts as well as other IP licensing and transfer contracts required by the Ministry of Commerce's TIER and other IP authorities.

8.2.3.3 Design the Manufacturing Process to Protect IP

- Compartmentalize critical steps in the design and production processes for IP-intensive products—and the equipment used to manufacture these products—to limit the likelihood that any one employee has access to all the information needed to copy IP.
- Consider incorporating into the production process technologies and techniques that are difficult to copy, such as chemicals, foils, inks, labels, papers, stamps, and threads.
- Incorporate IP protection needs into facility design. Some companies, for example, limit IP exposure by ensuring that sensitive information is kept in low employee traffic areas or behind unmarked doors.

8.2.3.4 Utilize Information Technology Tools to Track and Protect Information

- Consider tracking data flows and employee file transfers (both paper and electronic), engage internal stakeholders such as the human resources department in early conversations about developing and implementing policies that monitor employees in this manner.
- Closely monitor or prohibit the use of flash disks, portable hard drives, laptops, cell phone cameras, and other devices that could be used to capture and transmit sensitive information.
- Establish IT mechanisms to limit employee access to sensitive information, such as separate computer terminals or specialized passwords.

8.2.3.5 Focus on Human Resources

- Run background checks on key hires to check for any IP-related "red flags," and include non-compete and nondisclosure agreements in employee contracts.
- Educate employees regularly about the firm's confidentiality requirements, and about the practical and reputational consequences of IP violations.
- Delineate based on job title and function which employees have access to what types of information.
- Control and monitor employee access to sensitive equipment and facility areas based on job title and function.
- Conduct exit interviews with departing employees to recover any sensitive materials and remind them of confidentiality obligations.

8.2.3.6 Carefully Select, Monitor, and Engage with Business Partners

- Conduct comprehensive due diligence on suppliers and distributors prior to any agreement and on a regular basis thereafter. As part of that due diligence, investigate how those companies view IP, including IP they access through business partnerships and their own IP.
- Include IP protection clauses in all contracts and agreements. Regularly engage business partners to share the importance of those clauses to the ongoing business relationship, and ensure that partners fully understand what those obligations mean for both parties.
- Regularly engage business partners to reiterate the importance of IP protection, and, where appropriate, partner to boost IP protection efforts, such as supplementing monitoring resources or jointly engaging with government officials.
- Manage supplier, vendor, and distributor relationships through multiple personnel to limit the ability of local staff to abuse business networks.
- Review information that could be sent to third parties before transmission to ensure that it is not sensitive, or that the benefits of sending it outweigh the risks of it being leaked.

8.2.3.7 Build Internal Lines of Communication on IP

- Establish an anonymous internal hotline, as well as an outside hotline for confidential communication with suppliers, distributors, customers, and other third parties to report IP infringement.
- Build a database of company infringement cases and infringers and make it available to key employees across the company's China offices. Such a database can help educate staff about the types of infringement that a company may face, and increase the likelihood of spotting future problems.

8.2.3.8 Engage IP Enforcement Bodies

- Build relationships with government officials at multiple levels in IP-related government agencies and courts relevant to the company's industry, before any problems arise.
- Educate local officials responsible for allocating the resources for and enforcing IP protection about the company's IP protection needs. For companies facing problems with exported counterfeits, this includes recording IP with Customs in Beijing and educating local customs officials about the company's products in order to monitor for counterfeits.

8.2.3.9 Work with Outside IP Service Providers and Industry Associations

- Engage with industry associations, including IP-, industry-, and country-specific associations, to exchange best practices for IP protection, identify cases of infringement, and (if appropriate) develop collective strategies and actions to advocate on concerns.
- Build ties with, and conduct due diligence on, IP service providers and investigative firms to identify enforcement resources that fully comply with relevant Chinese regulations.
- Work with local and national media as appropriate to address negative publicity that could accompany an IP case against a domestic company.

8.2.3.10 Actively Monitor for Instances of Infringement

- Send representatives to look for counterfeiters at industry trade shows and trade fairs, such as the Chinese Export Commodities Fair (Canton Fair).
- Review distribution networks at all levels regularly for weak links and possible entry points for counterfeit products.
- Monitor IP publications, including the PRC Patent and Trademark gazettes, for new patents and trademark applications to see if they infringe on the company's IP.
- Establish and publicize clear reporting channels for outside stakeholders to report cases of IP infringement.
- Check the Internet regularly for infringing domain names and for websites that are used as platforms for counterfeit products. These include e-commerce sites such as Alibaba and Taobao.

8.2.4 Confront IP Infringement When Discovered

8.2.4.1 Contact Infringers and Their Service Providers

- Send cease-and-desist (C&D) letters to infringers. C&D letters can be a cost-effective way to stop infringement in some cases, especially those involving small infringers. These letters, however, also alert infringers that a company is aware of their presence, which could prompt them to move, change names, or otherwise alter their operations in ways that could inhibit a company's ability to gather evidence.
- Work with Internet marketplaces and Internet service providers, such as Alibaba and Taobao, to remove infringing goods or pirated materials from websites, and to take down websites providing infringing products or content.

8.2.4.2 Build Clear Cases Against IP Infringers

- Conduct a careful review of internal documents that can demonstrate infringement, including physical and electronic evidence. Companies should be aware that documentary evidence (as opposed to oral testimony or non-official documents such as marketing materials) carries more weight with Chinese officials.
- Work with vetted IP investigative firms to collect evidence on the company's behalf, monitoring firm activities to ensure that evidence is collected legally.
- Consider possible locations where the company could file an infringement case, and collect evidence accordingly.

8.2.4.3 Utilize Official Enforcement Channels to Pursue Infringers

- Weigh various channels available to halt infringement in China, including administrative, civil, and criminal channels. In determining a course of action, companies should consider company resources, timelines for action, and the strengths and weaknesses of each channel.
- Engage with local government officials to convince them to conduct enforcement proceedings. Consider using a company's contributions to local development or tying the case to larger goals such as product safety or public health, to illustrate to local officials the value of pursuing a case. Such ties can sometimes give companies access to additional penalties under other laws, such as the Food Safety or Environmental Protection laws.
- Consider "venue shopping," or bringing infringement proceedings in jurisdictions (and through enforcement channels) with a better record of IP enforcement.
- Consider using the new specialized IP courts.
- Consider using the new specialized IP appellate tribunal within the SPC.

References

Clayton, M. 2011. *Risk happens! Managing risk and avoiding failure in business projects*. London, UK: Marshall Cavendish—Business.

Gassmann, O., A. Beckenbauer, and S. Friesike. 2012. *Profiting from innovation in China*. New York: Springer.

Hopkin, P. 2017. *Fundamentals of risk management: Understanding, evaluating, and implementing effective risk management*. UK: KoganPage.

Keupp, M., A. Beckenbauer, and O. Gassmann. 2009. How manager protect intellectual property rights in China using de facto strategies. *R&D Management* 39: 211–224.

Keupp, M., A. Beckenbauer, and O. Gassmann. 2010. Enforcing intellectual property rights in weak appropriability regimes. *Management International Review* 59: 109–130.

Miller, K. 1992. A framework for integrated risk management in international business. *Journal of International Business Studies* 23: 311–329.

Olson, D. 2016. *Risk matrices in supply chain risk management*. New York: Business Expert Press.

Prud'homme, D. 2019. Re-conceptualizing intellectual property regimes in international business research: Foreign-friendliness paradoxes facing MNCs in China. *Journal of World Business*.

Prud'homme, D., and von Zedtwitz, M. 2018. The changing face of innovation in China. *MIT Sloan Management Review* 59: 24–32.

Prud'homme, D., and von Zedtwitz, M. 2019. Managing "forced" technology transfer in emerging markets: The case of China. *Journal of International Management*.

Prud'homme, D., von Zedtwitz, M., Thraen, J., and Bader, M. 2018. "Forced technology transfer" policies: workings in China and strategic implications. *Technological Forecasting & Social Change* 134: 150–168.

Schotter, A., and Teagarden, M. 2014. Protecting intellectual property in China. *MIT Sloan Management Review*.

USCBC. Best practices for intellectual property protection in China, available at https://www.uschina.org/reports/best-practices-intellectual-property-protection-china.

Yang, D. 2003. *Intellectual property and doing business in China*. New York: Emerald.

Yang, D., M. Sonmez, and D. Bosworth. 2004. Intellectual property abuses. How should multinationals respond? *Long Range Planning* 37: 459–475.

Yang, D., G. Fryxell, and A. Sie. 2008. Anti-piracy effectiveness and managerial confidence: Insights from multinationals in China. *Journal of World Business* 43: 321–339.

Chapter 9
Implications for Policymakers

In this chapter, we provide recommendations about ways to reform China's IP regime to make it more conducive to innovation. While many reforms could be suggested, we highlight reforms we believe are most important to addressing the issues discussed in Chaps. 2–7. These recommendations can serve as the basis for further discussions between academics and policymakers and other actors actively involved in China's NIS. The recommendations are grouped chronologically according to the chapter to which they correspond.

9.1 Recommendations to Improve Substantive IP Laws

- *Patent Law*
  - Pilot and conduct M&E on the methods of allowing provincial administrative enforcement authorities more power in enforcing patent infringement disputes as proposed in the current draft Patent Law before they are instituted as such into statute.
  - Ensure that provisions on de facto SEP licensing and SEP royalty-setting (which were included in the draft version of the Patent Law in 2015) are left out of the fourth revision to the patent law, as is proposed in the 2018 draft of the law. Leave regulation of such issues to separate regulations exclusively devoted to abuse of IP.
  - Accompany the joint liability provision in the 2018 draft for ISP, especially its "notice and take down" rule, with a corresponding "counter notice and replacement" rule to balance the interests of online sellers and complaints.
  - Allow protection of partial designs in the fourth revision to the law (as recommended in the 2015 draft of the law but not the 2018 draft).

The original version of the book was revised: Author's belated correction has been incorporated. The correction to the book is available at https://doi.org/10.1007/978-3-030-10404-7_11

D. Prud'homme and T. Zhang, *China's Intellectual Property Regime for Innovation*, https://doi.org/10.1007/978-3-030-10404-7_9

- *Anti-Unfair Competition Law and Procedures*
  - Introduce regulations or judicial interpretations to prevent the second disclosure of trade secrets during litigation.
  - Introduce an obstruction of evidence doctrine to punish those that intend to hide evidence and otherwise impede justice in order to alleviate the burden of proof on right holders with respect to infringing activities or damages calculation in unfair competition cases.
  - Better define the concept of "unfair competition" and identify and regulate new types of unfair competition activities in the Anti-Unfair Competition Law to avoid frequent application of the general principle of the law.
  - Introduce regulations or judicial interpretations to clarify the phrase "where laws and administrative regulations provide for investigation and punishment by other governmental authorities" in Article 4 of the present law. This would clarify the relationship between the enforcement of the Anti-Unfair Competition Law and laws regulating various industries.
- *UPOV*
  - Pilot core components of UPOV '91, including but not limited to the concept of EDV, to move closer to acceding to a UPOV '78 'plus'-style agreement or UPOV '91.
- *Law on Scientific and Technological Progress*
  - Further clarify, in statute or supporting regulations, circumstances under which Article 20 and 21 of the LSTP will be applied.
- *Trademark Law*
  - Further clarify, in statute, supporting regulations, or judicial interpretations the application scope of the likelihood of confusion analysis, especially its application to double identity cases and OEM cases.
  - Actively apply the principle of good faith and the newly amended provisions from 2019 to impede serious trademark squatting activities, and limit application of "Trademark Co-existence" and "Market Reality" theory in the adjudication process.
  - Clarify (in statute, supporting regulations or judicial interpretations) the definition and parameters of the following concepts proposed in the 2019 revision to the law: malicious trademark registration without real purpose to use the mark and malicious trademark litigation.
- *Copyright Law*
  - Introduce a rule specifying how to acquire a copyright license, exploit "orphan works", and deposit remuneration in today's Internet-intensive economy.
  - Narrow the scope of mandatory copyright licensing, and mandate copyright users to register their usage of work to facilitate the collection of remuneration.

- Improve multiple aspects of the copyright collective management system to better guarantee the interests of copyright holders.
- Adopt a more flexible fair use system.
- Provide performers an additional right to collect remuneration with regard to the renting and use of their "audiovisual works"; provide record producers the ability to claim remuneration if their phonogram is broadcasted or publicly performed.
- Increase the cap on statutory damages from 500,000 RMB to at least 1,000,000 RMB.
- Expand the scope of the Fault Presumption rule to all the users of copyrighted works when they cannot prove the legal source of infringing goods.

• *Geographical Indications*

- Take further steps to streamline and otherwise improve the efficiency of the new administrative system for GIs which is currently within the newly established governmental agency CNIPA under SAMR but currently still run by TMO, AQSIQ, and MoARA (with a possibility that SFGA will also be involved).

• *Integrated Circuits*

- Clarify that the scope of protection of registered layout-designs should be determined solely by written documentation submitted to SIPO rather than by a model or e-copy.
- Allow the ex officio invalidation procedure of registered layout-designs to also be initiated by third parties.

9.2 Recommendations to Improve Patent Quality

• Institute further central-level M&E to ensure that provincial and local levels in China are complying with SIPO's Several Opinions on Further Improving Quality of Patent Applications and other patent quality initiatives set-forth by SIPO.
• Consider requiring a mandatory Search Report (an opinion on the novelty of a patent) before or alongside granting of utility models, or require a positive Report as a condition for granting.
• Additionally, or alternatively, a third-party observation mechanism could be set up to provide a channel for the public to provide evidence about the novelty of a published utility model application. This information could either be used as a basis to reject utility model applications or simply published and used as a basis for third parties to initiate invalidation cases against utility models.
• Shift state financial incentives for patenting from focusing on costs of patenting to more so cover services that make patents commercially valuable—namely costs for services related to patent evaluation and due diligence, marketing studies, license drafting, feasibility studies, and proofs of concept.

- Better target government financial support and technical advisory services for smart management of IP at deserving technology start-ups. Provincial and local governments in particular should consider this recommendation.
- Further emphasize service/employee-generated invention patenting rather than utility model (especially non-service) patenting.

9.3 Recommendations to Improve Measures for Transmission and Exploitation of Technological Knowledge

- Consider that, as a rule of thumb, FTT policies will generally only contribute to sustained technology transfer if they do not deprive foreign firms of a minimum level of appropriability and allow them to at least somewhat benefit from technology transfer arrangements. At the same time, develop a cross-departmental taskforce to re-evaluate what technology transfer policies (all types should be considered) might actually effectively and expeditiously spur core and frontier technology transfer while also being in-line with international trading rules.
- Provide more detailed explanations about how the "essential facilities" doctrine in SAIC's Provisions on the Prohibition of Abuse of IPR to Eliminate or Restrain Competition will be applied in practice, or remove the doctrine from law and leave it to courts to handle relevant incidences of monopoly abuse of IP rights. Consider clarifying several other ambiguities in the SAIC provisions.
- Clarify what the term "强制" in Article 22 of the Foreign Investment Law entails, although non-exhaustive examples do not necessarily need to also be codified in law. In addition, further revise Article 22 of the new Foreign Investment Law to specify that it applies not only to ownership transfer/assignment ("转让") but also to all state measures/practices for licensing of technology not clearly in line with China's WTO obligations.
- Clarify the process for granting a compulsory license mentioned in the Regulations of National Standards Involving Patents, amongst clarifying other ambiguities in the regulation.
- Err on the side of caution and include provisions in the Foreign Investment Law and perhaps other legislation banning the most aggressive types of "forced-technology transfer" (FTT) policies. Consider that, as a rule of thumb, FTT policies will generally only contribute to sustained technology transfer if they do not deprive foreign firms of a minimum level of appropriability and allow them to at least somewhat benefit from technology transfer arrangements. At the same time, develop a cross-departmental taskforce to re-evaluate what technology transfer policies (all types should be considered) might actually effectively and expeditiously spur frontier technology transfer while also being in-line with international trading rules.

- Add further certainty to Article 5 of the newly revised Administrative Licensing Law by establishing a clear mechanism through which entities can object (ex ante and ex post) to the sharing of their confidential business information requested as part of the administrative licensing process.
- Further revise Article 31 of the newly revised Administrative Licensing Law to specify that it applies not only to ownership transfer/assignment ("转让") but also to direct and indirect pressure to license technology not clearly in line with China's WTO obligations.
- Rethink the centrality of statutory and judicial approaches to service inventor remuneration and rewards as part of China's state-led innovation strategy. Conduct further research about how the state can directly or indirectly support smart innovation-incentive management strategies within Chinese firms that are not necessarily related to immediate monetary rewards or remuneration (e.g., effective management structures, trainings, long-term stock options, etc.). If work on the draft Service Inventor Regulation is resumed, in order to avoid excessive service inventor remuneration claims: (i) do not allow high turnovers to be used for blockbuster inventions, and (ii) make it clearer in the regulation and/or via Supreme Court guidance that self-established remuneration systems can be only rendered invalid in exceptional circumstances and can otherwise significantly deviate from state-mandated terms.
- Clarify the legal rights of parties in patent commercialization arrangements (and the circumstances under which march-in rights will be exercised) in the Law on Scientific and Technological Progress.
- Develop a new taskforce to oversee the formulation of specific rules to implement the Law on the Promotion of Transformation of Scientific and Technological Achievements.
- Consider state-sponsored initiatives to require TTOs in Chinese universities and PRIs to draft better patent applications (and otherwise better prosecute patents), better patent licensing contracts, and better overarching patent management strategies.
- Consider revising the classification/lack thereof for certain technologies and definition of "technology import and export" in the Technology Import Export Regulation to make them less ambiguous.
- Consider shifting from financially supporting "indigenous IPR" to also allow local firms to use state funding for in-licensing foreign-owned IP/IP jointly owned with a foreign entity if the applicant can prove the IP will be absorbed and used to generate indigenous innovations.

9.4 Recommendations to Improve New/Experimental IP-Related Measures

- Rethink the centrality of statutory and judicial approaches to service inventor remuneration and rewards as part of China's state-led innovation strategy.
- Further clarify how the Opinion on Reforming and Improving Policies Supply Guarantee and Use of Generic Drugs will be implemented and monitor the impact of the policy to ensure it does not have the unintended consequence of restraining innovation in the pharmaceutical industry.
- Introduce measures to guarantee the quality of software patents and business method patents and help avoid the classic patent hold-up problem which stifles innovation.
- Increase transparency of the control of data flows in the domestic market and across borders and strike a better balance between national security and private interests in data protection laws.
- Further improve the drug test data protection system, building on proposals in the current Draft Anti-Drug Medical Equipment to Encourage Innovation and Protection of the Rights and Interests of the Relevant Policies.
- Clarify, in statute or judicial interpretations, how the rules on IP protection and unfair-competition in the newly legislated E-Commerce Law relate to China's core IP laws.
- Sponsor (and publish) more scholarly empirical research on the effects, including on technological innovation, of China's IP Demonstration Cities Program and other experimental IP programs in China.
- Cautiously develop and administer the blacklist system with legislation at a higher level than that governing the system at present, and better harmonize the implementation of the system to avoid misuses of administrative power.
- Provide additional clarity about how the system for "IP dishonesty" will be implemented, including but not limited to how it will be integrated with the blacklist system, and develop transparent protocols to ensure it is applied consistently and fairly.

9.5 Recommendations to Improve IP Administration

- Continue to strengthen the coordination mechanism for IP governance in China under the leadership of the State Council. Consider expanding the scope of one state body to enforce not only patents but also copyrights and trademarks.
- Develop a more powerful coordination mechanism to improve coordination of administrative IP enforcement in particular among enforcement bodies across China.

- Ensure the still disjointed management systems for GI registration and enforcement involving the vestiges of SAIC, MoA, SFA, and AQSIQ are better combined into one harmonized and effectively administered system under CNIPA.
- Continue to smartly manage the hiring of qualified patent and trademark examiners, as well as the overall infrastructure and management of IP examination.
- Reduce the number of malicious registrations of non-distinctive, generic or other illegitimate trademarks or offer a green/expedited channel to speed-up the cancellation of certain types of registered trademarks.
- Improve the transparency of the IP examination and invalidation process, and allow more participation from the public and requestors in parts of these processes.

9.6 Recommendations to Improve IP Enforcement

- Implement the recommendations proposed in Chap. 2 that relate to revising IP enforcement-related provisions in core IP laws.
- Ease the burden on IP enforcement bodies posed by an explosion in IP disputes by increasing the numbers of staff in courts and specific IP administrative authorities, establishing more specialized IP courts, and designing differing procedures for simple versus complex IP cases to speed up trials and conserve judicial resources.
- Cautiously maintain a healthy relationship between the newly established specialized IP appellate tribunal and SPC's IP Tribunal to ensure they remain independent from each other.
- Explore revisions to judges' performance evaluation criteria that could better address the reluctance of Chinese judges to confidently apply provisions on access to evidence, the admissibility of evidence, and enforcement of judicial orders or judgments in IP cases.
- Strengthen judicial enforcement of IP by applying fines and sanctions for noncompliance, improving the acquisition and admissibility of evidence, and increasing damages typically awarded due to IP infringement.[1]
- Use outside professional technical specialists more in order to address the capacity constraints in China's IP system.
- Limit blatantly unfair court rulings by including clear rules for moving court cases to third party jurisdictions; ensuring that appeals of court rulings are a viable option so that upper courts can address unfair rulings by lower courts; and develop further central initiatives to monitor and limit unfair court rulings.
- Strengthen the connection among various administrative enforcement authorities and the connection between administrative enforcement and criminal enforcement. To punish and discourage repeated intentional infringement, measures such as

[1] In order to avoid patent trolling due in large part to the design of the US legal system, we do not suggest that China copy US IP Civil Procedure verbatim. However, we do believe that awarding higher IP damages and introducing a moderate discovery procedure enabling collection of evidence by IP rights holders will improve IP enforcement in China without strongly encouraging patent trolling.

blacklists, higher fines, confiscating infringement-related accounting documents and others are also needed during IP administrative enforcement.

- Pilot and conduct M&E on the methods of allowing provincial administrative enforcement authorities more power in enforcing patent disputes as proposed in the current draft Patent Law before they are instituted as such into statute.
- Consider focusing insurance and other financing schemes for IP litigation costs, as well as technical advisory services, on deserving technology start-ups in particular.
- Invest additional resources in non-government arbitration and mediation for IP cases, and adopt procedures to encourage greater use of alternative dispute resolution mechanisms.
- Reform the Arbitration Law and enhance the level of autonomy of arbitrators in China. The level of autonomy in arbitration has been enhanced in certain FTZs such as Shanghai FTZ. Measures could be considered to gradually spread their experiences to other regions.

Chapter 10
Conclusions

China, which is currently an upper middle-income country, is currently grappling with how to best transition from an imitation-based economy to one driven by technological innovation. Smart choices are needed if China is to make this transition and, in the process, avoid the middle-income trap and catch up with forerunner nations. Over the last decade, China has embarked on a state-led indigenous innovation and intertwined IP development strategy; however, despite this new strategic approach to catch up, China has not yet landed among the ranks of high-income economies. The country has also increasingly found itself under fire by foreign governments, firms, and other stakeholders for "IP theft".

Amidst this backdrop, this book provides a timely and up-to-date evaluation of the risks that China's IP regime poses to innovation. Our central finding is that China's IP regime for innovation has improved notably over time, and therefore is more conducive to innovation than many believe, but it still poses noteworthy risks. In fact, there is currently a paradox in China: the country is perceived to be a high-risk area for IP infringement; however, it is also recognized to have an increasingly business-friendly, albeit imperfect, IP law and enforcement regime. At the same time, perceptions from IP rights holders indicate that China's IP enforcement institutions and practices as well as China's IP laws, policies, and regulations create various risks. The presence of these risks may, to varying degrees, negatively influence the innovation activities of both foreign and domestic firms, as well as other stakeholders participating in the innovation process. In turn, this poses a larger set of risks to China's national development.

More specifically, we argue that China still needs to address six main intertwined IP-related challenges to become a high-income country: (1) Creating a legal appropriability environment that is more conducive to R&D and other innovation investments, patent commercialization, and technology transfer/spillovers in industries that will sustain growth; (2) Proactively encouraging innovation investments, patent commercialization, and technology transfer/spillovers in an economy where firms are often reluctant or unable to do so; (3) Balancing the strategic goal of eroding incumbents' IP-derived barriers to entry with the reality that absorption of external resources from foreign firms alongside dynamic use of internal capabilities is needed for sustainable

D. Prud'homme and T. Zhang, *China's Intellectual Property Regime for Innovation*, https://doi.org/10.1007/978-3-030-10404-7_10

indigenous innovation; (4) Improving the quality of IP rights in order to limit transaction costs and barriers to entry inhibiting innovation as well as avoid path-dependency and increase the economic value of innovations; (5) Proactively developing valuable IP in promising industries; and (6) Ensuring that government resources are managed wisely and devoted to the most productive IP-related initiatives. These challenges are of course joined by others facing China as it seeks to avoid the middle-income trap that are not necessarily related to IP.

We explore each of these intertwined challenges in detail through the lens of several different aspects of China's IP regime: (1) Core IP laws (in Chap. 2), (2) Patenting trends and the role of the state (in Chap. 3), (3) Important IP policies for transmission and exploitation of technological knowledge (in Chap. 4), (5) Important new/experimental IP-related measures and programs (in Chap. 5), (6) Administration of IP rights (in Chap. 6), and (7) IP enforcement (in Chap. 7). Our main findings from this investigation are as follows:

10.1 Core IP Laws

China has established a relatively complete legal infrastructure for IP protection over the past 30 years. During this time, China's IP laws and regulations have become increasingly conducive to innovation rather than mere imitation. Many of these aspects of China's IP regime are currently broadly in line with international standards.

However, some aspects of Chinese IP law contribute to an appropriability environment that is below optional for enabling innovation. Potentially problematic provisions in the 2018 draft Patent Law include the expansion of power for provincial/local administrative authorities to determine patent infringement and the removal of protection for partial designs present in the 2015 draft of the law. Also, the draft law is still vague about the proposed discretionary privilege of an entity to dispose of its service inventions, the approach to ISP liability, the open patent licensing system, and patent misuse.

Despite being revised in April 2019 in a number of helpful ways, there are still sub-optimal aspects of the Anti-Unfair Competition Law, which governs trade secrets and other types of unfair competition. These include a lack of procedures to prevent second disclosure in litigation. The law also lacks a clear definition of "unfair competition activities", so even though the most recently revised version of the law includes a list of unfair competition activities it still does not effectively govern all potentially relevant behaviors. Meanwhile, enforcement provisions in the law, which involve different enforcement agents and administrative liabilities, are still problematic, which creates challenges in administrative enforcement of trade secrets and other types of unfair competition.

Several other Chinese IP laws offer sub-optimal appropriability for innovation and entrepreneurship. China's legal framework for plant variety protection is sub-optimal as China has not yet acceded to UPOV '91. The Law on Scientific and Technological Progress includes ambiguous provisions on situations where the state may restrict licensing of IP derived from state-funded research. In April 2019, the Trademark Law was revised to help punish serious trademark infringements and malicious/bad faith trademark registration and litigation; however, the exact standards to determine confusion, bad faith, and trademark use remain vague. Potentially sub-optimal provisions in Copyright Law include a low cap on statutory damages, limited rights for performers and record producers to collect remuneration, an unbalanced mandatory licensing system, a rigid fair-use system, and lack of an effective way to exploit "orphan works". A complex web of state administration for different aspects of GIs still undermines efficient and effective protection of the rights at present, although is slated to be somewhat better streamlined after the establishment of SAMR. Potentially sub-optimal provisions in China's integrated circuits legislation include ambiguous rules on the scope of protection of integrated circuits and the ex officio invalidation procedure for the rights.

In response to these challenges, several of the aforementioned IP laws should be revised. These revisions should make the laws more optimal by increasing damages for IP infringement, expanding appropriability afforded by several of the laws, and clarifying or removing ambiguous provisions in some laws.

10.2 Patenting Trends and the Role of the State

Chinese firms are inventing more than ever. Some Chinese firms are also innovating but, on aggregate, still not as strongly as firms from technological forerunner countries. The growth of patenting in China and by Chinese entities operating abroad has diverse implications for the direction of the Chinese economy. Some of the past increases in patent stocks have contributed to productivity growth and potentially stronger strategic competitiveness in Chinese firms. However, there are diminishing returns to some of the inventions in China, especially utility models which are being generated en masse.

Moreover, despite the surge in the quantity of patents in China in recent years, patent quality has not risen proportionately. Chinese state patenting targets tied to performance evaluations and IP-conditioned state financial incentives have contributed to this rising patent quantity at the expense of patent quality. On one hand, neither the quality of invention patents filed in China nor the quality of Chinese-owned invention patents filed abroad is alarmingly poor, although different patent quality indicators are more assuring than others and state-supported filings appear to be of lower quality on average. On the other hand, the surge in utility models in China—especially, but not only, those that are state-supported—appear to be dragging down the quality of the country's overall patent stock. This patenting trajectory can create path dependency on low quality inventions and unnecessary barriers to entry and transaction costs, which restrains China's ability to transition towards an innovation-based economy.

The Chinese state has undertaken a number of important recent initiatives to improve patent quality, which appear generally well-designed. Still, further reforms could be made.

10.3 IP Measures for Transmission and Exploitation of Technological Knowledge

The Chinese state has formulated a plethora of IP-related regulations and policies to try and increase transmission and exploitation of technological knowledge – including direct technology transfer, spillovers, and patent commercialization. Many of these measures are very recent. The measures include the technology import and export regulations (TIER), regulations governing Sino-foreign equity JVs, regulations governing the interface between anti-trust and IP/abuse of IP, regulations and practices governing the interface between technical standards and IP, other policies considered by foreign firms to "force" technology transfer, a draft regulation for service/employee inventor remuneration and rewards (draft SIR), laws governing scientific and technological progress and achievements, state-supported technology markets and funds for IP development, financial incentives for development of "indigenous" IP, amongst other policies.

The Chinese state currently faces the challenge of proactively encouraging transmission and exploitation of technological knowledge in an economy where firms are often reluctant or unable to do so. Further, the Chinese state faces the challenge of balancing the strategic goal of eroding incumbents' IP-derived barriers to entry with the reality that absorption of external resources from foreign firms alongside dynamic use of internal capabilities is needed for sustainable indigenous innovation. These ongoing challenges are reflected by the fact that parts of the aforementioned IP measures are arguably not optimal for encouraging innovation investments, technology transfer (especially of frontier technology), patent commercialization, or spillovers in China because they are overly ambiguous or burdensome. This raises transaction costs of compliance and otherwise creates an uncertain legal environment for innovation in China.

In 2018 and 2019, the Chinese state made several very commendable revisions to some of these measures, although additional reforms could still be made. Several ambiguous, overly-burdensome, or otherwise suboptimal provisions in some of the measures should be revised or removed entirely.

10.4 New/Experimental IP-Related Measures

The growth of Internet-intensive and other emerging industries in China has posed new challenges to governance of IP, to which the Chinese state has proactively responded. Such technological change has led to a sharp increase of IP applications and more IP disputes in China in these new areas of economic activity. The Chinese state has recently attempted to regulate corresponding business models and other commercial activities in a way that ensures healthy competition and safeguards public interests while also not restricting innovation. The state has expanded patentable subject matter in China (e.g., for graphical user interfaces, software, and business methods); better protected pharmaceutical and chemical test data; formulated a new policy towards generic drugs; protected data usage and storage; regulated e-commerce activities; regulated the sharing economy; expedited patent examination; drafted a SIR; administered and reformed the IP Demonstration Cities Program; and set-forth a blacklist for IP infringers and other initiatives to penalize "serious dishonesty" involving IP.

These state initiatives appear to be generally well-designed, although improvements could still be made. With the exception of the draft SIR and perhaps some aspects of the recent policy on generic drugs, the aforementioned experiments/new initiatives generally seem to be creating an environment that is more conducive for innovation in growth industries in China. Then again, there are still some shortcomings in the drafting and administration of several of the initiatives and close oversight is needed to ensure they are working as hoped. The Chinese government should continuously reform its legislative, administrative and judicial approaches to the initiatives as the industries which they attempt to regulate evolve.

10.5 Administration of IP Rights

Since the 1980s, China has gradually established a complex and complete system for administering IP rights. Following its accession to the WTO, one of the biggest challenges facing IP administration officials in China has been the rapid growth of IP applications and a shortage of IP examiners. This being said, generally speaking, China's government institutions for administering IP rights have become better managed over the years.

Still, some improvements can still be made to guarantee the efficiency and quality of administration of IP rights in China. Inefficient coordination among the many central, provincial, and local government bodies governing IPR in China poses a challenge to the state's ability to administer IPR effectively and efficiently to enable innovation and entrepreneurship. Some important initiatives have been developed to address these challenges, although it appears that further reforms could be useful. Specifically, the state should improve coordination of IP administration and enforcement (e.g., improve coordination/better streamline IP rights granting, for example for

GIs under a more established SAMR, and other IP administration aspects among state bodies; and enhance oversight of sub-central-level IP policy-making/strategizing). Also, the state should expand the size and quality of China's IP administration infrastructure (e.g., by increasing quality staff and quality management in IP administrations).

10.6 IP Enforcement

China's IP enforcement environment is extremely complex. The country has a unique model for IP enforcement in which many local administrative agencies are used in addition to those state bodies often used in other countries for enforcing IPR (e.g., the judiciary and customs). Coordination across this massive system has been challenging.

There are significant differences in the strength of enforcement of IP rights available in different provinces in China. Quantitative and qualitative research finds that provinces in the eastern coastal region of China tend to more strongly enforce IP rights. However, paradoxically, these areas are often also cited as hotspots for problematic IP enforcement. This paradox is likely partially explained by a causal chain where a significant amount of economic activity is centered in these areas so they are more prone to IPR infringements in the first place, meanwhile high corresponding caseloads may sometimes slow the speed of IP enforcement. Also, given that businesses often have the most vested in these regions, a less-than-optimal enforcement outcome therein (whether owed to protectionism or other factors) can have a more pronounced impact than a similar outcome in a region in which less is vested.

Based upon our quantitative and qualitative research, we find that, generally speaking, the courts in China handling IP disputes are more efficient and effective today than in the past. Most IP cases today do not face the "acceptance difficulty" and "overdue problem" that once plagued IP rights holders in the past. This being said, if litigation suspension occurs because of a corresponding IP invalidation case or from jurisdictional suspension issues, IP litigation procedures can still be lengthy in China. The win rate for plaintiffs in IP infringement cases in China, especially for foreign firms, is high. This being said, the majority of IP lawsuits in China end up ultimately being dealt with by meditation or are withdrawn.

Despite these positive developments in IP enforcement in China, the effectiveness of judicial IP enforcement remains undermined by the low damages traditionally awarded in IP cases. Suboptimal IP infringement deterrence in China can, to a great extent, be attributed to the fact that Chinese judges rely on statutory damages rather than other methods of calculating damages afforded by the law. Moreover, the statutory damages granted in most IP cases in China are far below the cap specified in the law. Although these problems are relatively well known, there is limited research properly investigating the real reasons why judges behave this way. We argue that the propensity to rely on statutory damages in IP cases in China reflects the reality that many parties in IP lawsuits in China fail to offer adequate evidence of damages, and given that IP rights holders themselves often request statutory damages. Further, and importantly, these trends are explained by the less-than-optimal design of some judges' performance evaluation criteria and the lack of discovery procedures and other insufficient procedures for challenging evidence in China. The state has made some recent attempts to address some of these issues.

Further, there is empirical evidence that local plaintiffs have a better chance of winning IP disputes in China than ones originally registered in different areas. Also, although not commonly reflected in available aggregate statistics, our consultations identify cases where the authorities intervened in IP judgements, rulings or acceptance of cases appeared intentionally delayed, and IP judgments were otherwise inappropriate according to the law and facts at hand. This type of protectionism can favor domestic firms over foreign firms, or one local domestic Chinese firm over another. Protectionism is always problematic because even a handful of significant protectionist judgements can completely block innovative firms out of the market. And, more generally, unfair court rulings intent on protecting local firms undermine the sense of fairness in China's IP judicial system which can ultimately restrain innovation investments. The state has recently launched some initiatives in an attempt to deal with this issue.

Only a small proportion of IP infringements in China end up in criminal courts. However, our quantitative and qualitative analysis finds that more IP criminal cases have been brought to the police, prosecutors, and courts in China in recent years, and the number of suspects convicted is also growing. Then again, in order to further disincentivize criminal IP infringements in China, more cooperation is needed between relevant administrative agencies, the police, and the prosecutors; and the performance evaluations of some of these authorities should be revised.

Improvements have been made to local IP administrative enforcement in China in recent years, although there is still a debate about how to best improve this type of enforcement. The number of disputes handled by local IP administrative enforcement authorities in China has risen rapidly in recent years. Measures for more severely punishing and otherwise enforcing IP rights, including by local IP administrative enforcement authorities, have been recently introduced in various Chinese IP laws. However, there is an ongoing debate about the extent to which the power of local patent administrative enforcement authorities in particular should be expanded given that patent matters that are quite technically complex and therefore require exceptionally well-trained experts to administer. Also, there continue to be cases of local protectionism by local IP administrative enforcement authorities—although some recent reforms have been proposed to help address this issue.

Several reforms should be instituted to address the aforementioned challenges to IP enforcement in China. First, the state should expand the size and quality of China's IP enforcement infrastructure (e.g., by increasing numbers of quality staff in courts and establishing more specialized IP courts). Second, the state should strengthen procedures and practices to make judicial IP enforcement more of a deterrent to IP infringement (e.g., in terms of procedures to deter local protectionism; access to and admissibility of evidence; enforcement of judicial orders and judgments, and fines and sanctions for noncompliance; and increasing damages typically awarded in practice). Third, the state should improve coordination of IP enforcement (e.g., better coordinate among local administrative enforcement bodies; and improve coordination of civil, administrative enforcement, and criminal procedures).

10.7 The Way Ahead

As repeated throughout this book, the Chinese state has made an incredible number of commendable reforms in recent years in an attempt to address the aforementioned challenges—which have now become risks to national development. Nonetheless, we argue that China's IP regime could benefit from the additional reforms that we have outlined in Chap. 9 of this book. In the meantime, we have provided several frameworks in Chap. 8 to help businesses manage these risks.

There are several aspects of China's political economy that could complicate the reform process that we are recommending. However, with sufficient buy-in from the state, we do not believe that these factors will prohibit a number of smart reforms from being made that may notably improve the ability of China's IP regime to foster innovation and entrepreneurship. China is capable of further building a world-class IP regime in the near future that can help it avoid the middle-income trap and become an innovation powerhouse.

Correction to: China's Intellectual Property Regime for Innovation

Correction to:
D. Prud'homme and T. Zhang,
***China's Intellectual Property Regime for Innovation*,**
https://doi.org/10.1007/978-3-030-10404-7

The original version of the book was inadvertently published with an error in the numeral "50,000" and this has been corrected as "500,000" in the chapters "Statutory IP Laws" (Page 36) and "Implications for Policymakers" (Page 217).

The erratum book has been updated with the changes.

The updated versions of this chapters can be found at
https://doi.org/10.1007/978-3-030-10404-7_2
https://doi.org/10.1007/978-3-030-10404-7_9

D. Prud'homme and T. Zhang, *China's Intellectual Property Regime for Innovation*, https://doi.org/10.1007/978-3-030-10404-7_11

Annex A
IP Lawsuit Damages Awarded in Different Regions in China

Beijing IP Court

See Tables A.1, A.2, A.3, A.4 and A.5.

From the data in Table A.1 it can be seen that the compensation awarded in the cases of first instance concluded by Beijing Intellectual Property Court in 2016 is higher than that in 2015, among which the compensation awarded in the patent-related cases is 2.9 times that in 2015; 1.3 times that in 2015 for cases pertaining to software copyrights; and 3.7 times that in 2015 for cases involving affirmation of well-known trademarks. Moreover, the support rate for compensation awarded in the cases about patents and software copyrights has witnessed a substantial increase.

From the perspective of patent cases, the compensation awarded in cases about patent for invention and utility model has witnessed significant increases in Beijing IP court, among which the compensation awarded in the cases about patents for invention in 2016 is 9.7 times that in 2015, and 15 times that in 2015 for cases about patents for utility model. Moreover, the support rate for compensation awarded in the cases about patent for invention has witnessed a substantial increase.

It can be seen that the cases concluded by Beijing IP Court about full compensation awarded in 2016 are twice those in 2015, and represent about a quarter of the total cases about compensation awarded. This suggests that the proportion of cases where full compensation is awarded in those concluded by Beijing IP Court in 2016 is high. Further, if comparing the amount of compensation awarded in the cases of second instance about civil infringement concluded by Beijing IP Court with that in the first instance by basic courts in 2016, the average compensation awarded and support for compensation awarded in the cases appealed by basic courts to Beijing IP Court have increased.

D. Prud'homme and T. Zhang, *China's Intellectual Property Regime for Innovation*, https://doi.org/10.1007/978-3-030-10404-7

Table A.1 Compensation awarded in first instance IP cases in Beijing IP Court (2015–2016)

Type	Content			
	Average compensation awarded (RMB)		Support rate for compensation awarded	
	Year			
	2015	2016	2015 (%)	2016 (%)
Patent	1,324,372	449,916	63.9	46.6
Software copyright	285,000	220,000	97.1	77.2
Well-known trademark involved	2,267,686	620,000	63.9	78.5

Source Judicial Protection Data of Beijing IP Court

Table A.2 Types of compensation awarded in patent infringement cases

Type	Content			
	Average compensation judged (RMB)		Support rate for compensation awarded	
	Year			
	2015	2016	2015 (%)	2016 (%)
Invention	6,037,713	623,886	95.9	52.4
Utility model	1,814,000	120,000	15.0	46.7
Design	121,556	292,271	23.5	36.2

Source Judicial Protection Data of Beijing IP Court

Table A.3 Cases of full compensation awarded in first instance by Beijing IP Court

Type	Content			
	Number		Proportion	
	Year			
	2015	2016	2015 (%)	2016 (%)
Invention	11	5	21.2	11.6
Utility model	2	0	28.6	0
Design	3	3	30.0	50.0
Total	16	8	23.2	15.7

Source Judicial Protection Data of Beijing IP Court

Table A.4 Compensation awarded in second instance IP cases concluded by Beijing IP Court in 2015 and 2016

Type	Content			
	Average compensation awarded (RMB)		Support rate for compensation awarded	
	Year			
	2015	2016	2015 (%)	2016 (%)
Trademark	114,177	292,716	29.3	32.5
Copyright	25,916	31,973	23.9.1	29.8
Unfair competition	113,065	346,422	9.8	22.1

Source Judicial Protection Data of Beijing IP Court

Table A.5 Ratio of total compensation claimed to total compensation awarded in Shanghai

Type	Number of cases	Total compensation claimed (RMB)	Total compensation awarded (RMB)	Ratio (%)
Invention patent	20	39,564,225.8	3,965,400.0	10.0
Utility model	13	14,946,325.0	1,693,668.0	11.3
Design	36	22,591,981.2	1,920,803.0	8.5
Trademark	228	100,629,679.1	11,462,555.7	11.4
Copyright	300	88,162,515.43	10,879,577.43	12.3

Source Shanghai IP Litigation Report

Shanghai Area

According to the Shanghai IP Litigation Report 2016, covering the period 2013–2015, the ratio of total compensation claimed to total compensation awarded is about 10%.

This low ratio implies that damages awarded normally are far below the damages claimed. The gap is partly because rights holders normally claim high statutory damages near the cap without evidence of actual loss or illegal profit and courts normally are reluctant to support such claims. Another reason is that although Shanghai or other Chinese courts are inclined to protect IP right holder by recognizing the establishment of infringement, courts also attempt to balance the interest by granting lower damages.

Annex B
IP Administrative Enforcement by Local Governmental Agents

See Tables B.1, B.2, B.3 and B.4.

Table B.1 Patent enforcement by local IPOs in China, number of cases by region (since 1985)

Region	Infringement dispute		Other disputes		Passing-off of patents
	Cases accepted	Closed	Cases accepted	Closed	Closed
Total	46916	41287	3950	3389	72079
Beijing	787	658	225	221	1170
Tianjin	329	302	36	33	1211
Hebei	1066	931	142	147	1553
Shanxi	116	82	52	38	123
Inner Mongolia	146	133	11	11	1829
Liaoning	462	439	230	197	1721
Jilin	297	287	60	52	266
Heilongjiang	670	618	309	278	776
Shanghai	929	871	79	79	318
Jiangsu	2755	2262	336	325	11651
Zhejiang	13675	13293	538	466	1459
Anhui	717	557	38	30	1623
Fujian	896	713	56	55	2709
Jiangxi	556	400	40	27	1337
Shandong	3168	2613	200	191	10903
Henan	2085	1491	163	110	3478
Hubei	1283	1015	232	178	3390
Hunan	1388	1094	437	397	10282
Guangdong	10592	9324	216	189	3792
Guangxi	201	169	55	38	762

(continued)

D. Prud'homme and T. Zhang, *China's Intellectual Property Regime for Innovation*, https://doi.org/10.1007/978-3-030-10404-7

Table B.1 (continued)

Region	Infringement dispute		Other disputes		Passing-off of patents
	Cases accepted	Closed	Cases accepted	Closed	Closed
Hainan	96	89	12	10	292
Chongqing	545	504	151	43	454
Sichuan	1345	1212	159	134	2440
Guizhou	255	200	25	21	3155
Yunnan	368	304	29	22	784
Tibet	11	9	0	0	10
Shaanxi	500	369	37	33	1972
Gansu	312	218	25	18	660
Qinghai	36	26	9	10	67
Ningxia	208	193	27	18	150
Xinjiang	1122	911	21	18	1742

Source Patent annual report (2015) from SIPO

Table B.2 Number of passing-off patent cases investigated by IPOs in China

Year	Closed cases of passing-off fictitious patents	Closed cases of passing-off "real" patents	Cases transfer to PSB
2004	1425	92	/
2005	2808	362	15
2006	933	33	12
2007	681	32	32
2008	601	59	21
2009	548	30	9
2010	728		/
2011	1704		7
2012	6512		/
2013	9161		/
2014	16259		/
2015	21237		/
2016	28057		/

Sources Patent Annual Report from SIPO, and China IPR Yearbook (The combined statistics from 2010–2016 vis-à-vis earlier statistics are explained by the fact that the third revision of China's Patent Law promulgated in 2008 and which became effective in 2009 combines what were previously considered types of passing-off crimes into one.)

Table B.3 Trademark cases enforced by local AICs

Year	Number of cases	Cases transferred to PSB	Number of Suspected transferred to PSB	Number of marks seized	Number of infringing tool seized	Fine (RMB)
2001	22,813	86	88	138,795,152	14,004	131,900,000
2002	23,539	59	78	78,979,514	14,882	135,610,000
2003	26,488	45	52	58,395,994	15,597	196,390,000
2004	**40,171**	**96**	**82**	**36,144,891**	**280,781**	**220,880,000**
2005	39,107	236	215	46,508,620	18,414	288,700,000
2006	41,214	252	263	28,019,264	2905	347,870,000
2007	42,314	229	228	27,400,110	4201	364,430,000
2008	47,045	137	145	18,506,514	16,773	405,800,000
2009	43,596	92	109	13,148,785	3409	358,390,000
2010	48,548	175	163	12,752,200	/	/
2011	**90,701**	757	/	/	/	507,718,100
2012	**120,400**	**576**	**557**	**11,047,944**	**2675**	**851,000,000**
2013	83,100	362	347	6,530,808	8566	1,121,000,000
2014	67,500	300	215	12,138,234	43,706	480,000,000
2015	27,400	164	171	3,912,398	10,310	367,000,000
2016	28,000	203	/	/	/	350,000,000

Sources China IPR Yearbook; Annual Report of China's IPR Protection Status

Table B.4 Number of cases in which punishment is imposed by local copyright enforcement bodies

Year	Number of cases	Cases transferred to PSB	Ratio (%)
2001	3650	69	1.89
2002	5250	136	2.59
2003	**21,032**	**224**	**1.07**
2004	**7986**	**101**	**1.26**
2005	7840	366	4.67
2006	8524	235	2.76
2007	9816	268	2.73
2008	9032	238	2.64
2009	9438	374	3.96
2010	**10,590**	**538**	**5.08**
2011	**12,070**	**508**	**4.21**
2012	**7908**	**823**	**10.41**
2013	7019	539	7.68
2014	4728	366	7.74
2015	3477	160	4.6

Sources China IPR Yearbook, Annual Report of China's IPR Protection Status

MIX
Papier aus verantwortungsvollen Quellen
Paper from responsible sources
FSC® C105338

If you have any concerns about our products,
you can contact us on
ProductSafety@springernature.com

In case Publisher is established outside the EU,
the EU authorized representative is:
Springer Nature Customer Service Center GmbH
Europaplatz 3, 69115 Heidelberg, Germany

Printed by Libri Plureos GmbH
in Hamburg, Germany